U of C Book Store
9/96
Day of Dad's Surg
Bill / Laurel / Stu
and me

WOMEN
and
STRESS

WOMEN
and
STRESS

Dr. Charmaine Saunders

Edited by Natalie Newton

CRESCENT BOOKS
New York • Avenel

Copyright © 1990 Charmaine Saunders
All rights reserved

First published by Angus & Robertson Publishers.
This edition published by arrangement with
HarperCollins Publishers Australia.

This 1995 edition is published by Crescent Books,
distributed by Random House Value Publishing, Inc.
40 Engelhard Avenue, Avenel, New Jersey 07001

Random House
New York • Toronto • London • Sydney • Auckland

Printed and bound in the United States of America

A CIP catalog record for this book is available
from the Library of Congress.

ISBN 0–517–14909–5

8 7 6 5 4 3 2 1

*To the memory of my loyal friend and companion,
Henry, who died in July 1989.*

CONTENTS

CHAPTER FIVE

CHAPTER SIX

CHAPTER SEVEN

CHAPTER EIGHT

CHAPTER NINE

CHAPTER TEN

ACKNOWLEDGEMENTS

There are many people to thank as no book is ever the work of a sole person although, sometimes, a writer feels totally isolated from everyone else.

First, my publisher, Lisa Highton, who conceived the idea in the first place. Then, to the editors who worked with me on the book—Susan Tomnay and Tracy Tucker of Angus & Robertson and especially Natalie Newton, who shared the work closely with me every step of the way and made it a much less lonely task. Next, the following people who contributed to the book, directly and indirectly:

Helena Ederveen of the Osiris Centre.
Patricia Cheong who taught me about numerology, reincarnation and myself.
Judith Hamilton of 'Career Change'.
Vivienne Lorrigan of KEAPS.
'Dr Disk', who bailed me out every time I got into trouble with my computer.
Wendy Munro of the Seekers' Centre.
Leila Williams, psychic artist.
Isobel Kerley of the Western Australia International Yoga Teachers' Association.
Lesley Hone of the Nerve Centre.
Kate Faraday of the Western Australian Breath Integration Centre.
My assistants, Katie and Nellie, who keep my mundane tasks at bay.
Finally, but most importantly, my close friends, Laura, Angie and Kim, who keep me sane when *I* get stressed!

FOREWORD

My aim in writing this book is to provide a reference point for all women in their quest for a richer and more fulfilled life. There are already many books in the marketplace on stress management but only a few that relate specifically to women. I'm not suggesting that women suffer more or worse stress than men, but only that they experience it differently, as indeed they do all of life.

The book sets out to achieve three ends: to examine the common and persistent causes of stress; to offer a vast array of stress management techniques, from the traditional to the alternative; to use case studies and personal anecdotes and experiences to unfold the full implications of stress in women's lives.

I suggest that you read it straight though and then, armed with pencil, return to the sections of the book that are relevant to you at this point in time. As much as it is a book about the life journeys of women, it is also a reference and a manual for you to work with and dip into at different stages of your life. I hope that you won't confine your usage of this book to crisis times or wait until you're feeling close to burn-out. Nothing would thrill me more than to think that you, your mother, grandmother and daughter(s) will take turns reading my book and that this sharing will increase the bond between you. When I get letters from readers of my first book describing the benefits they derived from the information and/or advice given, I am thrilled but also humbled because there is so much pain and loneliness in the world and my efforts are but a ripple in the pond. I believe in the strength and dignity of women and I see my book as only one of the many keys that are available for unlocking the magic within us all.

It also sets out to explode certain myths about stress and other aspects of human experience. Stress, for example, is not always a negative or dark force but can be harnessed for positive power. When a woman is feeling 'stressed', the chances are strong that she is living her life by someone else's rules and to someone else's schedule. The book takes the reader through a personal odyssey as much as supplying factual information. It is a step-by-step guide to dealing with personal identity, improving self-esteem and having rewarding relationships.

The case studies I have cited are actual women patients that I've seen over the past six years but of course the names have been changed to fictitious ones. Stress is the underlying theme and the explicit subject of the book but the life-experiences shared within run the full gamut of human activity and endeavour. There is a certain 'turn-off', I know, in the constant barrage of positive messages we receive these days but personally I can't get enough. I've had more than my share of the negative and it's wonderful to know that there are millions of people out there who want to be happy and enjoy fully our beautiful world. The affirmations at the end of each chapter will help you bring these belief systems into your life if you say them regularly and work with them sincerely.

In writing this book, I am less concerned with telling you what I already know than in sharing my learning process with you. I intend to be as honest as humanly possible, at the risk of being misunderstood or ridiculed. After all, I cite risk-taking as a key element in personal development. My gift to you is my whole life experience to this point and my hope is that, in sharing it, you will learn a lot more than just how to manage stress.

Allow yourself to enjoy the journey as you turn the pages ahead. I plan the book to be user-friendly. I hope that you'll laugh and cry and learn and get happy, for these are the true miracles of life.

Please put pen to paper and tell me your responses, feelings, stories and problems. Write to me at PO Box 637, Subiaco, WA 6008. I would truly love to hear from you and will send information on any topic covered in the book.

What is stress and how do we live with it?

Most people do not consider the insidious nature of stress when they feel 'bad'. Even when it is the most obvious cause of their ill-feeling and subsequent unhappiness, they usually blame everything else first.

Stress is an external pressuring force, or a catalyst resulting in tension. Tension is an internal force that builds up inside and is caused by stress. It is stored in the body as a result of unresolved angers, emotional stresses that have accumulated along with a hundred other daily aggravations. In this book, I will suggest practical ways in which tension can be released from mind and body. This regular release is necessary to avoid the complications that might otherwise arise.

We often hear and speak about such things as tension headaches, but too readily accept that these ailments are all part of modern living. Life in the 1990s can be relaxed and peaceful. This book will help you attain a relaxed state by teaching you how to use positive mind power, regular exercise, correct diet, and time management to achieve that goal.

Short-term stress can be easily overcome, but over a prolonged period the effects can be devastating. Long-term stress rids the body of its ability to fight off viruses and infections and has been strongly linked with diseases such as cancer. Once you are sick, the healing process depends not only on rest but on such factors as the presence of hope, belief in the ability of one's own body to defeat illness, and receptiveness to treatments. Therapists like the late Ainslie Meares, from Australia, have achieved wonderful results treating cancer with meditation. In the summary at the beginning of his book, he says, 'Life is better for us if we have a lower level of anxiety. Our mind has an inbuilt capacity to reduce the level of our anxiety; but our mind cannot exercise this capacity unless the circumstances are suitable.' Meditation uses the power of the mind and the psyche to free the body's healing powers.

In a nutshell, the surest way to avoid illness is by being happy, active, and actively involved in the process of living. Happiness breeds happiness. Mind and body in harmony provide all the necessary strength for happy, healthy living.

Knowing the signs

Does your life lack joy? Are you constantly fatigued? Does your life seem unmanageable? Don't wait until you are sick, depressed, or chronically stressed. Life should be enjoyed, not endured. Prevention is the key word, but we cannot prevent what we do not understand, so the first step is awareness. Try this— make out a list of all the major stress areas in your everyday life. First, make a list at random without giving too much thought to reasons or logical sequence. You may be amazed at your discoveries from this inner journey. For effectiveness, employ determination and honesty in this exercise. The results will make the time spent more than worthwhile. Armed with this new knowledge, you will be able to make real changes in your life. Otherwise, you may waste valuable time and energy working on a personal project that is not worth the trouble.

A patient of mine, whom I will call Margaret, consulted me about her stress problem. She blamed her job, which she disliked but felt she could not give up for practical reasons. She canvassed the various options, and after several weeks told me she had found a much better job. Then she said her stress level had not considerably decreased! Apparently, after altering the professional side of her life, Margaret found that her relationship problems did not evaporate as she had expected. Her job was a source of stress, but not the only one. By examining the, alternatives and being open to change, she resolved much more than she had expected. Many people cannot eliminate their sources of stress quite so easily, but by identifying them they can at least have hope of an improvement.

High levels of stress make you deeply unhappy and create sickness, but how do you recognise stress, and the damage it can cause?

The most common physical symptoms of stress are:

■ headache.
■ stomach trouble.
■ chest tightness.
■ lower back pain.
■ tension at the base of the neck.
■ chronic constipation.

Other stress symptoms can be:

■ insomnia.
■ loss of efficiency.
■ loss of concentration.
■ irritability.
■ breakdown in relationships.
■ lack of motivation.
■ general downturn in life.

You cannot expect to function well in any sphere of your life if you feel constantly stressed.

Stress in personal relationships

Imagine the scenario of a man who works long hours during the day and returns home hoping to find a peaceful haven, just wanting to put his feet up and relax. If his wife does not go out to work and has young children, she has probably been counting the hours until his return, only to discover that the last thing he wants to do is engage in social conversation. He may be happy enough to pass a few words of greeting, but not a lengthy conversation with his wife or children. He has had a whole day of decision-making as a boss or order-taking as an employee. Both are mentally exhausting and psychologically draining. His wife is also fatigued and wrung out after a demanding day with the little ones. Neither has much to offer and yet both need understanding and love. Stalemate! Who gives in? Should the husband grit his teeth and play with the children to relieve his wife when all he wants is a cool drink and a quiet read of the paper? Should the wife play the martyr and continue to smile bravely when she would really like to throw something? Answers later!

In this day and age, the above situation does not necessarily apply. The father may just as likely be at home when Mother walks in from work! More commonly, both partners work away from home and the children are cared for by others. These various combinations present infinite complexities within the psychology of the individual, as well as in relationships. Therefore, the threats to peace and harmony are greater as is the challenge of success. There will be plenty of times when one partner is more stressed than the other.

In a caring relationship, the less-stressed person would take over in the courage and stamina departments. That is called 'give and take'. If one partner does all the giving and the other all the taking, the relationship is out of balance and needs work. Of course, there are those extremely strenuous periods when both people are going through particularly stressful times, when neither one can offer strength. These times are the tests of love at the heart of the partnership. We either pass or fail, but 'failure' does not necessarily imply a poor marriage. The marriage simply needs both partners to communicate sensibly.

How does stress manifest itself in a relationship? First, communication breaks down. The stressed partner loses interest in talking or maintaining closeness. This, in turn, antagonises even the most tolerant of spouses, and the cycle begins. Resentment sets in, widening the communication gap. Many people have experienced this at some time. They feel awful without knowing why; they start acting badly, and this makes them feel even worse. Now they are at the point where they cannot talk about it at all. Everything feels bad. Sound familiar? Suppose for a moment you are the 'victim' of this picture; you have a partner who has turned from a reasonable human being into an ogre. No matter what you say or do, things just get worse. Now you are getting angry, too, and you don't even have a problem (that is, other than your grouchy partner). Soon, no one is talking, and, inevitably, the problem reaches the bedroom, in many ways the heartland of any relationship.

Can you imagine conducting even the most spurious of sexual interactions when conversation is almost nil, and resentment and barely disguised anger is constantly bristling between you? I doubt that the most cynical and expedient of us would enjoy that very much. The best sex occurs when people stay close *outside* the bedroom. Good sex is simply the expression of feelings two people have for each other. It is not a separate activity that takes on a life of its own. Sex is an extended form of communication and cannot be divorced from it.

After the more passive problems, the next stage is usually extrovert and aggressive. Behaviours such as snapping at each other, quarrelling, and, in more severe cases, vocal and physical violence. The entire family is affected, particularly any children, as they have no way of understanding why Mummy and Daddy are suddenly shouting and angry all the time. (These comments are levelled at the average couple, not cases in which the marital problems are chronic and fighting is the norm.) Under these aggressive conditions, partners become more and more defensive, accusations and criticism abound, and divorce seems the only solution. Each person wants to bolt, to run away from it all and get some peace and quiet.

Not a pretty picture, is it? Yet, it is so easily prevented, or rather, it is much easier to prevent than to repair. I wish couples seeking my help with marital difficulties would come in at the *onset* of problems instead of waiting so long and letting the damage go so deep. Remember that stress is an outside force. It surrounds you all the time, but you can be its master rather than allowing it to control you. If your personal relationships feel stressed, chances are that the origin of the problem does not lie in your marriage. You are, however, giving stress power over that particular area of your life. Stress can originate from sources that are years old; the root poison may have been left to fester for all that time. The pressure was accelerated and nothing ever resolved. Find the cause, call it by name, and you can eliminate it.

The term 'personal relationships' does not only refer to marriage or sexual partnerships but encompasses the myriad of human interactions we embrace in a lifetime. However, the marital relationship (including de facto and long-term dating) is perhaps the most challenging. This challenge is why it represents an interesting basis for the study of relationship stress. Simply sharing a home with another places one in a position of potential stress.

As this book unfolds, you will see the importance of having a positive attitude to what you undertake. That positive approach is the difference between success and failure. Much of what is said can also be applied to siblings, parent/child, boss/employee and friendships.

Stress in the workplace

The workplace and stress factors in your business life should also be approached with a positive attitude. Apart from the ravages of physical and emotional stress, there is also the effect on your mental processes, such as memory, decision-making, efficiency, motivation and problem-solving.

Telling a stressed person, 'Pull yourself together', or 'You'll be all right if you just stop feeling sorry for yourself', is pointless. Stressed patients often add that they feel disorientated and confused, so their thinking is likely to be irrational; negative remarks may appear to be the truth. This situation prolongs the pain, adding to the antagonism. If the person criticising is also in a position of authority, then the whole problem deepens.

A stressed person cannot just start behaving 'normally'. There is so much general talk about stress, yet the community lacks real understanding of its many faces and the depth of its consequences. The working environment must be pleasant and relaxing for a person to function well. I'm not suggesting that anyone can work totally without pressure—sometimes, that is just what is needed to get the job done, but a positive atmosphere is very important. Both boss and worker need to feel vital, connected and appreciated. When this state is achieved everything else hums along. There are workplaces where people contribute with love, and there are workplaces where self-serving attitudes and mean, small minds poison the creative fires. There is no comparison between the two.

Consider the following excerpt on work from Kahlil Gibran in his book *The Prophet*:

Then a ploughman said, Speak to us of Work.
And he answered, saying:
You work that you may keep pace with the earth and the soul of the earth.
For to be idle is to become a stranger unto the seasons, and to step out of life's procession that marches in majesty and proud submission towards the infinite.

When you work you are a flute through whose heart the whispering of the hours turns to music.
Which of you would be a reed, dumb and silent, when all else sings together in unison?

Always you have been told that work is a curse and labour a misfortune.
But I say to you that when you work you fulfil a part of earth's furthest dream, assigned to you when that dream was born,
And in keeping yourself with labour you are in truth loving life,
And to love life through labour is to be intimate with life's inmost secret.

But if you in your pain call birth an affliction and the support of the flesh a curse written upon your brow, then I answer that naught but the sweat of your brow shall wash away that which is written.

You have been told also that life is darkness, and in your weariness you echo what was said by the weary.
And I say that life is indeed darkness save when there is urge,
And all urge is blind save when there is knowledge.
And all knowledge is vain save when there is work,
And all work is empty save when there is love;
And when you work with love you bind yourself to yourself, and to one another, and to God.

Any of the following can and usually will create stress if continued over a long period:

- the wrong person in the wrong job.
- poor work attitudes (i.e. employees only concerned about breaks, holidays, benefits, etc.).
- boss who is a poor leader.
- unhappy work environment.
- positive feedback does not flow from boss to employee and vice versa.
- boss or employee feeling frustrated with roles.

If you identify with any or all of the above, then commit yourself to change. If you know that you're in a job that is wrong for you, then have the courage to look for another one. You will be doing yourself and the boss a favour in the long run. If you are a boss and you hate it, you may work better in a position where you take orders instead of giving them.

So none of the above applies, but you still feel stressed at work? Chances are your stress is unrelated to your job, but is manifesting itself there because you feel unable to cope generally. You are making more mistakes than usual; you are irritable with yourself and your workmates; you are tired all the time even though you go to bed early every night and are not going out much or drinking too much alcohol. You hate feeling like this, and you don't know how to stop it. Stressed people commonly complain of poor sleep and loss of appetite. Temper tantrums are frequent. The step to alcohol, drug-taking, violence and even crime is not a big one.

I am not attributing all of the evils of the world to stress. Stress is only a symptom and, as such, can be dealt with only after the root cause is unearthed.

Identifying your stress

What can you do about stress? First and foremost, identify the type of stress from which you are suffering. The underlying cause will take a little more effort and time—don't expect miracles all at once.

Ready? Armed with your pen? Mark off which of the following problems are your particular demon:

■ unresolved childhood experience.
■ a relationship with which you've never been able to deal.
■ a specific event or situation in your life.
■ a current relationship difficulty.
■ something doesn't 'fit' about your professional life.
■ being physically unfit (this one is relatively easy to fix as it can be identified and measured accurately, and many courses of action are open).
■ a learned pattern of negative thinking that is causing depression and, possibly, inertia.
■ a lifestyle that is out of balance.

Now that you have considered this list, your path is much clearer: you now know what stressful things irk you the most and in what area of your life. You are on your way to a happier lifestyle.

I'm going to work through these seven 'paths of pain' and help you start eliminating the stressful centre of your unhappiness. Is your stress physical, emotional, or professional? (See earlier in the chapter for professional stress.)

As an additional exercise you may wish to assess your personal stress with the following commonly used rating system.

Just tick off any of the twenty-four situations in this list which has happened to you in the past six months and add up the numbers to find your personal stress rating and what your score means.

• Your husband or wife dies	*100*
• Your marriage breaks up	*70*
• Your mother or father dies	*60*
• You fall seriously ill	*50*
• You get married	*50*
• You get fired	*45*
• Someone in the family is ill	*40*

9

- There's a baby on the way — *40*
- There's a new baby — *40*
- You've got sex problems — *40*
- You change your job or get promoted — *35*
- You take out a big loan/mortgage — *30*
- You're arguing with your partner — *30*
- The kids leave home — *30*
- You have problems with in-laws — *30*
- You achieve a personal ambition — *25*
- You move house — *25*
- Your working hours change — *20*
- You buy something on credit — *15*
- You go on a diet — *15*
- You get a speeding ticket — *15*
- You go on vacation — *15*
- You throw a big party — *10*
- You saw *Psycho* on TV — *10*

WHAT YOUR SCORE MEANS

If you've scored less than 150 you can probably cope with the stress and strain of your life quite well at the moment.

Scores between 150 and 400 indicate that you're in danger of going down with some stress-related illness if you're not careful. You need to reduce the stress in your life and learn to handle it better.

If you scored more than 400 you may already be showing signs of some form of stress-related illness. You might feel tired all the time, find it hard to sleep, get irritable a lot or have gone off lovemaking.

Whatever your score, don't panic. You can make yourself better by learning to handle all that stress.

Physical stress

Physical stress is, at least, more straightforward. Look at the following:

■ daily diet.
■ quality of sleep, rather than number of hours slept.
■ lifestyle habits, such as pleasure in all current relationships.
■ moderation in activities like smoking and alcohol consumption.
■ balance in your life—are you a workaholic or do you find yourself thinking unduly about sex or having a good time?

If your diet is poor, you can consult a physician or dietitian or simply buy some books on nutrition. Reasonable exercise should be taken three to five times a week and more if possible. The two forms of exercise I usually recommend to my stressed clients are walking and swimming. They are both gentle, can be taken at one's own pace, and, most important, are therapeutic for mind as well as body. They're also inexpensive! Once a certain level of fitness is reached, more strenuous programmes such as jogging or aerobics can be started. Starting slowly with exercise and building up is very important. Overtaxing defeats the whole point of combating stress!

Next is quality of sleep—it is important that you never take drugs for sleeping. Insomnia is most commonly a direct result of an anxious mind, which is created by, yes, you guessed it . . . *stress.* Get rid of the stress, and you will no longer lie awake at night worrying about what you have to do the next day or what you did wrong today. You will be relaxed enough to know that everything will come right, that worry is debilitating and totally self-defeating. You won't want to worry and, what's more, you won't allow it to invade your mind when you are trying to do something beautiful for yourself—drift into soothing, natural sleep, one of our greatest gifts.

More immediate measures include the good old glass of warm milk, some mild exercise before going to bed, or some people say nothing works like lovemaking. Whatever method you choose, there's still always going to be that moment when it is dark, the person you are with is asleep, and you feel wide awake. That is the time when you need to relax instead of tensing. Clear your mind. When you've learned that, your lids will start getting heavy; you'll snuggle under the covers and nature will take over. Sleep is always most elusive when the need for it is urgent. An expectation of insomnia will almost guarantee a sleepless night.

When you are sleeping for only a few hours a night, you will wake feeling tired if your sleep is fitful or dream-ridden. Also, stress itself makes you feel constantly fatigued whether or not you are sleeping properly.

Being moderate in the indulgence of such things as alcohol, cigarettes, sex, socialising, food and thinking of those things is commonsense. You cannot expect your mind and body to function healthily if you overload them with narcotics or chemicals and burn them out with overexertion. No one suggests that you give up the things you enjoy. In fact, that would probably cause you the most stress of all! Balance is the key. Ask yourself every day: am I doing too much of any one thing? Can I cut back or introduce something I do not do enough of or at all?

A good test of this is to attempt to feel satisfied. In every twenty-four-hour period, you need these four areas satisfied: emotional, intellectual, spiritual and physical. The self-questioning will ensure that at least your thinking is balanced. You may not be able to adhere to this checklist every day, but you won't stray too far away from it as long as you remind yourself daily. Getting out of balance is a sure way to allow stress into your life. Take the simple precautions I suggest, and stop the problem growing like a piece of knitting. If your relationships are not giving you pleasure, are you in the wrong ones or even unable to enjoy being happy? A look at the emotional causes of stress will provide some of the answers.

Emotional stress

The personality of the individual as created by genetic design and upbringing has much to do with emotional fortitude. Psychologists have argued for decades about the nature/nurture conflict. My feeling is that we come into this world with our basic natures stamped on us, but the critical early years help to form the adult person. Those first growing and learning years make the difference between whether we become weak or strong, achieve or stagnate, are positive about ourselves or negative. That puts a great deal of responsibility on parents who are, after all, only human. They not only have to feed, clothe and shelter their children, they are also expected to form happy, balanced individuals. No wonder so many appear to fail. It

is my task to help the products of parents' 'failures' to understand
the interaction between themselves and their families—the
complex relationships of mother to daughter, father to son,
sibling to sibling. The ambivalence of so much family love
makes a challenge for any student of human behaviour.

Stress first sinks its roots in all of those painful family
exchanges, tantrums, frustrations, quarrels and, perhaps worst
of all, silences. Much of adult stress of the emotional variety
began in unexpressed childhood anger. The child learns to play
the accepted game: Mummy shouts, and I stay silent even though
I haven't done anything. Any attempt to argue is met with
disapproval. Resentment has planted its seed.

One recent client, Sue, was worried about not being assertive
enough. She was the only child in her family and was very
strongly under the influence of her mother. After a series of
unhappy marriages, she was now married to a man that her
mother disapproved of.

Sue's mother subsequently died and left her full of unresolved
anger and guilt: anger because of never being allowed to speak
up as a child and still, after all this time, feeling that she did
not have her mother's approval; and guilt for the same reasons!
In addition, she carried the irrational guilts of marrying against
her mother's wishes and being alive in the face of her mother's
death.

These truths were slowly unearthed. One key image that kept
returning was of her mother often closing herself into her
bedroom and isolating herself from her child. Each time she
did this, she said she was disappointed or upset with the child.
Can the effect of such withdrawal on a little girl really be
fathomed? Such incidents are never forgotten; they are stored
away for later in life to serve as fuel for the fires of stress.

The smallest and largest incidents are stored away in this
manner. The more sensitive the child, the more is put away
for future reference. Of course, these are not conscious decisions,
and on the surface the child may seem perfectly happy. In fact,
the extrovert child who is constantly in trouble will probably
have fewer later problems. 'Naughty' children are getting their
revenge now!

The immediate solution is to clean out your emotional
cupboards. You need to look honestly and candidly at the past.

It is not necessarily a fearful journey, even though some may have horror tales to tell of violent parents or sexual abuse or emotional deprivation. Thankfully these experiences are still the exception and most people just remember lots of 'little' pains.

Unfortunately, though, these pains are remembered with the logical mind of an adult. You have to remind yourself that those miniature tragedies were experienced through the vulnerability of a child's mind. Thus, the grown-up rationale does not realistically apply. For instance, I have often heard the words, 'I didn't have it so bad really. Lots of kids I knew got kicked around a lot worse than I did.' People desperately need to believe that their childhood was good. Perhaps it's the last bastion of illusion left to us. Instead, you need to say, 'When such and such happened, it was awful. It really frightened me.'

I remember an incident when I was seven of being unable to get out of a public toilet because I couldn't work the lock on the door. All the years I was growing up, this incident was often mentioned and laughed about in my family circle. As an adult, I can laugh and say, 'Wasn't that silly?', but I still remember the panic and terror of that seven-year-old child who was me. If you do not look frankly at your own particular box of demons, they will continue to haunt you. The worst fears are those with no name—identify them and get happy!

In your journey backwards, you may uncover one especially unpleasant memory not previously recalled. Don't be afraid; it's all part of your psychological spring-cleaning. If you feel it is getting out of hand, you should enlist the help of a professional. If you are feeling very stressed you will need some guidance in such a quest anyway, as you may find it difficult separating the wheat from the chaff alone.

Stress, however, is not always created in the past. It could spring from a source occurring since adulthood—a very unhappy, emotional experience that is left unresolved. People who come out of broken relationships with dignity and love, for instance, have little to resolve. They can accept the breakdown of something they once had without shame or guilt. But most divorces and breakups are conducted in an atmosphere of anything but dignity and love. In these cases, there can be a legacy of bitterness and resentment.

Most societies do not encourage the expression of anger,

regarding it as antisocial behaviour. Children are rarely taught to deal constructively with anger; when a child shows anger in any form, a parent is usually immediate in negative response. Remarks such as, 'Don't show your temper to me, young lady' are common. Soon you learn that anger brings disapproval. When you grow up, things frustrate and anger you every day, and you become very efficient at disguising it. Notice there is a distinction between *anger* and *temper*. A well-balanced person does not usually lose their temper, which is one of the first lessons learnt in assertiveness training. Feeling a healthy, angry reaction at injustice or cruelty or indifference is surely part of being human. Without guilt, this normal reaction can be expressed positively—but imagine how much emotional tension is built up every time anger is hidden.

Take the example of the fellow just roundly told off by his boss for something that was not his fault. The unfairness of it! This fellow is bristling with anger, but dare not say anything for fear of losing his job. Honesty is not overly popular in modern society! Therefore, he goes home and he takes it out on his wife at the first opportunity. This reaction causes tension at home, and further stress is created. The chain, or hierarchy of anger can go on. The wife who was yelled at scolds the little boy who in turn kicks the dog. This scenario is the not uncommon extreme of misplaced anger.

The lesson from this story is to deal with the principal issues. If you try to resolve your pain and frustration by dealing with anything other than the direct cause, you will compound the problem instead of solving it.

Many emotions cause tension, yet emotions are an essential and important part of living. We should try to enjoy our emotional life while minimising the stress caused by tension.

Communication

Without doubt, the skill everyone needs most to master is communication. This word vies with 'stress' for being one of the most overworked words in modern language (next to 'sex' and 'love'). Everyone says they know how important it is to communicate well, but they either don't know how to communicate properly or don't really understand how vital it is. So what is good communication, and how can it be achieved?

Communicating within personal relationships is far more difficult than any other interaction—the adage 'familiarity breeds contempt' holds true. The more sure you are of your ground, the more likely you are to take liberties. Things you would never say to a stranger or friend, out of fear of disapproval or any negative response, you will direct at a spouse or lover because we assume that person will take it. As a result of this familiarity and yet in contradiction of it, you find that the more vulnerable you are in a given situation, the more inclined you are to be heavy-handed and botch things up. You are so busy making sure you do not get hurt that you quite often hurt the very person from whom you are trying to protect yourself!

Then there are the times when you care a lot about something, and you stand to lose if you do not succeed with what you are trying to achieve, for example, if there is a difficult issue you must discuss with someone close to you. You know how important it is that you get the words right, so there is extra pressure on your performance.

Communication is also vital in the workplace and can be just as sensitive as in personal relationships. Many problems can be prevented from escalating just by the anticipation of a potential crisis and a follow-up of communication. How many office problems can you think of that are a direct result of someone not speaking up?

Consider the junior assistant who thinks his shift is unfair, but fails to speak up, when all the time there was a good reason for asking him to take two evening shifts in a row. What about the secretary who thinks her boss is not happy with her work because he never praises her, the clerk who failed to mention that copier paper was running low and when it ran out and another worker was blamed, was too afraid to speak up. There are endless examples. Overstating is better than assuming something does not need saying, like the husband who assumed his wife knew she was beautiful but never told her so, until she ran off with another man because, 'He says I am beautiful!'

Of course, there are many ways to communicate without actually speaking. Non-verbal communication and body language can convey as much, if not more, than speech. Think of all the unspoken signals we give in everyday living that are understood by all people in the same culture—waving, laughing, winking and poking out a tongue. A smile means the same thing throughout the world.

You need awareness of your effect on people to become a truly good communicator. The greatest orators and those who have moved history through the centuries have all been people who possess what is termed 'charisma', a peculiar type of charm that reaches out to people and surpasses the normal barriers of language, physical attributes, culture and prejudice. A truly charismatic person could be speaking in a language no one in the audience shared, but that person would be understood. You and I may not be able to reach such exalted heights of delivery, but we can all learn to speak more effectively.

There are several important aspects to communicating well:

1. The quality of the voice is important. No one wants to listen to an unpleasant, non-melodious pitch or a voice too loud or too soft.
2. Be sure of what you want to say. Good communication comes from confidence in your own opinion and in the way you express your ideas.
3. Do not hog the conversation. A tasteful conversationalist has speech that is totally natural and effortless.
4. Listening is essential. It is not only polite and assures an audience for you, but should show you are genuinely interested in what the other person says.
5. Be aware of the signals you are giving out while you converse.
6. Be sure of your facts, and do not be beaten down by a more aggressive speaker. Confidence emerges quietly and unhurriedly.
7. Be convinced of the important nature of communication. Communication is especially vital in today's world when life moves faster than ever before, and the possibilities for misunderstanding are great.

Why is it essential that you master the art of communication?

■ there is a lack of cohesiveness in society, within personal interactions, compared to the simpler times of a world before wars, man landing on the moon, computers and nuclear weapons.

■ human beings are still interdependent and must learn to coexist in the world. Communication is a powerful tool for this task and for the reduction of stress at all levels of debate from domestic to political.

■ you need to make yourself understood even to the most basic degree.

■ communication reduces emotional isolation.

■ it is a necessary skill in many occupations.

■ it can make the difference between success and failure in personal relationships.

■ it can and does reduce stress between people.

Many centuries ago, John Donne said, 'No man is an island, unto itself.' If this still holds true, then you must bridge the gaps in whatever ways you can.

Stress prevention is extremely important and, as already shown, communication can only help. Other helpful aids, as has been shown, are personal identity, assertiveness, and self-esteem. Honesty with yourself and those around you is paramount. Do not be afraid to ask for what you want in life, accept failure, and take responsibility for your own actions. All these things are essential, but it is taking the first step that is the hardest part.

Sincerely wanting to improve will give you the necessary motivation. Make a plan, have a mental deadline, then set that amount of time aside. Couples wishing to reduce stress in their relationship, for instance, should make a specific time for each other and stick to it. It will become second nature to talk about the day's activities and share thoughts, feelings, dreams, disappointments and so forth. If you have problems in your job, discuss them with your partner and then push them from your mind—if you are thinking about business in your leisure hours, your life is out of balance.

Several areas of gratification and expression are needed in your daily life. Decide what your cut-off point will be, and make sure you adhere to it. If you wish to finish working on weekdays at 6 pm, give yourself a mechanical reminder around that time every day, such as a pep talk or a signal like a cup of coffee, then adhere to the following rules: no business talk after that time; no phone calls; no thinking about work decisions or problems. It is much easier to relax the body than the mind, so it is no good watching television if your mind is back at the office or at a meeting scheduled for the next day. Relaxation is hard to achieve, which may seem like a contradiction in terms, but you often have to work at being relaxed! Once you have learned the art, you can relax anywhere and at any time; you do not need to be on holidays, or a far away island or a sunny beach. Wouldn't that be wonderful? You can be calm and confident whether in the boardroom, the bedroom, or on the sports field.

Finally, don't let small problems build up; speak up before a molehill becomes a mountain. After trying some or all of these suggestions, you should be able to alleviate some of the stress in your life. If not, you may need some formal methods such as relaxation therapy, yoga, intensive programmes of exercise, meditation and so forth. There are many excellent books available on each of these disciplines (see Chapter Ten).

Deep breathing

The deep breathing technique is very helpful and can be practised by anyone wishing to feel calmer. A simple method is to sit or lie in a darkened room and concentrate just on breathing in and out. At first it will be difficult to sit for any length of time. With perseverance, the time can gradually be lengthened. The beauty of this technique is that it can be employed *at the point* of stress. I have found it helpful to impotent men in abating their feelings of anxiety prior to intercourse, and very effective for keeping a fiery temper in check or in coping with sudden bursts of pressure in the office, home, or behind the wheel of a car (where the true demon in each of us is undeniably aroused!).

Positive stress

Stress can be harnessed as a positive force when used in a beneficial way. Athletes, dancers and actors could not perform with any conviction if they were totally without stress. Activating the release of adrenalin is necessary to generate excitement and a high level of expression and achievement. A stress response causes adrenalin production, which stimulates increased respiration and heart rate. This increased energy can be used to function as a friend.

Sports psychologists help athletes of all kinds to build winning mentalities from the 'hype' they feel when they are nervous before a race or game. You can use this approach to help yourself in everyday life, rather than tuning in only to stress's negative signals. Let stress give you the winning edge. Instead of thinking, 'I've got so much to do, I can't get it all done', let the pressure stimulate you to do better and more efficient work. This can happen only if you have a positive mental attitude, good self-esteem and are physically fit. No single piece of improvement can operate in isolation. It is all interconnected, and you have to commit yourself to a total package of self-love and nurturing. You can have a life in which no negativity is tolerated, and you care enough for yourself to make life enjoyable instead of a struggle.

Time management

One method of stress reduction should be mentioned separately because of its importance, and that is *time management*. Not knowing how to manage your time each day and allotting it to the many and varied tasks that need your attention causes stress.

A simple plan is all you need. The use of a diary as a record of what needs to be done, what has been completed, appointments, accounts due, people to see, ideas you want to pursue and more is very helpful. Whichever method works for you is the best one, but the trick is to keep it basic. Some people think that if they use an elaborate system, they will achieve more, whereas the opposite is true. Having a tidy area in which to work is also essential. You must be able to keep documents, files and information of any kind available and easy to locate. Keep your work requirements in order; do not allow your affairs to become chaotic. 'Fixing it up later' is time-consuming and unnecessary.

Firmness with others is sometimes imperative. Say 'No' when you set aside time for work and are interrupted. If you are a slave to other's desires, you will never be able to set goals for yourself and stick to them, especially if deadlines are involved.

Now that you understand the true nature of stress and the strategies needed to reduce its effects on your life, the significance of the presence of stress in the lives of women today can be looked at. Women experience stress whether they work at home, out in the community, are bringing up children on their own, or are fiercely independent. In the next chapter you will start on the most interesting and demanding journey of all—into yourself. But first, to sum up, here are some mechanisms you can employ to reduce stress in a practical way:

- consciously separate work and leisure time.
- give yourself cushions of time during your daily schedule.
- be aware of stressful areas in your life that need attention.
- isolate people and situations that aggravate stress levels.
- exercise regularly.
- be aware of needs and priorities.
- seek balance and proportion in things.
- set limits on your giving and make necessary adjustments and choices.
- give yourself rewards at the end of the day or when you feel you have accomplished something special.
- use communication effectively to reduce stress.
- employ the formal strategies of relaxation, therapy and stress management if necessary.
- make plans and goals that are realistic and aid progress.
- adopt a time management plan and stick to it.

AFFIRMATIONS

I am what I am becoming.
Every day in every way, I'm getting better and better.
I am willing to release the patterns that have created limitations in my life.
My good comes from everywhere and everyone.

Chapter Two

Women and health

Women experience stress in different ways to men for a number of reasons: females are biologically different, live life from a female perspective learned from birth and function emotionally and psychologically in a uniquely female way. At first glance, this discussion may seem blatantly sexist: what happened to the neutral 'person' that is acknowledged today? That person exists in the realms of fiction. There are irrefutable differences between men and women that should be recognised and treasured. As the French say, *Vive la différence!*

The degree of difference is not important, what is important is the fact that everybody is not the same. Women do not necessarily suffer more stress or find coping with it harder. Men and women can find themselves equally ravaged with this modern disease. Factors of temperament, lifestyle, education, socioeconomic status, upbringing, occupation, quality of relationships and so on need considering. Why then is it worth looking specifically at women and stress? Women have their own history and story to tell in all civilisations and cultures. In Western countries, there has been a long and sometimes bitter struggle for recognition and respect. With the advent of women's liberation, much progress has been made. Some women would say, 'too little, too late', but scores of women have stood up with pride for the right to be different, and yet have been treated the same. Why would we want to be just 'persons'?

Until women love who they are and stop trying to compete with men as if males belong to a different species, they cannot expect to make the best of themelves. Women have a right to equal opportunities to prove themselves, such as in the workplace, but beyond that equality is a myth. Are all men equal? Of course they are not, nor women, nor any two people. So, in my opinion women should stop playing semantics and get on with the business of being the best individuals they can. There are plenty of women out there proving themselves everyday, working alongside men with equal competence, doing so-called 'men's jobs', and holding down senior positions in all arenas of society, not to mention the mothers and homemakers who choose to work in their homes rearing the citizens of tomorrow.

Why do women feel stress differently in this day and age? Biological considerations include these exclusive functions of women: pregnancy and childbirth; menstruation; menopause and the cessation of menstruation; breastfeeding, and such phenomena as breast cancer, cancer of the cervix, postnatal depression, and premenstrual tension.

These biological differences will be examined in detail in later chapters. Apart from the obvious external features exclusive to women, our whole physical structure is unique and brings about a set of complex and interwoven behaviours. These behaviours can cause their own special brands of stress.

Life from a female perspective

From the moment of birth and even earlier, a baby is gendertyped. A boy must have blue booties knitted for him and a girl pink and so on. When the child is born, this societal influence continues: children are dressed according to gender and certain toys and games are considered suitable for each one. Woe betide any nonconformist relative who turns up with a truck for a girl or a doll for a boy!

Some enlightened parents might consider these remarks exaggerated, but if a current survey were taken, how many 'modern' families would prove them wrong? Even today parents expect children to fit predetermined sex roles. Playing safe is better than listening to child development experts. Therefore, most girls grow up in an atmosphere of role expectation and conditioned behaviour. At school they are expected to play 'girls' sports' and study 'soft' subjects like language, history, business skills and home economics. Those expectations are fine for girls wanting to enter professions requiring these options, but are girls discouraged if they wish to take up metalwork or chemistry? (There was no such disadvantage when I was in high school. As it was a girls' college, however, perhaps we enjoyed more freedom of choice.)

More and more, women are pushing out the boundaries of their worlds and refusing to live with arbitrary limitations. There is no denying that here is another potential stress trap—how to get out from under the labels and restrictions that abound. By the time a young woman leaves school for tertiary study or the workplace, she is acutely aware that carving a path of achievement for herself means first encountering and conquering the demons of prejudice and suspicion surrounding her. She is caught in a paradox: how to be assertive enough to win without succumbing to the prejudice and suspicion.

A woman's emotional life and psychological make-up are also unique. This uniqueness is partly due to the biological differences that have already been discussed, but is due also to such matters as attitude, purpose, desires, interaction with others and choices—all very subjective and intangible yet they have a significant bearing on a woman's day to day life. General belief holds that women are more emotional than men, that women relate better to babies and small children, and that they operate more on instinct than logic.

For each true assumption, hundreds of women provide exceptions, but some generalisations must be made and conclusions drawn if anything at all is to be said in this book. I will look at many examples of female lives, examine the reality of being a woman in the latter half of the twentieth century and, hopefully, come to understand why women cannot experience stress as men do, just as they feel differently about life, death, sex, marriage, children, work and every other major issue. Now you know why there is the expression, 'the battle of the sexes'. The challenge is to live together in harmony, minimise the differences, and respect each other. That is the premise for this book; the focus will be on the female perspective and its link to stress.

How women experience stress

For women today, the sources of stress are essentially the same as those faced by men. The differences come into focus when the way in which it is felt and the methods of coping are examined. As was seen in the first chapter, the three main areas of human existence that are vulnerable to stress are: physical, emotional, and work-related.

Physical stress

How can specific physical and biological realities cause stress in women? If stress is not managed or there is not an awareness about levels of stress (just as we are now conscious of blood pressure and cholesterol), it simply gets out of control.

The rampant misunderstanding about stress makes the average person confused when attempting self-monitoring or seeking professional advice. You hear the lines: 'Everyone suffers from it', 'There is nothing you can do', and 'It's just the times we live in'. All of these lines are common catchcries in conversations about stress. Women are particularly prone to playing down stress levels and minimising symptoms.

Carol was in a highly stressed state. Despite the threat of losing a hard-earned pension, she had walked out of a government job only a matter of months before retirement because she could no longer endure the levels of stress under which she worked and lived. To make matters worse, her former department then wanted to deny her her pension entitlements. No question of such an action would have occurred had Carol contracted a disease or injured a limb, but because stress is difficult to prove it is often misjudged and viewed with suspicion.

Women and men are not living with any more stress today than they were in earlier periods of history but when roles are discussed later, it will be seen that much more is expected of women today. Once it was enough just to 'be'; now one must show productivity, results and achievement every day. Much more must be crammed into sixteen or so waking hours. Therefore, the basic matters of fatigue and stamina must be dealt with. Women are taught at an early age to cope, not to make a fuss. So they suffer in silence, pretending they don't feel irritable, tired, or tense. There are the chronic whiners, the hypochondriacs of the stress world, but in the main women get on with it. Women with children are often simply too pre-occupied to nurture themselves and give themselves adequate periods of rest and relaxation.

Men generally talk more about the pressure they work under and the responsibilities they have that create stress. Pressure is almost a source of pride to them. Many of them even insist they need high levels of stress around them in order to do their best work! That view is very limited and guaranteed to bring disaster in the long-term.

Emotional stress

The reasons for emotional stress in a woman's life are twofold: having to deal with her own identity, ambitions, and needs while coping with the demands of people and events; and all the various relationships that constitute her world, particularly the personal ones. They are the ones with which this section is concerned.

Much of the book will be examining the emotional pressures on women and how they compete for attention in a woman's busy schedule. It will also show that those women who feel unfulfilled suffer just as much stress, but of a different kind.

Work-related stress

'Work' has many different meanings for women, but it is the relationship of work to role that evokes the stress. For instance, a woman who is a working mother really wears about six hats through her daily business: wife, mother, employee, housekeeper, workmate and then her sundry personal roles such as daughter, friend, sister, etc. Each role requires a prescribed set of behaviours and creates its own stress potential. In the best of all possible worlds, women would be able to juggle all their duties, responsibilities and personal interests with no wear and tear to the psyche or the body, but in the real world the damage can be substantial if moderation and stress management is not practised. Even a woman with only one major role, say careerist, has to keep on her toes at least as much as her male counterpart. She has to endure the criticisms and sanctions of a society only too ready to find fault should she break any of its mores or fail in its expectations of her.

A very interesting case in point is that of the former Sarah Ferguson, now Duchess of York. By anyone's standards, she is a modern woman with many roles to fulfil and many obligations and responsibilities. When her first child was only a few weeks old, she had to leave it because of a conflicting set of demands on her time: she had to tour Australia with her husband, Prince Andrew.

So we see three distinct roles brought into play: wife, mother and public person. Placed in that dilemma she was forced to make certain choices, as we all are every day. The baby was left at home, and the parents went on with their professional and public duties. This decision was accepted grudgingly by the opinion-makers and general public, but a hue and cry went up when the Duchess of York extended her trip to have more time with her husband, which was perfectly understandable for a young, married woman. People immediately judged her decision to be a choice in favour of her husband and against her child. What they found most infuriating was the fact that she failed to look at all repentant or ashamed! Having taken her stand, she made the best of the situation. She did her job fully and with good cheer. If she had looked miserable and red-eyed, missing her baby and whining about it, she would have had the world's mothers on her side. Most of the criticism and mock horror came from women. Imagining themselves in the same position, they chose to believe that they would do the accepted thing, the idealistic action, no matter what the personal cost.

Now you must add self-delusion to your ever growing list of stress traps! Women are often not supportive of other women. In striving to have it all, a race of superwomen has been created, who flirt with dangerous levels of stress every day. You need to learn to take it easier on yourself and those around you. Stress manifests itself in a woman's life in several major ways and a thousand minor ways. The trick is to be aware of the danger signals and monitor the levels in order to reduce the negative effects.

The symptoms outlined in the first chapter apply for any woman who is unsure if she is suffering from the negative effects of stress. You should ask yourself if you are neglecting or overloading any part of your life. Does each day feel comfortable or does it feel like a strain?

Are you balancing your emotional, physical, intellectual, spiritual, or relationship needs? Commonsense and an honest approach will supply most of the answers you require. Professional or medical intervention should only be necessary if stress problems have been neglected over a long period of time and the cumulative effects are severe. Following are five associated conditions that are linked to stress, but which also have their own specific descriptions and consequences.

1. Depression.
2. Anxiety.
3. Fears and phobias.
4. Addiction.
5. Anger and violence.

Depression

In a way, stress and depression are opposites. Stress is a feeling of heightened experience; depression, of course, is one of being 'down', or low and flat—hence the word itself, 'depression'. Their common ground is their effects on ordinary individuals through their health and the way they function in their lives. Also, they both have discernible and definite symptoms. Those symptoms caused by stress tend to be more subtle and easily disguised. On the other hand, there is not much doubt when you see a depressed person. Picture a woman slumped over, with her head down like a marionette whose strings are cut. Her eyes have a glazed, far-off appearance; her speech is probably in a monotone. When faced with a person in this state, there is an inclination to shake her. She gives the appearance of being sleepy or inattentive, but this is no self-pitying performance for sympathy. There is a world of difference between feeling a bit 'blue', which everyone feels at times, and the type of condition I have described here. Chronic depression is crippling and debilitating.

The full truth of the differences came to me on one of the rare, depressive days that I have. I was experiencing all the usual unpleasant feelings and, by afternoon, was ready to give up on the day altogether. I sat outside in the garden, normally my sure-fire cure for anything, but still felt no better. A thought came clearly into my mind that I could pull myself out of the depression if I really wanted. As quick as a wink, the answer came back to me, 'But I don't want to!' I was enjoying it! How can being miserable be enjoyable? A colleague once said that no one is ever anxious, depressed, worried, or sad without reward. There has to be a kick from even the most negative behaviour. Otherwise, we simply would not do it—something to think about, isn't it? Of course this relatively innocent type of depression and the kind that is a psychological problem requiring professional treatment should be easily distinguished.

Before any behavioural change can be effected, there must be awareness and then desire. The 'how to' part comes later in an infinite number of ways. No book or therapist can help until a commitment is made by the individual seeking the change. Often, when I have worked with couples, one partner is only present for the sake of the other. At times, the unwilling person is openly hostile or sullen; other times, the person appears co-operative but it is clear that conciliation in the heart is missing—they are only going through the motions. Committing to change is as demanding as learning to play a musical instrument or studying a foreign language.

Many people seem to think that change is a matter of luck or that a person is born a good communicator, or confident, or secure. While some of these factors are innate, many are also learned behaviours (as examined in subsequent chapters). The learned behaviour can be unlearned—luck has little to do with it, motivation much. Unlearning poor behaviour is a goal that needs determination and stamina for success.

How do you fight apathy, discouragement, laziness and setbacks? How do you give yourself the best chance possible? In the case of depression, the enemy is the very nature of depression. One of its symptoms is lethargy. So, asking a depressed person to stop being depressed or 'buck up' or 'snap out of it' is like asking a sleeping person to recite the alphabet. It is illogical.

There are many techniques for stemming the tide of anger, anxiety, or a stress attack, but these fail with depression. In minor cases, the best defence is no defence. Give yourself an emotional day off. Indulge yourself. Apart from a long, slow chocolate bar, there is nothing so delicious as a good cry— especially when there is absolutely no reason for it! The fact that you want to cry is reason enough. Self-pity and hurling abuse at nothing at all are fun, too. The rather facetious message here is that most problems get worse because people take them far too seriously. Humour is a wonderful cure, and laughing at yourself is probably the best medicine of all. The next time you are depressed, go with it. You will not know you are having fun until it is over, but I guarantee the depression will not last. Just change your attitude about it and turn it from one of the bad guys into simply one mood in an endless spectrum of human emotions and experiences. Again these suggestions do not apply to patients with depressive illnesses or other psychiatric conditions. That is not the context in which depression is being discussed within this book.

What if you feel the incidence of depression in your life is excessive? What if it is becoming a habit or even a security blanket? If you get rid of your depression, what will you have?' Depression can become a friend not easily surrendered. Once the desire to change is established, the next step is setting a definite goal and a time limit for achieving that goal. Make a specific plan and keep the goal realistic. Plan for possible delays and setbacks, but ultimate success.

Two friends and I were speaking about achievement. One said that she tended not to see things through because of all the hurdles in her path. My formula for goal-reaching lies in the fact that I see the finished task, not the hurdles in between. Rethink your concept of failure. A bad day is a bad day. Why let it become two bad days or a bad week? Relate this to dieting: just because you weakened today and ate two cream cakes is no excuse to eat four cakes tomorrow!

Overlooking the little failures brings the big successes. Watch out for the hidden enemy that waits in every corner. Don't be eager to taste its dull poison—the poison of negative thinking. With the slightest crisis, we are ready to toss in the towel and say it was not going to work anyway. Self-doubt and lack of hope are also strong temptations. Trust your own instincts and judgments, and listen to the wise voice in your own head.

What about the experience of depression? Some women

describe it as being in a dark hole. Some say it is being surrounded by grey. Yet another common description is that it is like a weight upon the head, thus the bowed effect. Everyone agrees it defies complete definition. There are common characteristics, but each one of us endures depression in a sad, bleak place of our own making, a place deep in the psyche. The worst thing you can do is analyse it at the time it is happening to you. While depression is running its course, it makes little sense and is uncontrollable. Trying to understand the process and its reasoning will add to the pain and cause unendurable frustration. With depression, the line of least resistance is really the best way to proceed. If there is an underlying cause that needs examination and work, that can come later.

Drugs

Anti-depressant drugs may be necessary for a short period if the depression is so severe that a woman cannot function at all. Drug therapy should be the exception rather than the rule, though. The use of medication on a long-term basis for the average person should not be condoned. I have counselled women after they have been on drugs for up to fifteen years, and are hopelessly dependent chemically and emotionally. When I suggest a weaning off, panic fills their faces as they contemplate life without a crutch.

In the grip of depression, rule number one is: do not try to find reasons or blame yourself. Any self-hatred you possess will rear its ugly head at this time, but you can resist. Remember, it is all an illusion and no more real than the joy you may have felt yesterday. It is all mercurial, wondrous in its insight into the process of life and none the more or less desirable, except in our minds. Do not lose sight of the fact that these good and bad feelings are temporary. Depression has a rather unpleasant habit of feeding on itself, so do not help it along by your fears and doubts. Simply put, going with the flow of your feelings does ward off the demons.

One of the best 'cures' is a long, brisk walk. It works for two main reasons: exercise shakes off the lethargy and being around nature is healing in itself. If the thought of a walk seems too daunting, attempt one small act. Even making yourself a cup of coffee could be the first step in retrieving what otherwise might be a lost day.

Depression is a symptom and not a cause. Depression and stress become linked in a situation where, for instance, if a woman is sufficiently stressed over a long period, she may fall into a deep and prolonged depression. Whether a result of a chronic condition or a situational crisis, depression is a side effect of a stress no longer endurable. See the checklist at the end of the chapter to help identify your needs in relation to depression. Do consult a therapist or counsellor if you feel your condition is too severe or recurring.

Anxiety

What is the difference between worry and anxiety? If you have $500 in the bank and $800 of urgent debts, your concern would be classified as 'worry'. On the other hand, if you have $800 in the bank and $500 of urgent debts and are still unhappy, you are suffering from anxiety.

Anxiety may also appear in an anonymous guise: the vague sensation of tension at certain times or in relation to particular stimuli. Some women report a sense of disorientation for no apparent reason. They may find they are suddenly being forgetful, making small mistakes, or being clumsy. Much anxiety is directly or indirectly linked to a lack of self-esteem, the feeling of not being able to perform a particular task.

Anxiety is an unnecessary worry. In my opinion, all worry is unnecessary because it does not help any situation, and can even make things worse in many cases. Following are common forms of anxiety that many women suffer.

Agoraphobia

You don't need to have heard of it to be affected by it. The worst effect of agoraphobia, or the morbid fear of being in an open space, is the inability to deal with panic attacks. Research has not shown why one woman will have an anxiety attack over an occurrence or event that another considers the most ordinary thing in the world. Many agoraphobics perspire profusely at the thought of leaving their homes, getting into a car, or entering a shopping centre. These are mighty feats to be conquered for an agoraphobic. They feel safe only within the confines of their own world, usually their place of residence. If they venture out, they prefer driving themselves as another fear is loss of control. Without warning an attack can take hold, turning the supermarket or store into enemy territory. Due to this unpredictability, a sufferer often takes the path of least resistance by just staying at home.

Agoraphobia is difficult to diagnose and treat because the symptoms are often unclear or non-specific. The condition is a relatively recent addition to the identified anxiety types. Many women have at least been afforded the relief of knowing they are not alone in this type of suffering. Severe cases may even be treated with drugs, but many women just suffer in silence.

Obsessive-compulsive behaviour syndrome

The most amazing stories have been unearthed about sufferers of this condition, whereby some women cannot leave their homes without cleaning the same spot, such as a stove top or each doorknob, dozens of times.

Jane had a strained relationship with her mother and sister, a feeling of never being good enough. The eldest child, she felt the burden of extra responsibility and expectation from her parents. These feelings formed the nucleus of the original anxiety which was given impetus by a careless remark made in a medical situation. Now the demon had a face, Jane knew how to focus her anxiety—her focus became disease, illness, germs and dirt. In her mind, these things were the enemy, and the association with obsessive cleanliness began. Jane neglected other important tasks in order to accommodate the endless wiping and scrubbing and polishing.

Why didn't she simply stop? She obviously realised her condition. The power of her fear was stronger than her desire to live a normal life. An interesting by-product of this state was that Jane was unable to reveal herself to her family and instead, kept up a pretence of being a cheerful and in-control woman. Therefore, their visits to her home were literally a nightmare requiring even more hours of cleaning after their departure. I suggested telling her family as a means of severing the original bonds of disapproval. She was not ready to consider this strategy.

All compulsive behaviour is related to anxiety. I was a compulsive list-maker motivated by a strong desire to remember everything, but I have now trained myself to be less dependent on my lists. Lists are a tool of efficiency, but should not be allowed to control you. Women can focus their anxiety on anything from food to weight to clothes to family to sex to relationships in general. Once the focus is set, it usually becomes very intense and consumes the woman's interest on a daily basis. One of the best examples of this behaviour is in relation to body size and food consumption (which will be examined in Chapter Three).

Be aware of being confined by tunnel vision—everybody is capable of this type of behaviour, but depending on personality type, some women are more vulnerable to it. This condition does not always manifest itself in actions such as list-making or excessive cleaning; in fact, it is more likely to occur as thought processes. Consider a woman preoccupied with not gaining weight. This obsession will show up in the guise of weighing food and counting calories, but the thinking behind the action is the problem. Women in high-pressure jobs and moms at home with children do not function in a vacuum. There are times of relative stability, and then days or weeks pass with routine thrown to the wind. This occurrence is all right as long as some compensation is provided for the hectic stretches. Burnout occurs when the balance is tipped one way for too long. Some women never redress this balance, the 'I'll take a break one of these days,' syndrome. I have dubbed this type of general anxiety as 'focus on one'. After I had been counselling for only a short time, I found that most people's problems involved one other person or event in their lives, and it was enlarged to accommodate the subject's need for a focus. What else is the worn-out mother-in-law syndrome?

Hate focus

Christine possessed a hate focus. People in her life took turns at being the subject of her 'hate'; it could be a stranger or a close person. After a time, the focus faded and even the reason for it became obscure. Then another target would fall under scrutiny. She found sound reasons for all of her hate focuses and believed in the emotion totally, but once it passed she held no animosity for that particular person. It was quite extraordinary. What finally stopped this behaviour was the understanding that the people Christine 'hated' were really her mother in various guises. Her anger was for her mother. She had to resolve that relationship, let go of the anger, and then the behaviour would change.

Sleeping alone

Some women may experience an abject fear of sleeping alone in a house overnight. They do not trust themselves to deal with any fearful situation that may arise. When they are helped to see that they are perfectly capable and strong in resolve, their fears dissolve. The next step is to practise not being afraid, which entails sleeping alone for one night at a time until they build up their confidence.

A friend of mine suffered from a recurring nightmare depicting a very clear face of a man killing her. This led to an unnatural fear of being alone at night and being vulnerable in bed. She was 'cured' out of the necessity of being alone with her children when her husband's work took him away. Their need and her superior ability to protect them showed her the strength she possessed. Gradually, the fear and the dream faded.

Everyone has their demons. It is a bit like carrying a tight-lidded jar, in which you are convinced there is something unspeakable. All it takes is to open the lid and let out the horror, no matter how bad it is. Then it is released and you are free of it. You must identify your horrors. Then you can release them in stages; do not expect too much of yourself at once.

Fears and phobias

Tension emanates from the personality and results from the physical aspects of stress, which then may lead to fears and phobias. Here is an interesting definition of fear:

> False
> Evidence
> Appearing
> Real

People say there is nothing to fear but fear itself, but surely there are things to be afraid of in this world. If someone came at you with a weapon would you be immune to fear and panic? Could you face the reality of a frightening situation and say, 'This is just a figment of my imagination'? Of course not, but even in the most fearful confrontation, your attitude will decide the outcome. The way you regard your position in the social hierarchy will determine how you handle yourself. If you see yourself as a victim, as powerless, you will accept defeat more easily. Ultimately, you may be overpowered. Fear will either cripple you or spur you to defend yourself.

If you truly love yourself, you would be prepared for the possibility of attack. Secure your home. Lock your car when you leave it. Perhaps learn self-defence. As with so many things, you need to decide who's the boss. Assertiveness means, as much as anything else, letting go of fear as a way of life. Psychologically, fear is not so much about events in our lives as it is about the way in which we live. If you are taught fear as a child, it becomes a habit and colours the way you view all your life events. Fear, like depression, also feeds on itself. Before long, it pervades every corner of your mind. Fear is essentially a fantasy in that it exists in the mind and not in reality. Most of the fear that you experience in everyday life is connected to the future. You put yourself under tremendous stress by imagining all the things that could go wrong. It is like being in a perpetual state of waiting to see the dentist. Once you get there, any pain you may experience can never match the anticipated torment. If there is no pain, you cheated yourself by worrying for nothing. If there is pain, you have given yourself two doses.

Phobia is a more specialised and concentrated form of fear. Like anxiety, it is focused on one particular feature of life. The agoraphobia spoken of previously is a fear of open spaces. Other common ones are claustrophobia, a fear of enclosed spaces; hydrophobia, a fear of water and especially of drowning; and arachnaphobia, fear of spiders. It would be difficult to think of anything in existence that someone, somewhere does not fear. A cute pet to one person is a horror to another.

What makes a fear a phobia? Just to dislike something, for example dogs, does not qualify. Nor is it a phobia if you were attacked by a dog as a child and now freeze every time one approaches. A phobia is an irrational fear totally out of proportion to the stimulus. There may be a concrete reason for the original fear, but a phobia is more than that.

Lucy phoned a radio show I was on and said she had an uncontrollable fear of escalators. If an elevator was out of order, she preferred carrying heavy parcels down several flights of stairs to riding the escalator. The cause was known. As a child, her father hit her if she showed any reluctance to step onto an escalator. (For a child, this would be a normal fear rather than a phobia.) Not only did he teach Lucy to fear escalators, he instilled in her the knowledge that they were forever an object to be hated and regarded with suspicion. There was only one solution for Lucy, who had what is called a developed phobia. She had to face her problem head-on. I suggested liberal doses of escalator riding, initially with a trusted companion, and eventually alone. She had to learn first-hand that escalators possess no intrinsic fear value and then conquer her fear gradually.

One of the most interesting and unusual cases concerned a woman with a phobia of vomiting. Mary had a fear that was so strong, she had not allowed herself to vomit for many years. There must have been times when she had needed to vomit, but the mind is stronger than all other compulsions. She had programmed her mind as a child not to allow herself to vomit. Her body merely obeyed. As it turned out, the trigger was a very simple and innocuous remark made by her mother when Mary was eight years old. Mary took it to heart and committed it to unconscious memory. Once she recalled this remark to her conscious mind, she was able to make new choices for herself as an adult. Rationally, she understood that vomiting is a natural process. I did not suggest Mary rush out and try to be sick, but if the biological urge came in the future, she need no longer fight it.

As well as specialised phobias, there are also general fears—those haunting ones for which there is no name. Some women live their lives in perpetual fear of everything. They are timid, passive, even dominated. If things are good in their lives, they search for flaws they can turn into problems. This exercise justifies their timorousness. This type of behaviour is usually linked to a lack of self-trust and personal identity.

Fear, doubt and worry are the enemies, make no mistake about that. If you let them have a foothold in your life, they can become a major prop. Banish them altogether. Affirm every day that you live totally without them. 'Cold turkey' is the only way, as the effects of allowing these enemies to linger are insidious. The best way to combat fear in your life is to build up your inner strength. The demon's lair is within you, and that is where the battle must be fought. Develop strength of purpose. Too many women feel at the mercy of fate instead of taking control of their lives.

Fear has a number of perceptible characteristics: accelerated heartbeat; sensation of cold; perspiring in the palms, and stiffness in the limbs. In a crisis or under attack, the onset of these signs would be instantaneous. Even thinking about a fearful event or situation can produce them. The effect is similar with stress and anxiety. One way to hinder the progress of the undesired condition is by doing breathing exercises. Deep breathing from the diaphragm will help. Even four or five deep breaths can do the trick. As the old adage goes, count to ten if you feel you are going to lose your temper, or if fear attacks you.

There is a wonderful logic in the reasons for specific behaviour patterns. In all the cases so far, this theory is in evidence. Considerable digging is often required to unearth the kernel of truth, but the simplicity of the 'answer' is, at times, quite amazing. Even if you think your actions or thoughts are bizarre, your subconscious mind has a very clear reason for them. Learning to trust this deeper part of yourself is the first stage to a marvellous relationship.

Addiction

Modern psychology has identified a number of personality types. One of them is the addictive personality. (I must emphasise that I am not fond of labels. In our instant society, people feel more comfortable with ready answers and strict descriptions. People ask questions like 'What have I got?', or 'What is wrong with me?' People think that having titles for their discomforts will make them disappear. I was always reluctant to brand a client in this way, preferring to lead them gently to a better understanding of themselves. Therefore, my description of addiction is intended to be very general and merely a guideline to understanding and acceptance.)

An addictive woman tends to look for props in life. If it is not one thing it can be another, even though it is never thought of in such blatant terms. An addictive personality becomes very good at hiding the particular prop of the moment. While some may disagree with this idea and assert that alcoholics are quite separate from gamblers, smokers and drug-users, the truth is that the addiction is irrelevant; the need is the vital factor. Certainly, addicts are very protective of the monkeys on their backs and look down on sufferers with different monkeys. There exists a 'mine is better than yours' mentality.

One alcoholic patient showed extreme pride in giving up liquor and became fiercely opposed to all drinking. She subsequently became hopelessly addicted to gambling but insisted it was a harmless hobby. There is the essential nature of the addictive personality. To those people on the outside, addictions appear sordid and humiliating. In fact, dependence can be attached to virtually anything. Too much of anything throws life out of balance. Therefore, a woman can be addicted to food, church, or her furniture! Putting all her energy into one activity to the detriment of herself and her normal schedule is placing the power and control of a woman's happiness into external hands. This action is how dependence begins.

Addictive women tend to have undefined visions of themselves. They do not know how to get what they want from life. Therefore, they rely on an outside source for comfort and pleasure. Alcohol brings oblivion; gambling is a thrill; food is wrapped up in notions of childhood security, and relationships remove the autonomy of decision.

The first stage in killing the addiction is improved self-esteem. The addicted person has to get back into the driver's seat. Assertiveness training is advisable. It should be followed by a programme of meditation and relaxation so as to undo the patterns of negative dependence that may have been established.

Shifting the focus away from the object of addiction is most important. This shift in focus can come with a widening of interests and daily activities. Addictions often begin in childhood, out of boredom. Then they grow into seemingly unbreakable habits. If the habit is pleasurable, as in the cases of sex and food, it is much harder to break. I do not use the word *control* because controlling behaviour is a short-term solution. The real solution is to *change* the behaviour.

Addiction of stress

One of the overall messages of this book is that stress is highly addictive. I have coined the term 'stressaholic' to describe a person who begins to enjoy and need the kick stress gives. A jogger can get to a point where he keeps going even though the body is tired and overworked. Withdrawal symptoms can occur when the body does not get what it expects every day. The same applies to stressaholics, except that in the case of stress, the mind and body are both engaged. Stressaholics tell themselves they need pressure to do their work. Turning off stress gets harder and harder. That is why so many women in high-pressure jobs find switching off at day's end very difficult. The only answer is, as already outlined, an arbitrary cut-off time each day after which you refuse to think about or discuss work. Working couples have the most difficult battle as often they only have the time after work to discuss business decisions.

Interestingly, the body adjusts after several hours of stress. The longer the pattern prevails, the more comfortable the feeling. Unwinding becomes more difficult as months of stress pass. Have you ever noticed that sitting still to read or watch television after a hectic period in your life is torture? You just know a hundred things need your attention. Even though you are very tired and acknowledge needing rest, you still prowl around looking for things to do. These are the conditions under which insomnia can take root. If you cannot relax for five minutes, how can you drop off to sleep?

Stress conditioning also shows up on holidays. Say you have three weeks off. You are usually tense the first week. Gradually, your body gets the message that it is okay to stop thinking. As is so commonly heard, by the time you are fully relaxed, it is time to return to work! The key to this problem is balance. Do not neglect or overemphasise any one area of your life. Prevention is better that cure any day, so don't become addicted to stress!

Anger and violence

Although later chapters will examine various emotions more closely, anger is mentioned here in the context of women's vulnerable stress areas.

Anger is a deep-seated emotion containing repressed hostility, frustration and feelings of hurt and rejection. It is usually garnered during childhood and put away along with the toys. Unfortunately, it is not easily discarded. Rather it lies in wait like a predator, choosing its moment to leap. Anger is the signpost to those feelings of hostility, frustration, hurt and rejection and must not be ignored.

Identifying the cause of an onset of anger is important. Forget the type of anger that arises because someone spills coffee on your best dress. Anger here refers to that which appears to have no root, yet plenty of substance.

Hanna had an uncontrollable anger. She said it was like being in a trance; she could barely recall her words or actions during the episodes. According to her mother, Hanna's face became distorted during the explosive part of her attack. Then she would lie down for a long while before regaining her composure. Often, she could not remember the trigger for her anger. In Hanna's case, she was a second child who had been grappling with pent-up feelings of inadequacy and resentment for years. The pain had to be exposed and all the poison released in order for healing to take place.

Violence is a direct follow-on from this pattern. The accumulated aggression explodes and targets the nearest person, animal, or object. No one is capable of hurting, wounding, or even killing someone unless they are deeply in pain.

Society spends far too much time closing gates after horses have bolted, patching up social ills instead of looking for the root problems. Violence, crime, murder and drugs are symptoms of a mass community disease called human pain. They are generated by the needs of a society out of tune with itself, unhappy and lonely. You should educate rather than placate, heal rather than repair, and love rather than punish.

DEPRESSION NOTES

1. *Factors controlling depression*

a. Stress.
b. Coping strategies.
c. Self-image.
d. Focus of the anxiety.

e. Self-generating worry.
f. Insecurity/self-doubt.

2. *Symptoms*

a. Irritability.
b. Insomnia
c. Inability to relax.
d. Inability to concentrate.
e. Crying.
f. Dependence.
g. Withdrawal.
h. Inertia/lethargy.

3. *Strategies to handle depression*

a. Action.
b. Breathing space/distancing/centring.
c. Willingness to change.
d. Faith and positive thinking.
e. Physical health.
f. Attitude.
g. Share your problem.
h. Letting go.

- Make a list of things that make you happy
- Make a list of things that make you unhappy
- Diminish the negative: emphasise the positive
- What do you want from life?
- Unhappiness, though undesirable, is still comfortable—take a chance on change.

——————— **AFFIRMATIONS** ———————

I approve of myself exactly the way I am right now.
I create my own Reality and my Reality is beautiful and abundant.
I'm now perfectly attuned to my higher purpose and the divine plan of my life.

Chapter Three

Stress and health

Experts and their research tell us that stress, too much and for too long, causes harmful effects in the body and can even bring on disease. Like so much modern information, we are bombarded with it, and it seems to make precious little difference—smokers go right on smoking; drinkers drink happily; and the citizens of most Western societies continue to eat high fat and high sodium diets. The point is that there is limited value in telling people what they should or should not do in regard to their health. A highly stressed executive, for example, will only change her lifestyle if and when she becomes gravely ill; the warning signs along the way will most likely be ignored. Therefore, you should feel it for yourself. If you already have aches and pains that are largely unexplained, make a list of them as you read. Keep a diary of them for a week. Watch how and when they relate to the stressful events in your life.

My aches and pains:

Sunday:

Monday:

Tuesday:

Wednesday:

Thursday:

Friday:

Saturday:

If your spontaneous reaction was that you have no particular physical problems, then write down your vulnerable areas of stress—in plain words, what bugs you!—and the parts of your body in which you feel the most tension. You may get headaches, be prone to backache, or suffer stomach disorders. Identifying your particular weak point will not be difficult. Then you can put it together with your stress stimuli.

Stimuli   Part of Body

Who
What
When
Where
Why
How

What I REALLY hate:

If you are prone to headaches and are living within a difficult marriage, you should note the times and onset of your headaches in conjunction with quarrels, disagreements, or even the presence of your husband. Identifying a correlation may not be easy because stress is a subtle enemy. With patience and perseverence, the process becomes easier and clearer. To simplify further, think back to any period in your life when you suffered undue amounts of stress. Did you not feel ill after it was over, or at the very least weak and debilitated? What do people usually say when they get sick, especially with a relatively minor disorder such as influenza? 'I've been very busy lately; I got myself run down.' What does 'run down' mean?

Stress attacks the body's immune system and reduces its ability to fight infection and disease. Therefore, after a long period of stress, the body is virtually wide open to attack from biological invaders. Why else would one person in a high risk category for cancer, ulcers, or heart trouble get sick while others do not? The relationship between stress and disease is well documented, but it still smacks of quackery when I suggest to a patient that her asthma or stomach-ache or sore back is directly caused by stress. A flood of protest usually follows—I think because I am saying *she* can do something about it. Most people prefer to have a pathological reason on which to blame their aches and pains. It removes the onus of responsibility.

Here is the very core of the whole health issue and the centre of the debate that rages between traditional practitioners and alternative healers. They part company on the following points:

- people should be responsible for their own health and well-being.
- prevention is better than cure.
- look beyond pathology and symptoms.
- heal with alternative cures rather than chemical drugs.
- look at diet, lifestyle and stress levels for answers as much as the more obvious physical symptoms.

It is important to add, however, that not all general practitioners in modern medicine are against these five points. Some have merged the best of new technology with the wisdom of the ages and are working effectively in this manner.

In all areas of health, particularly stress, you should be your own monitor, assessor and healer. Check the pathology first, by all means; don't assume your problem is stress. I think you really do know, though, especially once you have had the experience of stress-induced illness—if all illness is not!

Some alternative healers take the argument much further. They say the body can store emotional tension for weeks, months, or even years. This tension is responsible for aches and pains that have no apparent cause, but relate directly to the event that initially gave it birth. In other words, a remembered childhood hurt may manifest itself in an adult body as a chronic backache or sore knees, the location also offering a clue as to the identity of the cause. I say 'remembered', but very often these culprits are only echoed in the subconscious mind while the conscious mind believes the body's ailments are brought on by outside intervention such as bugs, viruses, pollen in the air, germs, or people sneezing around you. Humankind has blamed such sources for centuries, although in the days before technology and drugs, more natural cures and remedies were offered.

To return to the question asked earlier, what is the reason for unexplained woes, i.e. why does one person who is exposed to a virus get sick and another remain unaffected? A good example is smoking. A woman who smokes two packs of cigarettes a day may live to be ninety, yet a young girl who has only smoked for a few years can develop lung cancer. Of course, it can be argued that other factors come into play, genetic disposition, for instance. Yet no research has given us an answer to this intriguing question. There are still no definitive explanations or cures for many diseases, notably AIDS (Acquired Immune Deficiency Syndrome) and cancer. In the case of cancer, the progress of malignancy can be arrested, slowed, and sometimes stopped altogether. It is much more interesting to consider why some people get sick in the first place. A naturopath once told me that, in over twenty years of working with cancer, he had never seen a single case where a massive stress event had not occurred in the patient's life prior to the onset of the disease. There are also links between stress and multiple sclerosis.

The spread of stress's cause and effect is wide and covers everything from the common cold to terminal diseases. Do not wait for it to happen to you. Take control of your life and your health today.

Ever since I can remember, I thought of myself as a sickly person. From the age of fourteen years, there was not a period in my life when I did not have some health problem or crisis. I developed tuberculosis as a teenager, at the same time dealing with the usual insecurities and emotional turmoil of puberty. I was hospitalised for six months. Fortunately, I was a bright student and my studies were not adversely affected by this long absence from school. Even after I was well enough to return to school, life continued to be a cycle of medication, injections, rest, tests and, worst of all, restrictions. Besides tuberculosis, there were gynecological disorders, a chronic bladder condition, and a bad back caused by a double curvature of the spine.

People often ask me how I could be so brave at such a tender age, but the human spirit is very resilient. I simply adapted and did the best I could to be happy in the circumstances. Horrors to other children became my daily companions as did pain and discomfort. I do not tell these things to gain sympathy, but merely in order to relate the full story.

My health problems continued through high school, my early working years, and into my marriage. At the age of twenty-three, my gynecologist recommended a relatively minor operation to unblock my Fallopian tubes and possibly remove one ovary. This operation was to relieve some problems I experienced with my menstrual cycle and the fact that I was having difficulty in conceiving. Unfortunately, both ovaries and both tubes were found to be diseased and had to be removed. I was thrown into surgical menopause and would never be able to bear a child. This news was a terrible shock. Apart from that, my body had to make an enormous adjustment due to radical changes occurring in my hormonal make-up, my emotions and the very essence of my womanhood. I felt like a freak, especially when told I would no longer menstruate. Many women feel this way after a hysterectomy. Even though mine was not a full one, I went through all the self-doubt, and grieved bitterly for my lost femininity.

A friend of mine finally put it into perspective for me. She walked into my hospital room and found me crying. I told her I was upset because the operation meant no more periods, and she came back, quick as a flash with, 'Really! Where do you line up for the operation?' Nevertheless, it was many months before I found my equilibrium in this new body of mine. About a year after the operation, I was put on hormone replacement therapy and am still on it. Many studies have been made on the possible side-effects of artificial estrogen. I will say more about this topic when discussing menopause specifically. I have adapted to being permanently childless and have lived a normal life in every other way. My health problems, however, were not finished yet. Eight years after the first operation, my uterus was also removed because my doctor feared the high risk I was under for cancer of the cervix and/or uterine lining. The second major operation was much less painful and traumatic for a number of reasons, notably attitude and better general health. Afterwards, my general health actually began to improve, and the chronic bladder infections decreased.

In addition to all of this happening, I had always been prone to coughs, colds, influenza, and bronchial conditions. I simply took for granted that I would be ill for several weeks a year with one of these complaints. Sometimes they were extremely severe, necessitating lengthy absences from work which are very inconvenient for a teacher.

Are you picking up the strong messages running through my story? I perceived myself as a sick person from an early age. I expected to be ill a lot of the time and accepted illness when it came. I put up with all of the inconveniences and restrictions and pain that sickness brought without fighting back. I gave a lot of power and rights over choices to my doctors. I took whatever drugs and treatments were prescribed without question. At one stage, in desperation, I wrote in my diary, 'My body is a temple of medical experiment'.

By this time, I was getting disillusioned about the wonder of my recoveries. Yes, I often thought myself lucky to be alive, but now I wanted more. I wanted to live, not merely survive, and spent years trying every new wonder treatment that came on the market—always the non-chemical ones. I took bottles of vitamins, consulted umpteen specialists, medical and other, but nothing changed until my attitude changed. This theme is recurring in my life, although the truth of it dawned on me only very recently. The catalyst for me was a holiday in Greece during which my bladder problem flared up badly. As any of you who have travelled know, toilets and such facilities abroad do not always offer the comforts of home. After three weeks, I developed a toxic condition in my bladder that required my hospitalisation. The specialist told me he had never seen a woman's bladder in worse shape. He described it as 'full of holes like a blown-out tire'. When my condition stabilised, I returned home with a catherisation kit. If things did not improve, that would be my fate until death. Even worse was the threat of bladder replacement which was the next logical stage.

At age thirty-five, the future looked bleak indeed, but this time I had a new weapon to fight with—my determination not to be ill. I practised the muscle-strengthening exercises the doctor taught me. Soon, I was urinating normally with no artificial help. I do have to take diuretics, drink more water, and eat less salt, but today my waterworks work fine! I have not had one ounce of trouble in six years.

The next thing to go was my propensity towards flu. I simply told myself that it had to stop. I have not had any serious colds or flu in three years. Now, if I feel any symptoms, I take extra vitamin C and natural garlic tablets and get on with it. I can be surrounded by sick people, cold germs, coughing, or get drenched on a freezing night and not have to fear the onset of illness. This knowledge is freedom of the first order. My success in this area has taught me so much about my own power and ability.

This long narrative was not told out of the need to reaffirm my conquest over sickness, but to illustrate in a real way how mind power works. You can adapt the method to your own needs.

Society's attitudes towards illness are quite ambivalent. They range from irritation to pity to disgust. Most of us are relieved that someone else apart from us is seriously ill. Those who have been smug about their good health change their tune if *they* get sick. There are some who boast of their various and bloody battles in the operating rooms. They gladly display their scars and wounds, no matter how terrible. Then there is the type of person who denies the need for medical intervention under any circumstances. They would literally prefer dying to admitting illness or pain. These symptoms are perceived as signs of weakness and vulnerability.

Having been at one extreme, I now counsel the middle road. Be cautious about your health, but not anxious. There is nothing to boast about, or be ashamed of, in being sick. Remember, the choice is always yours. Do not believe, as I did for half a lifetime, that you are born 'sickly' and there is nothing you can do about it.

This chapter will discuss various strategies and tips for better health, beginning with an honest look at lifestyle.

Lifestyle

Lifestyle comprises a range of things, the main ones being: work, relationships, diet, (general health), narcotic intake, (mental attitude), sleep, and leisure activities.

Work

The role played on the well-being of women by stress in the workplace and the importance of having a definite cut-off point at the end of each day has already been discussed. Here, the attitudes towards work will be approached. Kahlil Gibran said, 'Work with love'. To some, that would seem a contradiction in terms. You spend eight or more hours at your workplace because you have to, not because you want to, then you have the rest of the day to enjoy. You certainly have that drummed into you, and most people believe it. Add to it a generous dose of good old Victorian work ethic and you have an entire generation working without love. I once saw a man in a film sweeping a floor while loudly singing opera to himself. It was a most beautiful expression of *joie de vivre*. That explodes yet another one of society's myths: some work is important and some is not. Certainly, some jobs are by their nature more exacting and influential, such as being a brain surgeon or the president of a country, but where would societies be if every man and woman wanted to be a surgeon or a president? Who would sweep the streets and tend our public gardens and look after the sick? Think of the worst job you could imagine doing. Mine would be working in an abattoir because of my horror of killing animals. I also marvel at the patience of dentists and seamstresses, yet someone out there wants to do those jobs, and isn't that lucky for the rest of us?

Jobs seem to fall into three basic categories: important, drudge and glamour. Most people who work in so-called glamour industries will say it is hard work. Yes, they love it. In that respect, they are rewarded, but love can be hard work, too! We all think it would be exciting to be an actor or courtroom lawyer or pilot. Then there are all the occupations that appear downright sinful, but oh, the fantasies they create in respectable minds. We are back to 'attitude'. You can clean out toilets and be happy or have all the money and prestige in the world and be miserable.

Everyone in the world who works can probably be narrowed down as one of the following: those who work just for the money that labour earns and 'live' when not at work; and those who would work even if they were not being paid for it. Our choices are somewhat made for us by the realities of our background, education, family and intelligence. Why limit ourselves? More about career choices and changes in Chapter Eight; for now, just remember you own the whole twenty-four hours of each day. Ultimately, you decide how you want to spend your time. Do what excites you, something that gets you out of bed in the morning with joy.

Relationships

We have relationships with everyone we come in contact with, not just those few who are close and important to us. If you swear at the man in the next car who pulled out in front of you, you just had a relationship with him. Losing sight of this fact is why we treat each other so poorly. A very small minority of any community would knowingly hurt a member of their family or a friend. Yet that 'stranger' you are hurting belongs to, and is loved by someone. There really are no strangers— we are all bound by our common humanity. Of course, there are degrees of interaction and levels of communication. It is sad when people show one face to the world and another to their intimates, especially if those closest are getting the short end of the deal. The words of a song say 'You always hurt the one you love, the one you shouldn't hurt at all'. Don't forget that love can also be exploitation.

The way you interact with people is part of your lifestyle and affects your overall frame of mind and performance. You cannot expect to do well at work if you are having screaming rows at home every night, nor can you be a contented mother if you loathe and detest your next-door neighbour. Again, avoid classifying your relationships into important and unimportant. Don't think it doesn't matter if you get along with your milkman, or if you put on a false smile every time your husband's boss looks your way. Try being at peace with all the people in your life. That includes your most casual encounters. If someone asks you for directions, do not regard it as an intrusion. Tell them more than they ask for. Suggest they walk with you if you are going in the same direction, and give everyone your smile. You will give yourself a gift at the same time. This is not a 1960s 'Smile and be happy' philosophy. You will not like everyone you meet, but as stress preventers and managers, there are yet to be found ones better than laughter, smiling and feeling good about yourself. This feeling in turn radiates out to others and becomes one of your better habits, one to sustain you through the days without sunshine in the sky or in your heart.

Diet

This word should only mean the food you eat, but it has come to have so many other connotations. To most women, it has one overwhelming message—unpleasant restrictions. If a woman is thin, it denotes keeping weight off. If she is overweight, it is the enemy and a constant burden. Such stereotypical images should be immediately dispelled. For a start, most people who live in affluent, technological societies are overweight, pound for pound. What does that mean? Simply that for height and build, there is too much flesh. There can be many reasons, although the companies selling weight-loss programmes will tell you that there is only one reason—a woman's weakness for food (overeating). They have a vested reason for making this statement (the need to get you and your money) while capitalising on fear, vanity and insecurity. There are genuine and valid reasons for some women to carry extra weight, just as some women cannot gain weight even when trying. Wallis Simpson said, 'A woman cannot be too thin or too rich'. I have not made up my mind about the latter, but I certainly disagree with the former. If you have ever seen a young woman in the grip of advanced anorexia nervosa, you could never think thinner is

better. Striving for a body size that fits the frame we were born
into seems logical.

You do not need to look into a mirror or have someone
compliment you to know that you are happy with your body.
Your clothes tell you, as does your own sense of well-being.
When you have to carry too much weight around, you feel
sluggish and easily tired. Everything is an effort. In other words,
monitor your weight and eat sensibly for health reasons and
because you care about yourself, not so that you can look like
the models in the latest *Vogue* magazine.

The media in general has much to answer for in persistently
creating and promoting only one look—the ultra-thin woman.
Do not be unduly influenced by what you see as 'ideal' on
television and in newspapers and magazines.

I can almost hear the responses: 'I'm a size twenty-two, and
no matter what you say, I don't want to be this fat', or 'I'm
a size ten, and I certainly would not be willing to give up my
slim body. I would rather go on miserably dieting forever', or
'Every woman would rather be thin. There is no getting away
from it'. You cannot be dissuaded from your own point of view.
That is precisely what I *do not* want to do in this book.
Alternative ways of looking at ordinary, everyday things are
offered, leaving you to make up your own mind. On the question
of weight and the many other issues married to it, one thing
should be stressed: the whole question of eating and not eating
is a major contributor to stress in women today. Disagree if
you will, but consider the following.

First, remember that the word 'diet' literally means the type
and amount of food you ingest daily. Now, the other connotation
of the word diet is one that means restrictions, self-denial,
measuring, endless body weighing and food weighing and, worst
of all, guilt. It all sounds tedious, but the very notion of dieting
is psychologically unsound. When you tell a woman that she
is gross and unattractive, then put her on a regime of strictly
doled-out meals, a punishing schedule of exercise, and throw
in lashings of guilt and self-pity, how on earth can that be
good for her? How does any of this punishment enhance her
experience of life? Sure, this is an extreme case. There are
millions of women who happily follow diets, maintain weight
and enjoy life fully. There are equally as many women for whom

each day is an agony of loneliness and frustration, who cut every diet out of every magazine and bitterly tear it up after a couple of days. They long to be something they are not and hate what they are. These women do not need to be force-fed an endless stream of propaganda about how thin they must be to keep their men and how no one loves a 'fattie'.

It is revolting that organisations prey upon women such as these and humiliate them in front of peers, if they have not achieved their weight-loss goals for the week. This type of treatment may work as a form of aversion therapy, but the women lose much more than their weight. They lose their dignity and all that is special and beautiful about them. If anyone tries putting you in this type of embarrassing position, just remind yourself they are doing it for money, and love yourself enough to walk out.

Unfortunately, not only professionals can be tactless and hurtful about weight problems. Friends are sometimes worse even without meaning to be. What are the reasons for overweight? In my case, it is hormonal and dates back to my operation at age twenty-three. Prior to that time, I was pencil-thin, but by the time I reached twenty-five, my weight had become a constant battle. I did not know how to cope. Friends would not stop commenting on the obvious change in me, despite knowing the reason. One particular friend used to make a point of informing me every time I saw her whether I had lost or gained weight. As the years pass, new people come into my life who do not know my health background. Sometimes, they unwittingly make cruel observations. I rarely bother explaining, but am infuriated by the automatic assumption that I overeat. In fact, I eat quite lightly although by no means perfectly.

A few years ago, when I was much larger, I developed a 'fat mentality'. I thought of myself as a fat person and wore the obligatory caftan as a uniform of my allegiance to being overweight. Then I joined a health club and went on a heavy workout schedule. I lost about thirty pounds in six weeks, began to love working my body, and felt wonderful. Perhaps the most interesting aspect of that whole transformation was that my diet automatically changed. When I was drastically overweight, I developed a number of bad eating habits. When I got physically fit, my craving for sweet, fatty and starchy foods dwindled. My body no longer needed or wanted them.

Your body is its own best judge of what is best for it; let it guide you. It is a better teacher than any book, nutritionist, or doctor. I am not blinded by my training and I will continually throw the decisions for your life choices back on to you.

Another difficulty about eating and weight is that food has an emotional quality—not intrinsically, but superimposed by generations of conditioning. Food is inextricably linked to such matters as security, comfort, love, punishment, family, pleasure and even, sometimes, sexuality. Children learn their words for desired food and drink very early; their first memory is drinking from their mother's breasts or from bottles. Food is even given or withdrawn according to approval levels. So many family occasions revolve around the eating and sharing of meals. By the time we reach adulthood, we think of food as love. When we are miserable, all we have to do to feel better is eat.

The European attitude that food is a celebration to be enjoyed with others amidst much noisy chatter, great gusto and no guilt is a great one. Put food back into its proper perspective: remember that food addiction is one of the worst ones in society. As it only hurts the individual it appears less serious, but is not.

The emotional power of food was brought home to me a few years ago when I still scoured around for 'cures'. I saw a naturopath who told me that my system was grossly toxic. (I later made him admit that everyone is told this!) He put me on a strict diet of herbal medicines and told me not to eat solid food for a week, which I thought was rather severe. In my eagerness to improve my health, however, I paid out large sums of money and left with my various potions. By the second day, I began feeling awful. I telephoned an aunt familiar with naturopathy, and she assured me a week's fast was not that unusual. Thus assuaged, I continued the fast. By the third evening, I was crying and curled into the fetal position on the bed. Only the thought of food interested me yet I was not even hungry. I suffered from psychological deprivation rather than lack of food. After all, the stomach shrinks when taking in less food. Also, I was ingesting other nourishment so there was no reason for me to suffer, but I felt disoriented and on the brink of emotional collapse. Finally, a friend insisted on cooking a meal for me. I felt like a terrible failure for not being able to get through seven days without eating. Now I wonder why I put myself through such an experience. (The organisation was later discredited on a national television programme.) Fasting is a legitimate and useful tool for clearing toxins from the body and losing weight, but it needs proper supervision. When I recommend this course to patients, I suggest starting with only one or two days.

Food is so much a part of the rhythm of your day. You wake yourself up with breakfast, punctuate the day with lunch, and look forward to evening meals with your loved ones. This link between emotions and food must be accepted before discussing eating disorders. Not only does food associate in your mind with feelings and memories, it is often eaten *because* of emotions. There are the acceptable occurrences of this such as overindulgence at weddings or Christmas family dinners, but think of all the times you have eaten out of anything but joy.

The two best known eating disorders are anorexia nervosa and bulimia. Both are directly linked to low self-esteem. The anorexic cannot make herself thin enough in her own eyes even when she has so little flesh that her bones show through. There has been some recent findings to suggest that anorexia is a physical problem rather than an emotional one, but I've yet to read a conclusive report. Bulimia is a condition linked to self-destructive tendencies. Many women confess to eating out of boredom or to kill the pain of active self-dislike, but a distinction must be made between women who simply eat too much of the wrong foods and those who can be strictly classified as over-eaters or bulimics. How do you tell?

Bulimics binge; they swing from stuffing their faces with food to starving themselves. They induce vomiting after going on one of their eating attacks in order to expel all of the calories, losing all the nutrients at the same time. They get weaker and weaker with time. They live double lives as much as an alcoholic or compulsive gambler, doing their eating in secret, with no joy and with much guilt and self-loathing. Women I have counselled who suffered from bulimia constantly use the words 'disgusting' and 'ugly' to describe themselves. Each one carries the self-image of a stupid, plain and unappealing woman. This impression is often inscribed in childhood. One of my patients was repeatedly told during childhood, 'As you are so plain, we shall have to find something else for you.' Bulimics eat to fulfil this unpleasant view of themselves. They see a fat, ugly woman in the mirror, no matter what the true reflection. They signal themselves to achieve this state, and eating is the obvious way. The human psyche is very subtle and has its own brand of logic. When a woman is helped to see what she is doing and why, she will begin creating a person she can enjoy being.

Bulimia is said to be a particularly emotional form of eating. One woman described her binge as 'eating in a trance'. Bingeing is usually brought on by a particular stress event, such as a disturbing phone call. Afterwards, everything edible in the house is brought out and devoured with no thought of combinations or amounts. Only when the stomach is full to straining and the sufferer is surrounded by the debris of her attack does the self-disgust come. That feeling is quickly followed by the urgent desire to expel the food. Food itself never was the desirable entity, just the tool to bring on the maximum guilt and disgust. Once these feelings are achieved, the food is of no further interest. The whole point of the exercise is the guilt trip. Food, our servant in its simplest form, has been boosted to such a sophisticated level that its original purpose is almost forgotten. It does not need to taste good to do its job, but our palates have a learned need for new sensations and infinite variety. Add the associations I mentioned and you have a potentially lethal combination.

Can you do anything if you identify with this description of bulimia? Here are some suggestions:

- give yourself some pleasant exercise every day.
- work at your identity and self-esteem.
- join a group that supports and does not criticise.
- look closely at the areas of your diet that you would like to change without making it a burden.
- do not focus on food.
- surround your life with a variety of activities and people.
- do not wait for others to give you pats on the back; do it yourself.
- take control of who you are and where you are going.

- break the physical eating patterns you established if they are wrong for you.
- never shop when you are hungry.
- keep a daily diary of meals you eat. Write down everything before you begin eating. You can't do this exercise and binge at the same time.
- try giving up the one food you feel is your greatest weakness. Give it up for a week, then try another one. Do this in rotation, so you do not feel deprived or depressed.
- do not bring foods into the house that you know are tempting for you.

Above all, be kind and gentle with yourself. Many of the above suggestions are equally suitable for women simply desiring to improve their bodies, and are self-explanatory. But first, a little further discussion on exercise and 'diet' (in the sense of a formal programme of eating) is needed.

No matter what your reason for being overweight, exercise can help. Whatever form you choose should be pleasant for you. There is little credibility in the philosophy of 'no pain, no gain': a compulsive attitude towards jogging or aerobics or weight-lifting is potentially harmful. Killing yourself in the process of sport seems to defeat the purpose. Women less motivated will give up and add this failure to their already overflowing storehouses of defeats and guilts.

Physical improvement is a very good place to start your quest for a better life simply because progress in this area is easily measurable. Other areas like stress management and dealing with anger are more subtle; getting better sneaks up on you. Take pride in every small piece of improvement. Exercise is good for getting mentally and physically fit. It builds your confidence, helps control your weight and generally gives you an easy measure of improvement. One of the best exercises is dancing; it is fun and a natural expression of joy. You do not need formal lessons—just trust yourself enough to follow your instincts.

On the matter of diets, a lot of formal diets are not nutritionally sound. Instead, you should adopt a lifetime pattern of eating in moderation, checking your food groups, and trying to balance your daily intake. Keep meals light and enjoyable. Even if you have to eat more vegetables and fruits for your body's sake, do not feel you must surrender your favourite treats.

There is no need to complicate life more than necessary. A positive attitude goes far towards obtaining your goals. If you focus on food and all of its various implications, concentrate on your shortcomings, compare yourself to women much younger or with slimmer bodies, then you will never be content. 'Count your blessings' sounds old-fashioned, but it works, because life is the only focus worth your energy. Wanting to be like someone else is futile. The ageing process is a reality; you cannot continue to have the face and figure of a twenty-year-old forever. Does it matter? Forget the mystique. All you need to do is eat the things you like in a balanced way. If you work at feeling good inside then your outside shell will reflect this.

To sum up, overweight can be attributed to: eating the wrong foods or too much food; glandular or hormonal conditions; medical problems such as a sluggish liver which can cause an inefficient metabolism; and insufficient exercise for the amount of food intake.

Narcotics

The term narcotics here will refer to cigarette smoking, alcohol and drugs as they are the main ones affecting modern women. 'Drug-taking is a modern epidemic and whether our chosen chemical comes in pill, syringe, bottle, capsule, cup, or cigarette, the vast majority of us are drug-users. Many of us will, at some time in our lives, misuse a drug; some will become drug abusers; some will become dependent on a drug'—Liz Byrski, *Pills, Potions, People*.

Smoking

Cigarette smoking is a very personal thing. No matter how much educational and advertising material is released by health authorities, women will continue to smoke out of enjoyment or an inability to quit. In fact, statistics show that women smokers are on the increase, approximately thirty per cent in the last ten years. The following programme was devised by me for use by individuals and groups who wish to stop smoking.

This series of workshops aims to encourage the smoker

to examine her reasons for smoking, how and why she began and her emotional contact to cigarettes. It is not intended as a deep therapy programme, but rather as an examination of motives and goals in the pursuance of what is one of the most common social habits. The programme is designed around six two-hour sessions, which allows for a brief lecture followed by questions and a sharing of ideas and methods.

1. The origins of the habit
a. At what age did I begin smoking?
b. Was it my own idea or who got me started?
c. How did I feel when I first began to smoke?
d. Did my parents smoke?
e. Did the friends in my group smoke?

2. Motivation for the habit
a. What do I like about smoking?
b. What do I dislike about smoking?
c. What do I dislike most of all about the feedback I get from my non-smoking friends?
d. How many do I smoke in any one given day?
e. Where and when do I do most of my smoking?
f. Is there a link in my life between stress and smoking?
g. Is there a link in my life between eating and smoking?
h. Is there a link in my life between alcohol and smoking?
i. Do the people I see most smoke?
j. Does my spouse smoke?
k. How do I feel about my children smoking?
l. Do I smoke at my place of work?
m. Do I resent the amount of money I spend on cigarettes?
n. Do I worry about my health because of smoking?
o. Do I suffer any physical symptoms because of smoking?
p. Have I ever had an embarrassing moment related to smoking?

3. Goals for kicking the habit
a. Why would I like most to give up smoking?
b. Of all the people I know, who tells me the most often that I should give up smoking?
c. Am I influenced to give up smoking by the media?

d. What do I fear most about having to give up smoking?
e. How do I think I am going to feel for the first few days of withdrawal?
f. How do I think I am going to feel if I successfully complete the withdrawal process?
g. Am I worried that I am going to gain weight if I give up smoking?
h. Have I got anything in mind that I can do instead of smoking, for example at a party, pub or at work?

4. Self-image versus social image
a. Do I like myself; do I think I am a good person?
b. How do I think I feel in a crowd?
c. How do I feel at a party if I don't know anybody?
d. Does smoking give me confidence?
e. Am I worried that I am going to look stupid without a cigarette in my hand?
f. Is smoking a way to pose, to look cool?
g. Do cigarettes help me to make conversation, for example offering a cigarette or offering to light a cigarette?
h. Am I a nervous and restless person?
i. Am I a tense person?
j. Do I worry too much?
k. Do I get bored easily?
l. Do I actually feel better after smoking?

5. Coping with withdrawal
a. Practical tips and ideas for quitting (exchange and discuss).
b. How to alleviate stress during the crucial first days— relaxation, meditation and massage.
c. How to develop 'distractions', particularly keeping the hands busy.
d. Occupy the time when you would normally be smoking, for example, at the pub, play darts while you're having a few drinks with friends.
e. Develop an attitude of self-love so that smoking becomes undesirable because it doesn't nurture the body but rather harms it.

f. Most importantly work at fitness of the body, as exercise relieves tension and also a healthy body craves less the dependencies of such things as tobacco, alcohol, drugs and excessive food.

6. *Roleplaying and summary*

a. The groups will act out a variety of roles within everyday situations, exploring the role of cigarettes in society; the problems associated with smoking; and the withdrawal process (the psychological and physical aspects).

b. Final discussion and exchange of ideas on the programme and quitting in general.

This programme considers the chemical addiction and reasons for smoking in the first place. Most women started smoking at school because of peer group pressure to try something daring, but continued for reasons other than the addiction. Ironically, stress is often offered as an excuse.

Drinking

The same thing goes for alcohol: it is a prop for what ails you. The problem is that it creates more 'ailments' than it could ever cure. Women drink if they feel depressed, lonely, or sad. After a while, the reason becomes unimportant. They begin to enjoy the loss of inhibition, and a false sense of confidence takes over. Instead of building their lives on a solid foundation of achievement and self-esteem, they are left with the never-fulfilled promise of a bright morning after.

There is nothing wrong with social drinking and occasional overindulgence. If the habit becomes obtrusive and excessive, you need to ask yourself why you are drinking so much. Do not fool yourself with such fabrications as, 'I don't need to drink; I just enjoy it.' A good test question to ask yourself is, 'Do I like myself better when I've had a few drinks or am I hiding inside a bottle?'

Drugs

Drugs in this context can range from speed (amphetamines) to Valium to aspirin. Developing an addiction to any of these is relatively simple—only three conditions have to be present:

taking a drug for the wrong reasons for too long a period; looking for solutions to a problem through an external source; and being unhappy with yourself and your life, or not loving yourself enough to stop abusing your system. The next time you take two pain killers because you are 'not feeling too good', try to find a more positive remedy for your symptoms.

Many people take drugs because they feel isolated and alone. Ironically, they only cause more alienation. Is anyone more anti-social than a 'stoned' person?

This is not to underestimate the drug problem in today's society, but this book will offer many strategies for you to use in order to live drug-free. If you are already addicted, there is no quick and easy answer. Study the earlier section on addiction, and get professional help. Withdrawal may be hard, but it is worthwhile when you can again smile at yourself in the mirror. Most importantly, find out what got you hooked in the first place. Make it an adventure.

Sleep

The human body requires six to eight hours' sleep a night in order to function at optimum efficiency. Do you want to give yourself the best chance of having a good day? A sad feature of human experience is that so many of us put obstacles in our own paths, seemingly making life as hard as possible.

Sleeping well is possible with practical management. Being at peace with yourself and your world certainly helps. Being able to sleep effortlessly and well is one of the greatest blessings and assets—to be able to switch off, no matter how much is on your mind. Sleep is a great healer, and makes any problems much easier to deal with the next day. Sound too good to be true?

What is the reason for poor sleep, and how do you deal with it? There is only one key reason you are likely to suffer from insomnia—the inability to relax. Insomnia strikes in one of three ways: inability to drop off to sleep; waking several times during the night, or sleeping fitfully. If you ask an insomniac why she cannot sleep, the answer will always be, 'I have too much on my mind.' If you are lying there making mental lists for the next day or going over that fight you had at work, you are never going to drift easily into sleep. You have to consciously clear your mind and relax your body. There are a number of things you can do before getting into bed. Did you relax when you got home or run around doing household chores? If you have too much to do and feel that you can't sit around all evening, then it should all become part of your stress management programme.

The worst thing you can do is get anxious. Try some warm milk, watching a little television, mild exercise, deep breathing, or meditation. Once the light is off, your attitude is most vital. Stick to the same routine every night. If you sleep best on your right side, wait until you are just about to drop off and then turn. It is like a signal to your body and works well when done naturally. Before turning, relax each separate part of your body. A relaxation tape is useful, as is soothing music. Keep a notepad by the bed, then if you think of something to write down, you will not have to get out of bed. Sleep is one of the most wonderful of the natural therapies and divides our days into workable units.

Leisure

Leisure falls into the same category as exercise. Learn the art of entertaining yourself and have fun trying different activities.

Would you be bored in the company of your favourite person? Of course not, so be your own best friend. Loneliness will soon be in your past. After all, you will always have yourself!

Let your body serve as a blueprint that you can consult for signposts to better health; keep in tune with its processes and the natural balance of your life. When you are unhappy, your body will register the stress and warn you with symptoms. Your external and internal worlds cannot be divorced. The challenge is to keep a healthy balance between them. The negative effects of stress often show up long after the cause. They gradually break down your resistance to disease, energy levels and general fitness. While you are busy 'coping', stress is doing its ugly work. Have you noticed you rarely 'crack up' in the middle of the pressure? When it is over, the avalanche of stress symptoms overwhelm you.

Be aware. Care for yourself, and use all of the preventative methods within your grasp.

———————— **AFFIRMATIONS** ————————

I am the power in my world and I choose to be free.
I let go of all limitations in my life.
I am at peace just where I am.
My mind is a tool I can choose to use in any way I wish.

Chapter Four

The seven ages of woman

Much about the influence of childhood is mentioned throughout this book, but it is necessary to discuss briefly now the stress experienced in childhood, specifically by girls.

The key to most childhood stress is powerlessness. Even with the best parents imaginable, a child has little or no autonomy over her own life, very little choice and little control over decision-making. At the same time, the quality of her life is totally determined by the rules set down by parents and the decisions they make for her. Wise parents institute the minimum number of regulations and involve their child as far as possible in the planning and activities of the family. This involvement not only gives the girl dignity and respect for herself, but also teaches a crucial life-lesson. The home environment is best for the learning of such skills as the art of conversation, how to give and accept affection, how to share and how to learn from criticism.

The old maxim that 'children should be seen and not heard' is not appropriate today. A system of exchange and mutual understanding would be more relevant. Parents need their privacy and time alone or with other adults, just as children need their own space and the right to do the things they enjoy, as long as they hurt no one else.

A good example is the child's bedroom. A bedroom should be a personal sanctuary, a place to drop all inhibitions and be oneself totally. If a child wishes to be untidy within the boundaries of her own bedroom, it is unfair to impose family rules in her miniature 'queendom'. Parents shouldn't feel compelled to pick up and tidy in the child's room. Has anyone ever really been taught to be tidy or do naturally untidy children simply conform for the sake of peace? Cleaning up after oneself in the communal sections of the house can be mandatory. Also, children should not feel free to barge into their parents' room without knocking.

This discussion brings to mind these words from Cat Stevens' song, *Father and Son*: 'The moment I could talk, I was ordered to listen.' How many of us remember childhood humiliations such as being told off in front of friends? Sometimes natural curiosity was taken for wilful disobedience. Our world was so narrow and the terrain so slippery.

Childhood

I was a very timid child and, apparently, used to run and hide when a visitor knocked at the door. I would only come out after my mother found me and assured me everything was all right. I did not recall this behaviour until many years later. I had always been puzzled by the fact that an unexpected knock at the door startled me and at my reluctance to open the door until I knew who was there. This behaviour seemed irrational to me as I am not usually a jumpy or nervous person. I still do not know the original cause for this carry-over fear from childhood. Remember the patient with the vomiting phobia? Many adult fears and phobias are directly attributable to childhood activities or messages.

Heather was brought up with three sisters. All slept in the same room for the entire period of growing up. A light was always left on in the landing to keep the girls from being frightened, but this well-meaning gesture had an unfortunate side effect. It left Heather with a chronic fear of the dark. She was unable to sleep in any room with the lights completely off, an inappropriate fear for an adult.

A more unusual example was one involving Ruth who was

unable to relate normally to men because of an incident in her youth. A boy in her class liked her, but she was very shy and kept her distance. One day he offered her a ring which she declined. The boy made a terrible scene and got rough with her. Of course, the whole thing died down, but the episode was firmly implanted in her mind. The idea stuck that any man who liked her was going to become a bully and embarrass her. So, as an adult, it was easier to simply avoid contact with the opposite gender.

Only when behaviour is understood in adult terms can the childhood fears be relinquished. How much worse it is for children who grow up with violence, alcohol, constant criticism, extreme anger, rejection, punishment, or a lack of love? Only sufficient self-love in adulthood can undo the damage and restore dignity.

I was in a shopping centre recently and found myself walking behind a family comprising a little boy of about four years being held on one side by his mother and on the other by his grandmother. He was just the height of the large rubbish bins placed strategically around the arcade. Looking around, he walked straight into one, making a loud cracking sound. To my amazement, the older woman shouted at the boy, 'Now look what you've done!' The trio stopped while Mom glanced around self-consciously, obviously embarrassed by her son. She then scathingly said, 'If he had a brain, he'd be dangerous.' Neither adult thought to inquire whether the boy had hurt himself. Worse than that, they were teaching him that whatever happened to him in life would be his fault.

CHILDREN LEARN WHAT THEY LIVE WITH

If a child lives with CRITICISM,
he learns to CONDEMN.
If he lives with HOSTILITY,
he learns to FIGHT.
If he lives with FEAR,
he learns to be APPREHENSIVE.
If a child lives with PITY,
he learns to feel SORRY FOR HIMSELF.
If a child lives with RIDICULE,

he learns to be SHY.
If a child lives with JEALOUSY,
he learns to feel GUILTY.
If a child lives with TOLERANCE,
he learns to be PATIENT.
If a child lives with ENCOURAGEMENT,
he learns to be CONFIDENT.
If a child lives with PRAISE,
he learns to be APPRECIATIVE.
If a child lives with ACCEPTANCE,
he learns to LOVE.
If a child lives with APPROVAL,
he learns to LIKE HIMSELF.
If a child lives with RECOGNITION,
he learns it is good to HAVE A GOAL.
If a child lives with HONESTY,
he learns what TRUTH is.
If a child lives with FAIRNESS,
he learns JUSTICE.

Dorothy Low Nolte

Kahlil Gibran said, 'Your children are not your children. They come through you, but not from you, and though they are with you yet they belong not to you. You may give them your love but not your thoughts for they have their own thoughts.'

Growing pains

Judging from the stories of children that most often appear in counselling, family stresses are the most severe of childhood. Looking at the average family unit, the years before school are relatively pleasant and carefree for a child. The main preoccupations are in learning basic skills, first words, and the rest of the time lost in play or parodied dreams of the future. At six years of age, I would teach an imaginary class by the hour, according to my mother who watched around the corner. The students were my various dolls placed on chairs around the room. With a long ruler, I would rap menacingly on any available surface near the head of an inattentive pupil.

Apart from the usual spills and ills, nothing too traumatic is allowed to cloud over the bright days of a pre-school toddler.

Therefore, she is totally unprepared for the shock of the first day at school, which has to be one of the most stressful events of our entire lives. For a five or six year old, it is a very frightening experience—the strange environment, a new adult in charge and a roomful of boys and girls all competing for the loudest scream and longest cry (what other weapons does a little child have?). This day is the first encounter with a world of strangers, new challenges and many skills to learn. Making it in this scene may mean, for a girl, having her hair pulled by the class bully, being so painfully shy that the simplest request from the teacher is impossible to answer, or developing a mad crush on the handsomest boy present.

Children with learning difficulties or other disabilities have a greater challenge in assimilation within the school system. An unkind teacher or a particular subject can be torture for a child going through those all-important foundation years between five and thirteen. Anxiety is often prevalent among primary age children. I have been consulted by mothers regarding stressful behaviour in girls as young as eight years. The cause is inevitably one of the following: unhappiness within the family; trouble at school with the work or the teacher; peer group pressure; or emotional difficulty of some nature. Young girls are being pressured much earlier these days in regard to socialising, alcohol, drugs and sex. Parents have to accept this fact and speak to their daughters about such matters as menstruation, boys, sexuality, contraception and personal hygiene. These talks are probably best coming from mothers to girls, but with so many single-parent families, fathers sometimes have to fill the role of educator. I suggest these talks should not be left any later than ten years of age. More will be said on this topic in Chapter Five.

Emotional problems can manifest themselves in such behaviours as bed-wetting, tantrums, sulking, antisocial actions, or poor school performance. These symptoms are really a miniature version of the adult scenario—you cannot be happy at home if you are struggling with stress at work or school. Many children feel out of their depth in various areas of their young lives, but do not know how to express this impotence. As with adult stress, the overload can explode quite suddenly and dramatically. The argument could be made that too much emphasis on stress is also unhealthy—if a child appears balanced and happy there is no need to look for trouble but if your child seems overly detached or temperamental, look beyond the physical possibilities to the stress traps beneath.

The more serious the event, the more likely the negative stress reaction. The loss of a pet dog can be quite traumatic. Entire books are written about the effect of a parent's death on a young child. Also, people rarely get over the break-up of their parents' marriage if it occurs while they are young children. In counselling, these grown children recall the exact time the family split. A child's world is wrapped in the security blanket of family love and the strength of the marriage bond that keeps parents and children together. When this security is threatened, it can be likened to an emotional earthquake.

Another situation that causes children stress is constant moving during their formative years, especially in the case of regular uprootings such as for the families of army or navy personnel. The children of these families develop high socialising skills, but report that they rarely make lasting friendships and can be shy and introverted as adults.

Some children appear to have 'difficult' personalities or display signs of wanting to behave in an unorthodox fashion. Easily misunderstood, the worst reaction is to try beating or nagging the child into conventional attitudes. Who knows— you may have a future scientist or novelist on your hands. Originality and high intellect is often perceived in childhood as 'being stubborn' or 'insisting on having her own way'. Very bright children are easily bored and need constant, fresh, mental stimulation. Forcing them to keep pace with the average child will cause grave stress and damage the relationship between parent and child.

Exponents of astrology will say that incompatibility of the child's star signs to those of other family members can also create tensions, perhaps explaining why certain people in a family never seem to get along and suffer from what is called a 'personality clash'. The metaphysical has quite a lot to teach us (see Chapter Ten).

Parental pressure would have to be one of the most taxing of stress problems for children. A little girl may feel out of place with her siblings, or out of touch with Mom or Dad or both. There may be pressure from one particular source, such as a bossy older sister or brother, a nagging mother, or a father with unrealistic expectations of his daughter's achievements. These situations can cause tremendous conflicts, a tug of war between the desire to please and the confusion about the crossed signals being received, love versus criticism.

All of the above are the generalised and more common forms of stress, but there are the unspeakable horrors that some children endure such as sexual abuse, seeing physical abuse between parents, witnessing parents or other family members bitterly quarrelling, or a drunken parent. This type of situation can often cause long-term emotional scarring. Some children can fight back and express their frustration and anger immediately, while others internalise the pain which takes root in future nightmares.

Sibling positioning
The child's positioning in the family is significant. There are distinct personality types for the first, second and third positions as well as one for the only child. Check your position and see if it matches the characteristics isolated by extensive research. All of the studies examined the three-child interactions. After that, the details simply recur. Of course, there will always be variations caused by such factors as the number of years between siblings and whether there was a long gap between one lot of children followed by a 'second family'.

First child: this child tends to become a dutiful, controlled, organised person, prone to bossiness, and will grow into a woman who will always be the first to volunteer her services for whatever needs to be done. On the surface, she will appear forever balanced and able to cope under any conditions. In fact she is strong-minded and capable, but also the perfect example of the woman taking on too much and running the risk of stress overload. She will tend to take poor care of herself and be there for everyone else. If and when she does crack, however, this type will suffer badly due to accumulated stress and her humiliation that she was unable to overcome her problems on her own, without any fuss. A leader in her family and the community, she always goes along with others' expectations of her. Parents put all of their insecurities and inexperience into a first child. There is always a special bond there that no future children can ever quite match. The problem is that the child will follow the parents' example and continue to drive herself after she grows up, and be too hard on herself. In nine out of ten cases of male impotence I counsel, the man is the first child in the family. These first children tend to be perfectionists and suffer mistakes very poorly, their own or anyone else's.

Second child: Traditionally known as the 'sandwich' child, a better term would be the 'shadow' child because no matter what she is or does, she is and will always be in the shadow of the first child. She came second; no power on earth can change that fact. Look at the second children of the royal families. They have all lived out of public attention, mainly because they are of little interest. Some of these children have been tragically lonely, some hostile, some ignored. They have the freedom to be more individualistic, but they cannot escape the constant comparison with 'Number One'. Second children need much more reassurance and praise as they develop inferiority complexes early in life and believe themselves to be inadequate and unworthy. Thus, a second child tends to be rather introverted, insecure, and nervous.

Third child: By the time the third child comes along, parents have more practice, money is more plentiful, and they are older and mellower. Parents tend to be easier, more indulgent, and less rigid as disciplinarians. Therefore, this child will get away with things that the older ones could never have done. She will be a freer, less conventional personality, much less concerned with what people think of her or the rights of authority figures. Overall, this child has the easiest time of growing up. She is often 'spoiled' and doted on by parents who either chose to have a third child or, if unexpected, becomes the 'apple of her family's eyes'. Sometimes, she is resented by the older children, but this fact will not unduly concern her. She enjoys her position as the 'baby' of the family and demands the right to do as she pleases.

Only child: An only child is independent, self-motivating, and prefers solitary pursuits. In adult life, she will be self-reliant, reluctant to ask for help, and fond of her own company. Boredom will never be a problem for her; she will tend not to join in communal activities. Having her own space is essential. Close, demanding relationships are difficult. An only child feels more comfortable giving love than receiving it; her deepest emotions will be expressed in private. She will have only a small circle of friends in which she confides, and she will tend to get along better with older people than those people in her own age group. This position is naturally the loneliest of the four, but also the maker of a strong and courageous person.

Remember with all of these descriptions that there are exceptions to any rule.

Teenage years

Much of what was said in the last section can also apply to the stress of teenage girls. Specific aspects of life for girls between thirteen and nineteen that can and will cause stress if allowed free rein are: puberty; sexuality and relationships; peer pressure; identity; drugs and alcohol; and incidence of suicide.

The onset of puberty in girls occurs at an earlier age than in boys. Body changes become evident around ten years of age, e.g. many girls have to start wearing a bra by age twelve years, and it is not uncommon for menstruation to begin as young as eleven years. These hormonal changes create certain biological pressures and cause the intense and conflicting emotions that we associate with puberty.

The peak of this intensity takes place at fourteen to fifteen years of age. As anyone who has ever had to deal with a teenage girl of this age will tell you, she is utterly 'impossible'. If you try to help or advise her, you are interfering. If you are an adult, you are the enemy. She is a mass of contradictions and very difficult to love. She wants to experience everything that life has to offer in one split second and will not tolerate your trying to slow her down. The next time you feel like throttling your teenage daughter or student, remember how it felt to be that age.

I used that strategy to good effect when I was a teacher. My students often commented that many of their teachers acted as if they were never teenagers themselves, all their pranks and misdemeanours lost in the memory of time. Somehow, I could not help identifying with their struggles, and I loved them for their relentless honesty. They were nothing if not unpredictable. At the very moment that you are ready to throw in the towel and give up on a teenage girl, she will turn around and do something devastatingly lovable, and your heart melts yet another time.

No one would deny that this is a difficult time. It is ironic that a young girl with so much to be happy about has to endure some of life's most testing lessons at this time. As Bernard Shaw said: 'Youth is wasted on the young.' The teenage years should be the most carefree and uncomplicated, but unfortunately, the very opposite is true. Teenagers are so eager for life, so unspoiled, they have so much ahead of them and so little wisdom to work with. It is undoubtedly a stressful time, even for the more adaptable and easy-going ones.

Almost *everything* at this age brings on stress, but in reality it comes down to the *perception* of stressful situations. To a teenager, good is bad and bad is good; it's all the same. If a girl likes a boy and he smiles at her, she goes into an apoplexy of anxiety—what will she do? What will she wear? What will she say the next time he looks her way? The excitement is going to kill her anyway, so these questions are all academic. Then if that boy *doesn't* like her, well, that can be reason enough for a week-long binge, not to mention a full-blown anxiety attack.

Statistics show that teenage girls are the population sector most vulnerable to eating disorders, particularly anorexia nervosa. There is a specific personality type associated with this condition, namely, an overachiever: too eager to please, desperate to win at all costs, and seeing herself as never good enough. Every failure is magnified out of all proportion and stored like negative treasures to be trotted out as the need arises.

Sexuality

Separating puberty from sexuality is impossible as one heralds the beginning of the other. A girl may well have tried out her sexual wiles on men long before this age, but it is usually not understood as sexual behaviour. Now she begins to understand what it means to be a woman; her body is developing and she sees the effect it has on the opposite sex. There is often pressure to experiment sexually. It would be nice to think that with the availability of much more education, literature and free discussion these days, girls have clearer choices. Girls, on the whole, have a much stronger sense of who they are than when I was growing up. We were more inclined to accept our parents' views and the voice of authority in our teachers and older relatives. If we did not do the wrong things, it was often because of fear and not morality. Feeling strong sexual urges at thirteen or sixteen is normal, although it is inappropriate to give in to them. Therein lies one of the main dilemmas of this period— all the fire and nothing around but rules and restrictions. Life seems to be one long car chase with every light a red one. (See Chapter Seven for more about sexuality and the potentials for stress.) Physically, it all begins during the teenage years, and its importance to girls growing up and dealing with normal tensions cannot be overlooked.

Every book on teenage boys will speak extensively on masturbation, wet dreams and guilt. These things are largely ignored in female therapy as if, somehow, sexuality does not exist for girls, overtly or within. In fact, girls are highly sexed at this age. In many cases, this energy is diverted to other pursuits such as study, sport, or friendship. Teenage girls love with great intensity, and the objects of their feelings can very often be their best friend or a beloved teacher. In other words, love and sexuality merge and feelings are not necessarily expressed externally in a sexual way. Having worked for years in girls' schools, I feel I know their behaviour patterns very well and understand the workings of these emotional subtleties. I used to be appalled when the girls would complain to me that their house-mothers accused them of being lesbians because two girls would shower together or want to curl up together in bed. That showed an utter lack of insight into the nature of the teenage girl. If anything was going to drive her into sexual experimentation, that sort of limited thinking would.

But sexual or highly emotional relationships are not the only things vital to a girl's maturation process. Another very important arena of her life is within the family home. As already stated, the quality of family relationships can make an enormous difference when it comes to the stress issue. Teenage girls are by far the noisiest and least restful of all creatures; do not expect much peace when one is around. If they are not giggling, they are crying or screaming—even their depressions are loud. They are not only noisy, they are emotionally disruptive, so all other family members have to be tolerant. In the worst possible scenario, Mom's going through menopause, Dad's got a mid-life crisis, and younger brother's wetting his bed all at the same time! Then the family's in real trouble. In a case like that, you can expect the teenager to be the least sympathetic, not because she does not care but because this period is one of the most self-centred times she will ever go through. Life is totally experienced through her tunnel vision of needs, desires and mixed emotions. She literally has no room to consider anything or anyone else. Once this fact is absorbed, relationships are less strained all round.

My mother, myself

The mother/daughter relationship, which is one of the most complex of all human interactions, really becomes highlighted at this time. It can make or break many teenage girls. If a teenage girl has her mother's love and understanding, her stress burden will be considerably lighter. If not, the relationship will serve as a major contributor to stress in both parties. Most women complain that they do not understand their teenage daughters and girls find their mothers' attitudes restrictive and prescriptive. The problems, in fact, run far deeper than that. There is usually a good deal of competitiveness and rivalry between the two women and the weight of the generation that separates them. It may not be malicious and overt, but, even at its most subtle, it is a very real barrier to positive interaction. The older woman is well aware of her fading looks and of her daughter's fresh beauty; the younger woman envies the 'grown-up' things she wants to do, such as dressing up and making love, as well as her mother's relationship with her father. In the absence of loving communication, these petty jealousies can fester into resentment and unspoken anger.

Many middle-aged women still speak of things they disliked about their mothers in childhood or teenage years. Remember that mothers are only human and, therefore, prone to many rearing mistakes. Not all mothers, if any, are the Madonna personified: everloving, understanding and patient. Some are selfish, cruel and even ruthless. There are lessons to be learned from our parents, and wise parents realise that they can learn from their children.

One thing I particularly disliked as a teenager was being constantly compared to my mother, who was beautiful, talented and popular. In her presence, I felt I paled into insignificance. She was young and vibrant where my schoolfriends' mothers were grey-haired and sedate. In many ways, she was like my older sister and I played the role of the insecure second child, always in her shadow. Therefore, establishing my own identity was more difficult than for other girls. I presented all the events of my life to my mother for approval. As she was so critical and her expectations for me so high, I nearly always felt that my offering was inadequate. After her death when I was twenty-three I felt released from a prison of love, at last able to be myself, whatever that meant. That is the core of the mother/daughter conflict. Children want to be recognised for *their* accomplishments and not expected to be a carbon copy of one or both parents. A child cannot ape their parents' achievements and successes, and most women would not say to their mother, 'I am just me and that's great. I want you to love me, not study me and pick out all the things you'd like to change. I'm not a toy sample that you and Dad devised and are still trying to perfect!'

Many personality defects and behaviourial problems stem from teenage years. A good idea for adult women who have not resolved their various issues with their mothers is to bring the subject into the next conversation and allow no stalling or avoiding. Once the demons are killed off, the relationship can only improve. This can benefit and improve a mother/daughter interaction even if the daughter is in her forties and the mother her sixties. (More specific information about relationships will be given in Chapter Five.)

I believe a girl should be able to go to her mother if she is in any kind of trouble, whether it is to do with sex, a boyfriend, drugs, or school work. Unfortunately, however, the mother is usually the last choice for confidante, not always because of fear of disapproval but very often because she is seen as an unsuitable candidate for discussion of these subjects.

Rebellion or SOS?

The much talked about 'peer pressure' means that young people feel compelled to do what their friends and classmates think is 'cool', 'in', or acceptable. This feeling applies to everything from clothes to relationships to smoking. Very few young girls have the courage to stand on their principles and risk being the odd girl out. These days, many teenage girls are pressured by their boyfriends to give them sex. These girls simply do not feel ready. Younger and younger girls are experiencing sex and fewer are having to live with the consequences because of the accessibility of the pill and other contraceptives.

More education is a good thing, especially in regard to hygiene and prevention of disease, but the correct values still have to be instilled if sexual behaviour in teenagers is going to be significantly modified. Relating back to the point made earlier: young girls are hungry for life and will entertain no lectures on 'waiting till you're ready'. They want to taste as many dishes as possible in life's rich menu, and the banquet will comprise not only wholesome components. This fact must be accepted. There is no point in trying to shelter young people unduly or prevent them from growing up with their eyes wide open, but they need the equipment and maturity to handle all the stimuli coming at them. Most of all, they need healthy role models. We cannot present a case of 'Do as I say, not as I do.' A reasonable amount of experimentation is good. A teenager will only get hooked on drugs or alcohol if she is unhappy with some other aspect of her life, if the channels of communication are closed when she *does* want to confide in her parent(s), or if her parent(s) are getting drunk or stoned every night and telling her to stay off the stuff!

Suicide is the ultimate protest, the final scream in the dark to an uncaring world—at least it is in the perception of a teenager. Teenagers are full of bravado, but are dealing with more stress than most adults can remember having to handle. They do not really feel as strong and as confident as they make out—whatever negative strokes they give should be met with love and reassurance. Most importantly, they need to know that however unreasonable or unlovable they get, the love of their family is unconditional and constant.

The teenage years bring the first real identity crisis of human development. For the first time, teenagers actually *identify* themselves as being separate from their parents or siblings. That is why they become rebellious and resentful if told what to do.

They desperately want to make decisions for themselves, to try their wings. Wise parents allow their teenage children to fly and are ready with a safety net if they fall, giving of their counsel without forcing their ways or opinions on their offspring. Many parents are not aware of the stress their teenagers are living and working under because of the effective mask worn by young people to disguise their myriad conflicts and confusions.

The only answer is to overcome your own prejudices and pressures, break down the walls that divide you, and love each other through all the crises and dramas of any human lifetime.

The twenties

A woman enters her twenties with a lot of enthusiasm. She has got through the turmoil of being a teenager, left school, and is now either working, studying, or in some cases married. This decade is a practical one. Statistics indicate that the average age for a young woman to marry in Western countries is twenty-three to twenty-four, making a large majority of the female population no longer single by their mid-twenties. This age is also a time of enormous change for women—ten years of building a career, a bank balance and a relationship, often all at once.

Marriage

First, a look at marriage. If a woman marries early in her twenties, she and her husband will either decide to work and establish a firm family foundation or they will want to have children immediately. Young women have a lot more confidence at this age than their male counterparts, by the natural laws of maturation. They have lots of energy and want to take control of their lives now that they are finally out in the world. Nevertheless, it is a shock to the system when a woman finds that she has to carry two jobs or take care of a husband and children, run a home, balance a checkbook and do count-less other things. What happened to her carefree life? That disappeared when she walked down the aisle, signed a lease, or began to work. Yet a characteristic of this age group is that women cope very well with all of their duties and responsibilities. Rebellion comes later!

The younger a woman marries, the more of her youth she

erodes away. Certainly, there is a tremendous adjustment. Clothes do not magically get picked up, washed and put away. Cupboards do not miraculously fill themselves—you have to go to the supermarket after work and lug bags of groceries home on the bus. All the wonderful gadgets and appliances in your parents' house cannot necessarily be afforded in your own home, so dishes are washed manually and clothes rinsed and squeezed out in the tub. Boy, independence sure is fun!

Wise young couples should save up their money first, plan their wedding date prudently, and then enjoy a few years by themselves before having children. However, this is not an ideal world. You cannot be expected to conform to standard behaviour patterns all of the time.

Unwed mothers

Some young girls make their lives harder than they need to, though. There are those who get pregnant as teenagers and find themselves mother to a small child by the time they are in their twenties, usually with very little money and a dim future. This lifestyle would have to be one of the most difficult ones that a girl can choose. I do not accept that she finds herself in this position out of bad luck but rather out of ignorance or bad management. We all have choices, and we make them consciously or unconsciously, then we live with the consequences, pleasant or unpleasant.

As already discussed, a girl is often pressured into sex before she is ready to understand what it means or take precautions against pregnancy. She may then find herself in the invidious position of being pregnant and deciding to terminate, or having the baby and losing the last vestige of her youth. The issues of abortion and adoption are two of the most sensitive subjects in the spectrum of human concerns. They are highly personal and involve a complex set of moral values. Without detailing arguments for and against, it is safe to say that a young woman who has to come up against either or both of these is put under tremendous stress. Many never get over it and spend the rest of their lives regretting the loss of a child by these methods.

Single women

These women form the minority—women who, by choice or circumstance, stay single through their twenties. They will live a very different lifestyle to the others; they will obviously have much more freedom, more personal money, and be able to travel or do other things for themselves. If they do marry later in life, they will be even more committed to making a success of it. Never regret any decision you make, even if your marriage ends in divorce—you will learn so much about life that you would not have known otherwise.

A second rebellion

One interesting phenomenon that belongs to women in their twenties is the second major identity crisis (after puberty) which usually occurs at about twenty-five. As with all identity crises, this one asks, 'Who am I?' If a woman is married at twenty-five, she questions the good sense of being married, even if the relationship is normally a happy one. If she is not married, she envies all the women she knows who are tied down with screaming children and a million bills. She's fed up with the job or profession she has and wants to change her looks. Unlike the thirties crisis, which brings radical thought and action, this one is more gentle and can be satisfied with a few minor adjustments. Often, women at this age will start to want more out of life and either decide to change occupations, take on a study course, manage their time better, do more exercise, or whatever it takes. This crisis will be marked by bewildered husbands and boyfriends exclaiming that their ladies are 'different', more difficult to please, or displaying uncharacteristic behaviour.

One fellow said his wife started a new job in the travel industry and began working a lot of overtime, took to going out for drinks with clients and flirting with her co-workers. When she did arrive home, often late in the evening, bitter quarrels would ensue. He was afraid that their marriage was over. As extreme as that might sound, his wife's behaviour had nothing to do with their relationship—this stage of development belonged entirely to her. It would run its course, die a natural death, and his wife would very likely be more devoted and attentive than before. What can kill a relationship in this type of case is the husband who loves his pride more than he loves his wife and refuses to be understanding. He will make threats, issue an ultimatum and generally cause so much pressure that the marriage cracks under the tension. This episode need not be an overly stressful one for a woman or her loved ones if she understands what is involved and has the loving support of those around her.

So a woman's twenties are an active and varied time, full of new experiences and constant opportunities for growth. The growth is largely unconscious because this is not a particularly psychological time. The lessons she learns have a cumulative effect, and she enters her thirties armed with a lot more knowledge and curiosity and a lot less illusion. She often does not realise how much she has changed until she is faced with some of the challenges of the thirties, and she can look back on a decade of colour and activity.

The twenties are also very busy. Life screams out to be lived at full pace. So much is missed along the way, but signposts are left for a future passing. A woman only has to return for the precious gifts she overlooked the first time. This view may seem romantic, but if you remember back to your twenties, you will recall that you tended to be constantly on the move, never stopping to pick flowers or have a conversation unless there was some point to it. You were a young person with goals and important things to do.

Ultimately, the function and purpose of an identity crisis is to teach us more about ourselves by challenging us with the unknown frontiers of our personalities. It is called a 'crisis' because it usually happens without warning. It brings in its wake a lot of painful soul-searching, resulting in a period of time during which we feel disorientated and at odds with the rest of the world. Once our personal microcosm tips up the right way again, we can pick up the pieces and move on, safe in the knowledge that we have survived and are wiser for the experience.

The thirties

The next major identity crisis for a woman strikes in her early thirties. Just turning thirty is a crisis in itself if what I felt was typical and all the women in my acquaintance report accurately. The leap from twenty-nine to thirty is gigantic! Youth is over—there is no longer any way to avoid facing the fact. Thirty is viewed by some as the beginning of the end.

These melodramatic notions indicate the way that women seem to generally feel about turning thirty, and yet, when you think of it, thirty is far from old. In many ways, the years of the thirties are the most vibrant decade. A woman has the most freedom and is more poised and confident in herself. The truth of this statement begins to sink in after the first two or three years, but if a woman thinks she can settle down for a long and cosy ride, she's in for a huge shock. The thirties syndrome is about to rear its ugly head. So what is this crisis and what does it mean to a woman in her everyday existence?

Thirties syndrome

I believe that this set of behaviours occurs at around thirty-two to thirty-four years of age because it is almost exactly a decade after a woman enters a twenties commitment, be it marriage or a job. This identity crisis is perhaps the most uncomfortable; it shakes the very foundation of a woman's life, everything she values has to be re-examined and discarded if necessary. It is akin to going through the experience of a tornado sweeping through your life clearing all the debris, but also some of the things you like, the safe and comfortable components. One thing that the thirties syndrome will never let you be is complacent or staid. It is all about change and new beginnings. If you are going through it now or have already been through it, you will know precisely what I mean.

I have counselled so many women in this age group with exactly the same 'symptoms' that there is no possibility of mere coincidence. A patient walks in; she is thirty-three. She begins to tell me how she feels as I ask questions. Within a few minutes, she wants to know if I am psychic. How can I possibly know all her symptoms? Isolating certain recurring characteristics is not difficult, especially when some of the descriptions are worded in exactly the same way.

Here are some of the distinctive behaviours. It is now roughly ten years since the average woman married or began her career seriously. She has played the game, fulfilled her obligations, and developed the sort of lifestyle she thought she wanted. Realistically, what does a woman know of herself and her long-term desires at the age of twenty-three or twenty-four? Sure, she thinks she knows a lot—one graduates from high school with the sure and certain knowledge that all of life's questions have been encountered and answered. Consider this saying: 'Just when I thought I had all the answers, I found there were only more questions!'

At eighteen, the world is your oyster. Everything is possible and the years stretch long and unencumbered ahead. You believe that all you have to be is a good person and life will be simple and successful. Then disillusionment sets in when your plans do not work out. You seem to struggle endlessly, shedding more and more of your dreams as you get older. A forty-year-old head on a twenty-year-old person would teach that life does not have to be difficult, but how would you learn your lessons along the way and get to know so much more twenty years later?

Thus, a woman of thirty years is living with the choices of a much younger woman, a woman she hardly recognises any more, and one that she undoubtedly no longer wants to be. What does she do? Discard the husband and children she loves simply because she feels differently about herself? Not possible, so the simple answer is to ignore the rumblings in her mind and the disquiet in her heart. She gives herself a pep talk and gets on with it. This crisis, unlike the one in her twenties, will not go away by 'coping' or pretending. The analogy of the tornado was offered as a deliberate choice. Like a major natural disaster, the signs manifest themselves for some time before the full onslaught, giving time to 'batten down the hatches' and make preparation to ensure minimal damage. In emotional matters the warning signs also appear, but women choose not to examine them and reinforce their resources. Hence, when the full force of the crisis hits, a woman is in the eye of the storm before she has the chance to catch her breath. 'Suddenly' she is acting differently; her family finds a stranger in their midst. Life becomes a veritable smorgasbord of emotions: hubby's defensive (What have I done?); children are bewildered (Doesn't Mommy love us anymore?); the woman at the heart of her family's pain is going through an agony of guilt (Why am I doing this?) All she knows is that there is no turning back; the process of extreme change has inevitably begun.

This rather gloomy picture may seem exaggerated. To the men, women and children who go through it every day it is probably understated. The worst part is that the participants are acting out a drama that has no meaning for them. The pivotal member of the family is no longer the security centre of the home. Their foundation is shaky and no one knows what to do about it. Mother seems remote; she is out a lot more; when she is home, she no longers wants to do the chores. Her manner is different, somehow sharper and firmer. For obvious reasons, many marriages sail into uncharted waters at this time. Some women opt out altogether, leaving the family for the sake of their own sanity and their family's happiness. When husbands consult me after this occurrence, I counsel extreme patience. As with the twenties crisis, women are out there on their own, unable to allow anyone from their 'old' existence to help them, for fear of being hindered. You see the real dilemma lies in the fact that a part of the woman likes what is happening. She enjoys her new-found independence which only adds to the confusion.

What the thirties syndrome essentially does is 'rock the boat'. It causes a shake-up of old ways of functioning and traditional beliefs. Not only will the external woman change (new hairstyle, make-up, clothes, etc.), but this time the metamorphosis will include the whole person. Husbands and boyfriends should not expect the woman they knew ever to come back. After this upheaval, no matter what the outcome, wives and girlfriends will be irretrievably altered. If handled correctly, this is a time of tremendous potential growth for both the woman and her loved ones, because the ultimate picture will be of a woman in a lifestyle chosen for herself, not one she has by default. Therefore, relationships can and will be much more 'real' than in the past. Too often, pride and ego get in the way, but a fresh new beginning is now possible. Another reason why the image of the tornado is so applicable to this situation is that, after the event, there is little of the former left standing. How do you survive without the trappings of your known life?

Therein lies the first lesson of the thirties syndrome: you are not any of the components that make up your life. There is strength inside you that you did not know was there until the testing started. Now, why wait till you're in trouble to call on this inner power? You have it at your disposal all the time, from birth until death. You are never powerless. The key to recovery, as with any other identity crisis, is to assess the progress made in your life and decide where you want to go from here. Human beings generally fear change. When things are going smoothly you leave well enough alone, thinking not to tempt fate with musings of your good luck. When you are in a life struggle, you grit your teeth and wait for the end of the bad time. Voluntarily appraising your life and looking for areas of improvement is too frightening. It also might mean that you have to take up the challenge and find a more efficient way to operate. Better just to not think about it until you must.

For myself, I needed to find a better way to function within my close personal relationships. A subconscious part of me knew this fact, so I 'allowed' a lot of terribly painful things to happen in my life. I somehow knew I had to go through the fire in order to grow and be stronger, just as steel is reinforced in the heat of the flame. A decade has passed since that period of my life, I see only the benefits I accrued from those losses, even though my conscious mind would have never willingly gone through the pain.

For various reasons, some women go through the thirties syndrome in their *late* thirties. In many of the cases I have seen, this delay happens when women marry later, say twenty-eight or twenty-nine. Once through the fire, a woman is very much the stronger and better. She may be left standing alone and bereft of her previous props, but in most cases she will no longer be afraid or uncertain any longer.

The forties

If entering the thirties is terrifying for a woman and appears to signal the end of her youth, the gap between thirty-nine and forty seems to yawn a little less wide. 'Life begins at forty', the saying goes. Perhaps we have heard this adage so often that we have been indoctrinated by its message. I actually looked forward to turning forty as the time drew near. No shudders or wishing time to stand still as in the case of my thirtieth birthday. This sentiment is shared by most of the women I've quizzed on this subject. Generally, turning forty is a landmark in one's life, like reaching the age of maturity at twenty-one and being officially given a key to the front door, even if you have had one since you were sixteen!

What door does one's fortieth birthday unlock? I sum it up thus: the twenties—building and practical; the thirties—psychological and learning; the forties—freeing and spiritual.

The age of spiritual growth

Your forties can be everything you might have expected and more, a time to engage in a programme of self-expansion and enhancing your awareness. Let yourself be led by instinct to the temple of knowledge. If you are wondering where that is, it resides within you. Many of these truths are available to us from birth, but we either choose not to embrace them or we reject them out of fear and ignorance. There is a saying, 'When the student is ready, the teacher appears.' Certainly, it happened that way in my case. Whatever your personal circumstance when you turn forty, you will have greater opportunity for spiritual growth, and I mean that in the broadest sense. This time in your life will be an exciting journey of discovery for you.

At forty, a woman has weathered a number of crises. She may or may not be with the same man she married in her twenties; she may not be with any lover at all. The forty-year-old woman could be an outstanding businessperson or a bystander in the commerce of life around her. A woman of this age often desires to return to university or the workforce. If she has had children, they are now self-sufficient, quite likely living away from the family home. She and her husband, if still together, are companions and friends before lovers, or she may be in a subsequent marriage and working hard to ensure it is her last.

There are as many circumstances as there are different women in this world. The details are not important. The common denominator is a subtle yet undeniable sense that this is now *her* time. She has done the dishes, helped with the homework, loved her husband, and helped make her boss rich. Now she wants something that has no purpose other than to fulfil her. Finding this fulfilment is the first challenge. I usually suggest to women that they think of something they always wanted to do, and disregard the fact that it might be totally impractical. If money is not an issue, pursue an activity purely for love. Often, that type of thing ends up as a paid job.

Empty-nest syndrome

Should you expect a forties crisis? If there is one, it will again involve confronting identity. Some women do not find the prospect of more time and freedom attractive. They dread the long, empty hours ahead. Where once the shouts and laughter of children filled their days, now they have to paint in the pictures themselves on a seemingly endless canvas. This is what therapists refer to as the 'empty-nest syndrome'. If a woman's whole *raison d'être* has been her family and caring for them, she now feels cast adrift, unnecessary, out of a job. Some women get very bitter and try to cling to their maturing children, using emotional blackmail to keep them close. For such a woman, turning forty is a symbol of a very different kind of loss, not of youth but of purpose. There is little joy in it. Loneliness and boredom are a real trap, but again, awareness can prevent the problem becoming too great. Look ahead. Do not just let this stage of life creep up on you. Be the driver of your own life, not a passive passenger willing to be delivered to destinations of another's choice.

A job is not the only answer; in fact, it may not be at all right for some women. If finances permit, a woman who has worked all of her adult life may need to give up going to paid employment and spend more time on a hobby, develop an artistic skill, or travel extensively. Neither men nor women should have to wait until they 'retire' to free up their schedules for the things they love doing. Society's idea of retirement is 'enforced pleasure'—you have earned this time, so get out there and enjoy it if it kills you! No wonder that in so many cases it does. Some people die soon after retiring because they lose their meaning of life, which was prescribed for them at their place of work over several decades. (More on this later.) The important fact to keep uppermost in your mind (after the cake and the party have disappeared along with the last strains of 'Happy Birthday') is to see the time ahead not as empty, but unexplored. There are late-bloomers like me who have more plans and ideas than they could ever implement if they live to be two hundred. Therefore, your fear should not be running out of meaningful things to do, but running out of energy before you get round to all of your projects. Remember to identify your own particular demon, and then send it packing with a good swift kick.

When I was a teenager, turning forty seemed like dying! Did anybody actually live to be that old? At the very least, it is the beginning of middle-age, but you can choose to say that you have already lived half of your life or that you have another half a lifetime to go! It is the old 'is the glass half-empty or half-full' argument. The answer you choose is dictated by your philosophy of life and reflects your attitude to a lot of things. When I turned twenty-one, I remember thinking, Well, this is it; time to grow up now and act like an adult. Somehow, I could not pull it off. Something inside me was not yet ready to relinquish the trappings of youth. At my fortieth birthday party, I wore a ribbon that read, 'I may be getting older but I refuse to grow up.' That says it all. Why should you have to behave as age dictates, as long as you act with decorum? Obviously, there are some behaviours that are inappropriate for an older woman, but on the whole one should have the maximum freedom of choice.

All birthdays are cause for reflection, but more so the 'special' milestones like eighteen, twenty-one, twenty-five, forty and fifty. They are times to look back on achievements, mistakes, lessons, experiences and blessings and to give thanks for all of it, even the difficult patches. These are the three gifts of life that I cherish the most: the value of enduring friendship; learning it is okay to make mistakes; and understanding that wishes really do have the power to come true. The people we have around us mirror our successes and our attitudes, so look hard at your companions and the details of your life as it is lived every day. That is one of the better side-effects of getting older—the gift of clarity that is afforded you via hindsight. A woman's transformation begins in her thirties and is continued into her forties. It can only be complete when she comes to terms with the changes and starts to feel comfortable in her new skin. In our twenties we take our good looks for granted, then we experiment and toy with various versions of ourselves. The not-so-subtle effects of the thirties syndrome paves the way for a mellower existence, if we learn to age with grace and not reluctance.

For those of you who are under forty, sail forward with anticipation and no negative preconceptions. If you are forty and not enjoying it, discover the reason and do something about it. Find a niche for yourself that is uniquely yours. Pull apart all the components of your life, find out what's missing and how to get it. Most of all, enjoy the woman that you have earned the right to be.

The mature years

During the course of her forties, a woman will gradually learn to enjoy being the mistress of her own fate in a way that would not have been possible earlier in her life. You may well protest that not all women are restricted by family and obligations that prevent their personalities from fully developing. That is true, but practical hindrances are not the only consideration. This chapter is not simply about getting older. It is primarily about psychological maturation, learning and growing.

Each decade brings its own wisdom, and there are no shortcuts. Certainly, some women develop at a faster rate, either by choice or by circumstance. If a girl suffers a painful experience early in life, this may force her to grow up sooner than her contemporaries. Recalling what was said about the only child, she is often perceived as an 'old' type because she tends to give out an air of seriousness missing in other children of the same age. This 'air' is usually because she spends more of her time around older people and has learned to adopt their style of behaviour rather than acting as a child. She will be less boisterous, less restless, and more content to sit with adults or amuse herself in a quiet way. Another example might be a young woman who has a deep desire to gain self-knowledge early in her life. We all do in one way or another, but some people feel a stronger compulsion to read, discuss and even meditate in their teens or twenties, while the rest of us are too busy living life to study it. As you go through your own journey, it is very important to know that there are no experts in living. We are all amateurs thrust into a complex world where we have to learn everything from scratch.

Even as you pick up information you are aware that you can never catch up, so you wrongly elevate your elders to godlike heights when in fact you are a fellow traveller stumbling in the dark and trying to gain a foothold. What you should respect about the senior members of your society is that they have made it to where they are. Age by itself does not guarantee wisdom. There are just as many ignorant older people around as young, but the mature men and women of this world have a lot to teach if they have learned their own lessons well. I love to see young people getting along well with the aged and sharing their various viewpoints. The generations can be linked with tolerance and love. So, when you get to be fifty, remember that you do not deserve a medal or a free ride just because of your age. I have seen so much bitterness and regret because people who have not earned their children's love and respect through the years are left lonely and isolated in their old age. There are always two sides to every coin. You reap what you sow in life.

The psychology of ageing

It's a misnomer to speak of 'ageing' as the stage of our lives when you noticeably get older because 'ageing' starts from the moment of birth. Also, some people never appear 'old' while others behave in an elderly fashion when they are in their youth. At what moment do you actually sense the passage of time? Is there a first time that you look in the mirror and notice wrinkles, lines, and grey hairs? They say that the years speed by more quickly as you get older.

Perhaps they do because time grows more precious with every passing year. You are more aware of the gift of life and the finite nature of your human existence. If these thoughts occur to you when you are young, you can brush them off as philosophical ideas, abstract at best, but by the time you reach your forties and fifties, the whole issue is becoming more personal and specific. For women, ageing is inextricably tied up with notions of losing one's looks, being unattractive to the opposite gender, and no longer being vital and sexy. Thank goodness for famous fifty-year-olds like Linda Evans, Jane Fonda and Joan Collins who have given older women new hope. Not only might life begin at forty, it can actually get better. Listen to a few interviews with women who are over forty and they will all say much the same thing: they feel so much freer, able to fully be themselves, unafraid to explore new careers or relationships.

What then are the stress traps, if any? Again, it depends on a woman's marital state. If she is married, her stress or lack of it will be shaped by the success or otherwise of her marriage.

By this age, a man and woman who have been together since their twenties or thirties will know each other pretty well and be able to live together within reasonable bounds of civility and understanding, even if the flush of passion is no longer present. (Of course, there are those mature relationships which are highly sexual.) Unsuccessful marriages will tend to have sorted themselves out by now. Many women who endure unhappy relationships for years, often for the sake of keeping the family together, find the courage to break away in their forties or early fifties. That choice is another characteristic of the period. It comes largely from an increase of self-esteem and the realisation that women have a right to consider their own happiness as well as their family's.

A woman who finds herself alone in her later years may have a difficult battle with stress. We live in a society of couples. If you are not one of a pair, you are 'out', at odds with the community at large. People do not always like to invite a single person to dinner because they have to make a choice between having an odd number around the table or finding a mate for the unattached woman and being accused of 'matchmaking'. A woman who has never married is regarded with suspicion. Is she so unattractive that no man has ever asked her, is she a closet lesbian, or is there something wrong with her? (See Chapter Six.)

Loneliness is a real issue for older women who either live alone or who simply do not have a close friend or lover with whom to share their lives. Over the years, the people they have known move away, marry or die. Suddenly they realise that they are no longer young, and the chances of meeting new people get slimmer every year. Think about it. Most of your lasting friendships are made at school or work, when you are in the formation stages of your life. You may add one or two friends to that original supply, but as you age, you also grow more difficult to please, more discerning about who you want to spend your time with. The days seemingly get longer as you find less to fill them. Many women find themselves widowed at this time and having to endure the bereavement process on their own. Making a fresh start isn't easy even for young people, but it gets harder as you age because you also become more inflexible.

Your personality changes. Older people can sometimes be

very stubborn, wanting things done their way, forgetting the pressures their younger relatives are up against. Obviously, if an ageing woman is ill or incapacitated in any way, special consideration must be given. Otherwise, it is important to keep in mind that relationships at all ages are a 'give and take' business. There has to be two-way interaction or it is not a 'relationship' in the strict sense, just indulgence on one person's part and tyranny on the other.

If there is no one to care for her, a woman may find herself at sixty or seventy, having to give up her marital home and move (with or without husband) to an aged peoples' home. To some women, this move is worse than dying. The stress of this loss of independence can be likened to the stress of retirement. After all, a woman may have worked in that house for thirty or forty years. Now she is being put 'out to pasture'.

Stress management at this level is just as essential as it is at any age previously. Life can still be full and rewarding, with new things to learn and fun challenges. It may only be learning backgammon, but in my opinion, more people die of boredom than any other single factor. My recipe for a long and happy life is to always stay in touch with the joy of every day, the possibilities and the magic, whether it be having your favourite meal, playing with a child, or watching the sun set. There is magic all around you, but you might sometimes forget to look. What has age got to do with the beauty of the moonlight, the miraculous sound of laughter, or a gentle breeze at day's end? Stay in touch. Don't let anyone tell you that your life is over or you have nothing to contribute—you have as much as you always had. If you were an uncaring and selfish young person, that's how you will be when you are old unless you consciously choose to change. If you love life and love people, living will be joyous for you at any age. It is your decision.

The potential for stress during the mature years can thus be summarised as the following:

- fear of ageing.
- relationship problems.
- loneliness.
- widowhood.
- personality changes.

■ moving house.
■ boredom/emptiness.
■ feeling useless.

There is no reason for a woman to feel rejected or unloved if she has to live out her days in a nursing home or hospital. If she has always been a vital part of her family's life and the interaction has been positive, the situation should continue in the same vein. A lot of criticism is levelled at families who place their aged relatives in homes. It is not the place that is important but the quality of life, and that largely depends on the woman in question, her family relationships and the choice of institution.

No discussion on ageing in women would be complete without the mention of the following phenomena: menopause/sexuality; mid-life crisis; and death.

Menopause

Menopause is a biological and emotional experience, unique to women. I have sometimes argued that men do go through a type of menopause, but the major difference lies in the fact that men do not undergo physical changes which are tantamount to a reversal of puberty. Just as in puberty, when girls have to deal with hormonal activity and a whole mass of conflicting emotions, so do their middle-aged counterparts during menopause. What men experience as 'menopause' is closer to a mid-life crisis, which women have as well!

In simple terms, menopause is a slowing up of all the processes that characterise a woman as distinctly female: her menstrual cycles will decrease and eventually stop altogether; she will gradually lose her ability to get pregnant or bear a child; her libido may lower and certain physical signs will signal the bodily changes that are taking place, for example, a dry vagina during intercourse.

One of the difficulties in coping with menopause is that there is no set age at which all women pass through it; it can begin as early as the late thirties or not until the fifties. The whole process can also take place over a number of years so that adjustment to the experience becomes a tedious and protracted business. Some women can actually have the symptoms for years before realising that they are experiencing menopause. If they have not kept themselves well-informed in their earlier years about their bodies and stages of development, they can feel very frightened and disorientated, not confiding in anyone because they think they are alone in their suffering. Ignorance in the community on this subject also leads to further isolation for women attempting to come to grips with their 'change of life', as menopause was called for many years. Even doctors are sometimes unsympathetic, telling women that they are simply bored because their children have grown up and that they should take up a hobby and not concern themselves about sex anymore or trying to stay young, none of which is basically relevant.

With the advent of more knowledge and education on human development issues, many subjects like menopause have been pulled out of Victorian closets and looked at in the light of a twentieth-century day. Women who want to understand what is happening to them at any stage of their lives and who want to take responsibility for themselves now can. They can help themselves by reading, studying and sharing on the issues that are relevant. Hormone Replacement Therapy, or HRT as it is known, has a valid role to play in controlling symptoms and allowing a woman to continue a productive and happy existence while her body progresses in a perfectly natural way. As mentioned before, there is a certain amount of controversy surrounding the taking of artificial hormones by medication. Having been through the pros and cons in my own life, practically as well as theoretically, I can say that this issue must be one of the least agreed-on topics in modern medicine. On no other subject have I heard so many conflicting opinions, and because everyone feels very strongly about their own argument, it's hard to disseminate all the information and know what's best. The most honest practitioner was the one who told me that the reason for all the differing views is simply that no one, not even the 'experts', really knows. That does not inspire a great deal of confidence in the advice given, especially when you are suffering seemingly unbearable symptoms. Having to make allowances for medical ignorance or error is frightening.

To illustrate with just one personal example, during the early period of my HRT treatment one highly qualified specialist in this field advised me to try a different combination of hormones because he did not agree with what I was given by another doctor. I duly went onto the new drug with the understanding that I may feel a 'little blue' until my body adapted. Four months of crying, irrational behaviour and emotional hell later, I ended up in the hospital and was told in no uncertain terms by the consulting gynecologist to stop taking the new drug. It is easy to forgive the doctor who put me through that unnecessary suffering because he was genuinely trying to help. My point is that the patient is ultimately the only expert: Now I take what suits my body and I do not consult anyone on my progress as long as I am feeling good.

One of the biggest battles is with tension, which is part and parcel of menopause. It feels like a severe form of PMS (Premenstrual Syndrome), added to which are the famous 'hot flashes'. The other unpleasant realities are depression, the disintegration of the bones known as osteoporosis, and loss of sexual appetite. HRT can relieve all of these and restore balance and harmony to a woman and her family.

What of the minuses? Researchers cannot seem to agree on whether HRT increases the risk of breast cancer or actually makes a woman immune to it. Then there is the risk of thrombosis, which is a very real one as I know someone who died from it very suddenly and swiftly, as a direct result of HRT. I have been told not to allow varicose veins to form in my legs as they could be dangerous sources of clotting. From a practical point of view, one of the worst side-effects of HRT is weight gain due to fluid retention, but that can be combated by a regular and rigorous exercise programme.

Hopefully, what is presented here is an honest and balanced picture of both sides of the HRT issue. Having been through the mill on this one, I would have to say that I am prepared to take whatever risks are involved in order to enjoy the quality of life that is possilble with HRT. I have lived with the alternative, and for me that's not an option. There are many other factors involved in the incidence of sickness and disease. It is a question of moderation and commonsense—it is not wise to be overly concerned with one's health, nor should good health ever be taken for granted or abused. Faced with the choice of whether to have HRT, weigh your symptoms against the risks, read up on the latest research and then make up your own mind. Do not be scared off by the fearmongers, and don't take any expert opinion as gospel.

And the panic comes

There is no need to say very much on mid-life crisis as the name speaks for itself. It is a blanket term for the transitional period in the middle years when a woman has to adjust to ageing, menopause, the empty-nest syndrome and all the other developments discussed earlier. One thing that does need mentioning is the fact some women have what is commonly known as a 'change-of-life baby' during this period. It usually happens because a couple become a bit lax about contraception once a woman starts to enter menopause. A baby at this time of life is often seen as a last grasp at womanhood. The child is loved as a special gift of nature, but if you have specific reasons for not wanting another child or if you think you could not cope after years of mothering other children, then keep in mind that menopause can continue for many years. Do not come off your chosen method of contraception until you are absolutely sure your body is beyond conceiving a child.

Ageing—angel or devil?

The ravages of bereavement will be spoken of more fully in later chapters. For now, a brief word needs to be said about personal mortality and how to deal with it conceptually as well as emotionally.

Death is one of the subjects that has been taken out of the closet in recent years together with incest, homosexuality and orgasm. Unlike these others, death will happen for all of us, without exception, and is a purely natural process, as much a part of life as birth. It remains an abstract notion until such time as it touches one personally. That is what most people do—only think about a thing when it affects them personally or if there is a reason. Obviously, one of these times occurs during the mature years.

The most comfortable image for death is to think of the whole of life as a journey, like travelling by train. You get on at a certain point and travel for a length of time. During that time, you may get derailed more than once, there will be detours, stops and starts; mostly, the journey will proceed in an uneventful, monotonous way with occasional points of interest as you pass some unusual or exciting terrain. Then, finally, you get off. Keep in mind that your getting on and off does not affect the train's continuous travelling. Whatever you leave behind or take with you will be a direct result of your own efforts. After you disembark, you may wait for another form of transport to take you to further experiences or you may walk awhile before setting off on new adventures. There could be someone or several people waiting to greet you or you may need to journey on before meeting up with familiar faces. Seen in this light, there is nothing to fear about death because it is no more than the end of a journey.

It is terribly sad when aged folk feel that after a certain age all they can do is sit around and wait to die. Having done battle with my own scary visions of death, I see now that it has no power over me because I will give myself freely into its arms when the time is right. The only tragedy in life is to hold on to something that is outdated, out of fear and loneliness. The greatest blessing must surely be to die with peace and a smile on your lips. It is achievable. As with everything else, you only have to want it badly enough to have it.

There is nostalgia for the passing of youth. Yet, that is the very nature of life—transition, colour, change. The best thing about growing older is slowing down; youth is exhausting. It is nice to feel good about staying home on a Saturday evening, to take time to enjoy a sunset without rushing off to the next activity, to take nothing for granted and to know that life gets better every day. No matter what your age, enjoy it to the hilt. Do not let people dictate to you what you ought to be doing or feeling. Most importantly, stay in touch with the child within you, your truest and wisest inspiration.

AFFIRMATIONS

I trust the process of life.
Getting there is much better than being there.
Life is good inside me at every moment.

Chapter Five

Relationships

Q uite a lot has already been said about relationships. This
chapter will look specifically at all the different types
of roles that each of us play on a daily basis. While
applying labels to relationships is not desirable, they are
unavoidable in a discussion on human interactions because,
as social beings, we function very much within the boundaries
of appropriate behaviour for specific roles. For instance, a
mother/daughter interaction follows the pattern that has been
formed over the years they have shared; two strangers have no
history and, therefore, must play a different game until a
comfortable relationship is set.

Eric Berne spoke of 'the games people play'. Those of you
who aspire to honesty and being 'real' like to think that you
do not play games in your daily dealings. The truth is that
games are unavoidable. That does not mean you are false and
living your life behind a mask; rather, relationship games are
the texture of the patterns that exist between people.

Compare the concept to a board or card game—there are
certain rules, moves and an overall format. To veer off these
established components is to no longer be 'playing the game'.
In the same way, relationships must operate on agreed-upon
ground rules. Blood relations tend to find their own levels
without the need for discussion, while friendships and romantic
alliances have to be more formally structured. Some people may

find this structuring terribly cold and mechanical, but if you think about it, most difficulties between people are caused by a lack of understanding and communication.

This chapter will include a study of marriage and parenting, the stresses and problems, remedies and positive strategies to gaining more effective relationships. Within these two examples are all the ingredients necessary for a full examination of the main relationship issues. Although not all of us marry, we are all someone's child, and many women bear children in and out of the marriage state. Unwed mothers are becoming increasingly common. We actually play many roles, including sibling, aunt, neighbour, grandparent, godparent, cousin, mother/father, boss, employee and many possible others. Moreover, we need to understand the relationships we have with ourselves. The whole concept of role has to be explored before going any further into the chapter.

What determines role? Apart from the ones we are born into or choose for ourselves, the acting-out of social roles is linked directly to the very important issue of identity. Initially, your identity is stamped on you by all the factual data that surrounds you from the moment of birth: who your parents are, where you were born, your race, religion, colour, the country you belong to, the area you live in, the school you attend, your intelligence and physical characteristics. A thousand other small details come into play as you move through your life, from your parents' social standing to your personal choices in clothes, music and food.

Every crossroad you come to and every path you take adds another dimension of identity to the emerging picture. By the time you are ready to go out into the world in your own right, you are a walking mass of statistics. As the world gets more complex and technological, the database on individuals is broadening. Feeling like just a name and number within your community is easy. This de-personalised era we live in offers a challenge to each of you to develop your own uniqueness and special qualities. Automation is all around you. Everything comes in instant form, and sometimes you forget that relationships and gifts like love cannot be bought over the counter at a discount store, nor can there be any shortcuts to success. Things may be quicker and easier now with modern conveniences, but essentially, the important things in life have not changed. Money still cannot buy happiness; success still has to be earned; simple joys are still the most rewarding. If you do not value yourself, it is easy to get lost in the crowd, especially if you live in the alienation of cities or the mediocrity of suburbia.

Identity is the outward stamp; role the outward behaviour. When an actor takes on a 'role', he/she must learn the chief characteristics of the person to be created or recreated—body language, mannerisms, gestures, voice patterns, idiosyncrasies or habits, dress, walking style. In everyday life, a phenomenon exists known as stereotyping. It causes us to judge each other by a series of conditioned responses. If a millionaire enters a room dressed in rags, the people surrounding him would assume he/she is a bum, unless they know differently. In Western societies, you are judged very much on your appearance—you are 'identified' by the external trappings that are visible to others.

Another major yardstick by which you are judged is your occupation. This is why many unemployed people feel so worthless. They feel they have no identity upon which to meet their fellow humans on an equal basis (see Chapter Eight). What is the first question one is usually asked on a social occasion? 'What's your job?' If you happen to have a job that sounds too much like fun, the rejoinder is something like, 'Oh, that's nice but what do you do for a living?' The implication is, of course, that jobs must meet certain criteria and the approval of social standards. That is one of the areas of this identity business that can cause stress—the feeling that one must conform or risk censure and even ostracism.

The other major stress trap is the conflict between external and internal realities. As you get older, you may wish to discard the identity(ies) that have been imposed on you. The original factual details cannot in the main be altered, except for such things as hair colour and choice of religion. One key example of desired change is in the area of personality, which will be explored more fully in Chapter Nine, but it is important to know for now that personal growth entails a heightened awareness of inner harmony and increased desire to outwardly express this tranquility. Thus is personality transformed. Even a very shy and introverted child may blossom into an assertive and dynamic woman through improving self-esteem or life-skills education. Unfortunately, family and friends are often uncomfortable with new images, as was seen in the last chapter about changes taking place in a woman's thirties and forties. Those close to you can feel threatened as can people from your past. I was quite amazed when I met an old friend at a party; our conversation got around to the intervening period in our lives since we were together. I had been through my thirties crisis by then and was proud of the progress I had made, so I expressed this to him. He refused to accept what I was saying and kept insisting that I had not changed a bit! He was not a superficial type of guy, so I can only assume that he had an emotional investment in an image of me which he was not about to have tarnished.

As you grow and change, people, especially family members, will expect you to retain characteristics or personality traits that you had as a child. Breaking them out of that expectation and getting them to accept you as a unique individual can take many years. Interestingly, when your family starts to adapt to changes in your behaviour and attitudes, you tend to still try and conform to those discarded expectations. This psychological quirk is subtle yet complex and, in essence, a self-sabotage. A lot of stress problems relate in one way or another to identity struggles. They are the starting points for self-improvement, followed by two other stages: self-knowledge and self-love (awareness/acceptance).

You need to be able to come to terms with your inner changes and display them more openly and freely. Learn to form a new identity for yourself that is appropriate to your stage of development and try to build more and more self-knowledge. To accomplish this, I have devised an exercise I call 'Identity Strategies', a self-monitoring system of self-actualisation. You cannot love something you know nothing about. Just as you set about to learn a foreign language or musical instrument, you need more information about yourself as a person before you can actively change the things you do not like and enhance the qualities you cherish. I suggest you try this exercise for a period of approximately six weeks, using a diary to record your insights and observations. You will be surprised at how much you learn about yourself.

Identity strategies

Monitor the following:

1. Your intuitions in given situations.
2. Your own speech, particularly in anger.
3. What other people say to you.
4. What other people say about you.
5. Your reactions and behaviour in given situations or around certain people. Be aware of flashback emotions, such as taking an instant dislike to someone you have never previously met.
6. Your dreams, particularly recurring ones.
7. Other people's reactions to you.
8. Your body language in given situations.
9. Tensions within your own body.

Keep a journal of thoughts, ideas, and feelings as they occur to you, and try to identify any patterns that are obvious.

Make a list of the following:

- qualities in yourself that you accept and ones you do not accept.
- things in your life that make you happy and things that make you unhappy.
- all of the things you want in life TODAY.

To explain each of the above nine points a little more fully:

Our sixth sense

1. Intuition is usually regarded as the province of women and is often spoken of in a patronising or deprecatory way, as if it is a minor tool or skill at best. In fact, intuition is a very useful aid in self-education. If you can learn to trust your inner voice, you have a direct line to subconscious riches of knowledge and power. The easiest way to describe 'intuition' is to say that it is a sense of what the right thing is to do in a given situation, a gut reaction that comes from deep within you and has no rational foundation.

I pride myself on being a logical and intelligent person, but I also have a healthy respect for seemingly unexplainable phenomena. Together with a reasonable amount of scepticism, I add a generous dose of belief in the existence of magic in ordinary lives. 'What works must be real' basically holds true for me. I suggest you try my ideas for yourself and adopt them when you have proven them to your own satisfaction. Work with your intuitive processes and build up a friendship with that truest part of you—your inner or higher self.

Listening to the grapevine

2. Your speech reveals a lot about you to others and also adds to your bank of self-knowledge. Chapter One outlined the desirability of clearer and more honest communication. As you grow stronger in your sense of identity and more truly assertive, your manner of speaking changes. You will notice this change as you grow. It can be quite disconcerting, especially to those around you. A quiet, mousy woman may develop a loud, booming voice; a shy, passive one could suddenly appear demanding and overbearing. This exaggeration is only because you are initially uncomfortable in your new role. It is possible to overdo assertiveness to the point of aggression until you learn to like the image you now wish to project. Gradually, people around you accept the changes without having to be hit over the head with them. When you are in the grip of a powerful emotion, the true things that you may not normally reveal can come blurting out. Statements you make when you are angry usually tell what you actually feel, yet anger is used as an excuse: 'I didn't mean it. I was angry.' Instead, you could benefit from taking note of what comes out and learn from it. It is like the pieces of a jigsaw puzzle; with every piece added, the picture becomes clearer and emerges further. Also true is that 'many a true word is spoken in jest'. If you are unsure of how a remark will be received, you tend to play safe by sugaring the pill with humour and laughing as you speak. Then, if the receiver reacts negatively, you can say you were only joking.

Once you start to work seriously with these identity strategies, you will find it difficult to lie to yourself. At first, working with them is a mechanical exercise, but it gradually becomes second nature, and you do it without having to think about it. Eventually, the whole process is internalised and becomes a way of life.

Another circumstance that can bring out the relentless truth in your speech is a state of inebriation. Alcohol breaks down the normal inhibitions to which social beings adhere. It gives you false courage and allows you to exhibit facets of your personality that are kept hidden when you are sober. Even though getting drunk is not a desirable method of self-development, it is worth noting how you behave and what you say if you are ever in that position. Listen to the reports your friends give you the next morning!

Avoid making blanket statements about yourself or judging others by your rules because, invariably, the truth lies somewhere between the two extremes. Self-delusion is a direct consequence of not knowing yourself. You delude yourself as much as you delude others. You might be afraid to explore yourself or experiment with anything that may take you to the outer reaches of your personality. Therefore, you continually limit yourself in your thinking, ambitions, dreams and relationships. The most important thing to believe is that you do have a choice; you are not totally a product of your environment, upbringing, or family background.

Everything that happens around you every day is worth noting. If you miss the signs, you miss the opportunities to learn. One thing you are trying to do is confront and integrate the two halves of yourself, the inner world with the outward manifestation. As you become more in tune and more balanced, the differences lessen; the external personality becomes simply a projected picture of your true self. Conducting your life this way is wonderfully fulfilling and sincere, but it is very threatening at first. It can make you feel so vulnerable and exposed that you welcome the return to your persona existence, saving the deepest parts of yourself for a selected few and, sometimes, not even then.

Speech is a gift of communication. Although not the only one, it is the most conscious and commonly used, and you learn early in life to manipulate what you say to get the desired effect. When you do away with these pretensions, speech becomes a valuable tool of expression for your real feelings, your original ideas, opinions and thoughts. Originality and spontaneity can then become possible. Look below the surface and behind the words, beyond semantics to messages from the heart. Therein lies the path to being a well-rounded human being and woman.

Masterminding a personality lift

3. and 4. In the same way as your own speech is revealing, so is the conversation directed at you or around you. It widens the horizons of your self-perception. Relatives or friends may comment on a particular quirk of your personality which you may not have noticed in yourself. Rather than be offended by these remarks, let them teach you something about yourself.

You cannot worry about what people say concerning you when you are not present, but when comments filter back to you, do not waste your energy overreacting. There may be a grain of truth in what is said. No one likes to be the recipient of harsh judgments from others, especially people who do not know you well enough to be accurate in their assessment. Take notice of the choice of adjectives and phrases that are chosen to describe you, whether you agree with them or not. You will begin to discern a common thread running through descriptions and comments about you. For instance, a particular adjective may be used time and time again and will most likely represent the image you are primarily projecting.

Just as you need to express yourself clearly to others, you also have to make allowances for the gap between what you hear and what you perceive. Like it or not, everyone is a victim of labelling. If you are comfortable with the image that people generally have of you, then you can choose to accept the standard set of labels which are applied to you, even if they are not all complimentary. Otherwise, you can practise giving out new signals so that people will see you in a different light.

Learning to be objective about yourself puts the reins of your life firmly in your own hands. There need be no excuses or cop-outs, no confusion, unhappiness or doubt, no blame to apportion and no guilt or torturing yourself. You are free of all negative things.

Tapping your personal power

5. Think of yourself as a stress gauge. Like a geiger counter, the signals inside you will sound off loud and clear when you are with a person or group of people who trigger stress reactions in you. The same applies to being in certain places or performing particular tasks. Those who believe in reincarnation would say that these occurrences are linked to memories of past lives and that unhappy or painful associations that crop up cause you to relive those same experiences.

Whatever the reason, everyone has experienced it—a sense of uneasiness, sometimes even claustrophobia. I get it if I am in a public place and for one reason or another, cannot leave. A type of anxiety takes over and I feel as if I want to run out or stand up and scream. This anxiety must be akin to what agoraphobia sufferers feel, but mine has no element of fear in it, only an unpleasant, shut-in sensation.

Over the years, I have come to respect these impulses and simply remove myself from the event as quickly as possible after the onset of the anxiety. You should become acquainted with your reactions in this way. Do not just sit and endure it or tell yourself you are being stupid. There is a good reason for the way you feel. Not having knowledge of the cause in your conscious mind is no reason to dismiss it.

So-called personality clashes occur in much the same way. You meet someone and for no reason that you can judge, you feel an instant dislike for them. This is invariably because the person you cannot stand from the moment you set eyes on them possesses a similar personality to yourself, especially if the trait displayed is one you would rather not acknowledge. For instance, you are aware that your voice is a bit too loud; your friends have been teasing you about it for years. You go to a party and from across the room, a woman's voice can be heard booming out as she laughs at someone's joke. You immediately tend to think that that woman is unpleasant. Must she laugh so loudly? It is as if you have looked into a mirror and do not like what you see.

Take advantage of this insight. Learn about yourself. Add another piece to that puzzle. It will also help you to get along better with people as you no longer look for faults in them and categorise them into types you do or do not like. You begin to realise that the power is entirely in your hands. Therefore, when you smile, you find everyone around you is also wearing a cheerful face; when you are sour, grouches are likely to surround you. Personality clashes are no more than the result of insufficient self-knowledge, as are so many other negative behaviours.

You hear or say the words, 'the vibes I got'. These vibrations are simply the manifestations of your inner feelings. No matter how hard you try, you cannot totally disguise them. People can read off your signals or sense them in some way, even when you think you are giving out nothing. Body language is more specific (see point eight), but this is a more emotive, more personal aura which, in fact, can be seen by means of a special kind of photography because it has electro-energy. Just as you give them out, you can also sense them in other people. It relates to the chemistry you feel towards some individuals in a sexual way, some in a hostile way, and some people that you feel you have always known. These signals and those you give out by your body language are vital factors in your interactions at all levels. By studying them in yourself, you are able to make active choices regarding the way in which you want to be viewed by everyone around you.

There is another factor in all this that cannot be ruled out. Remember the profound influence of your childhood experiences and how events and incidents can stay with you long into adult life? When you find yourself at the wrong end of a very strong emotion and cannot easily explain the response, it can be the result of a 'flashback emotion'. This is an associative emotional response; in other words, you are literally being transported backwards emotionally, back to a time when a similar event distressed you or excited you or horrified you. This reaction happens commonly when you meet a person for the first time and immediately feel a strong emotion, completely out of proportion to the current event (how can you 'hate' someone you've just met?).

So, stay alert in order not to miss the continuous stream of information that is buzzing around you all the time. It takes a bit of time at first, but the rewards are great. Whether you react positively or negatively is not the issue. Try to avoid making value judgments about yourself in situations and concentrate on stepping back and being an observer. Only by objective appraisal can you ever see the truth, as, when you stand too close, your view is distorted. Awareness of your reaction makes all the difference to the way you handle stress. When you are working on your self-esteem and gaining inner strength, you feel protected, not behind a wall of defences, but in a fortress of your own making. You are of the world, but apart from it; with people, but separate from them; no longer vulnerable because you are free from all doubt and fear. All it really means is that you keep your own power unto yourself and give none of it away. Give of yourself, give love, give of your energies and talents, but your personal power is not for sharing. Offer that and you are issuing a licence for everyone to take advantage of you. No one should ever be able to make you feel inadequate or stupid or inferior; neither can anyone subject you to stress unless you yourself have chosen to live your life in that manner. Remember that stress becomes a bad habit and has to be discarded just as you would give up smoking or biting your nails.

Own your bad habits and give away neither your power over personal choice nor the making of mistakes. When you try to pin the blame for a mistake you have made on to another, you are wasting yet another opportunity to grow. Saying others are causing you stress is incorrect. They do what they do, and you must do what you do. If you choose to feel stressed, that is your business. This philosophy may seem rather harsh, but if you adopt a new slant to your relationships and the roles you play within them, life can quite subtly alter for the better.

Take the case of the neighbour you cannot get along with. Just seeing her across the fence is enough to put you into a bad humour for the rest of the day. Your strategy is usually to pretend you have not seen her to avoid having to speak. Why not turn that strategy around and give her a big hello, wave fondly, and rush over to chat at every opportunity? She will be so amazed you might find her annoying behaviour (whatever it is) will alter, or, in any case, you will begin to feel quite differently about her. Of course, if someone in your life is very negative or destructive and you can keep them at arm's length, it may be wiser to do so lest you absorb their vibes. If you simply find someone that you cannot get out of seeing difficult, your best bet is to keep your power and do a lot of smiling! Monitor your feelings and reactions around people, particularly those you see a lot of or who play a significant role in your life. They are the ones that matter most. The way you handle these interactions will make the difference between a happy or a stressed you.

Life's a dream

6. Dreams are the realm of fantasy, the symbolic language of your subconscious mind. They are essentially your communication link to your inner world. On that basis, you have much to learn from the messages and insights they offer. As a tool of self-knowledge, they are one of the most valuable. Dreams can offer help to someone going through a crisis or simply in the process of building self-esteem and enhancing personal development.

When Elaine lost her mother, she was left with the feeling that there were many unresolved issues between them. After counselling, Elaine began to understand herself as a child and to forgive her mother for her failings. Then she had a very significant dream in which she sat by her mother's bed as she lay dying. In the dream she felt grief and did not want her mother to die, but Elaine told her mother goodbye and very firmly stated to her that she, the mother, had to go now and leave her daughter to get on with living. This dream left Elaine very sad, yet it also marked a whole new beginning for her.

People who do not get a chance to say goodbye to loved ones at their death have a second chance through dreams. For several months before my mother died (she had cancer for two years so her death was not unexpected), I had recurring nightmares. Never before or since have I had bad dreams, but these were truly dreadful. Every night I was a sleeping witness to horror heaped upon horror—war, murder, torture, killings, mutilation, death. It was as if all my unspoken fears trotted out as I slept, in defiance of my stubborn silence during waking hours. I had no conception of the gravity of this event called death and my mother, whom I had believed invincible, was now going through it without me. Nothing I did would change one moment of her pain or prolong her life by one hour. So, young and inexperienced in tragedy, I continued a normal life by day while my subconscious, ever vigilant and close to the heart of all existence, forced me to look at the way I really felt during sleep.

Dreams can be relentless purveyors of truth as well as blessed bringers of comfort. A good example of the latter occurred to one couple whose marriage was very unhappy and on the verge of collapse. After a few sessions of counselling, the husband (who basically needed to do the most personal work) had a dream that he and his wife were with me and I asked him to tell me about his childhood experiences at the hands of his stepfather. In the dream, he poured his story out; then, he woke up crying. His wife comforted him, and in the pain of that moment their rift was healed. Years of anger, resentment and unresolved hurt washed away. They stayed up all night talking in each other's arms, and as husband and wife shared, they let down barriers and allowed each other in again.

Some metaphysicians believe that everyone is protected by an individual spirit guide, sometimes many. Your dream guide has the special task of walking with you through your sleeping hours, guarding you from nightmares and helping you to connect with your dreams. Never underestimate the power of dream activity. It is not hocus-pocus, but has been scientifically researched and clinically tested. In fact, more and more amazing results are being uncovered all the time. One recent documentary showed experiments in dream-sharing where people can inhabit each other's dreams after making a pre-sleep arrangement to meet *inside the dream experience*. As well, scientists are looking at the possibility of communicating with dreamers by giving them commands to perform during sleep or telling them to respond to specific stimuli. It opens up many more horizons for dream experiences. To those who might say, 'what's the point?', the point is that we sleep for more than a third of our lives on earth. That time is not blank. We are not only resting our physical bodies, but also our minds and emotions. Dreaming allows us to go over the events of the day in a cleansing fashion. Most dreams are of the garden-variety type, yet some are prophetic and creative. Receiving stories, songs, poems, designs and ideas of all sorts during the dream state and remembering them on waking is quite possible and there are many famous examples throughout history.

Explaining how people can learn of a relative's death or predict a disaster through dreaming is also difficult. There can be no satisfactory scientific explanation, but neither can it be mere coincidence. As with everything else suggested in this book, try it for yourself. The best way to work with dreams is to record them on a daily basis for a set period of time. Dream study is the anchor and foundation of a spiritual programme. The more you tune into your night-time psychic activity, the more accessible it becomes. How far you go will depend on the level of mind expansion you have reached and your personal belief system. Keeping a pad by your nightlight on the bedside table is advisable, especially at first, so that you can jot down the main images of your dreams during the night. As you train yourself, you need less and less to wake up and write details down; you will find that your recall is quite clear the next day. First, you will find that a pattern begins to emerge. Symbols recur such as insects, climbing hills, or particular companions. Once you learn the art of interpretation, you will come to understand the significance of these symbols and what they mean in your life. Not all dreams are important but you will learn to distinguish between the ones you ought to study and those you can shrug off. Accuracy of interpretation comes with practice. It becomes a compulsive hobby after a time and really adds to your body of self-knowledge.

Take this example: you are experiencing difficulty in a current relationship; the reasons for the problem are troubling you and you naturally take these anxieties into sleep with you. During sleep, your psyche will work on the various angles of the problem and provide you with guidance towards a solution. The well-known American therapist, Dr Joyce Brothers, suggests that if you have a nagging problem with no obvious answer, address it to your subconscious mind before falling asleep. The very first thought that comes into your conscious mind when you wake the next morning should provide the solution you seek. Perhaps the best way to make this whole process clear for you is to illustrate with a specific example taken from my own learning process. Remember my story about being locked in a toilet as a child? For years I had a recurring dream of searching for a toilet and being desperate to pass water. I would always have a lot of trouble finding a lavatory and, inevitably, my search would take me down, down, into horrible, dark, scary dungeons. I would find toilets, but as I entered each one, I could see that they were too filthy to use. My dream always finished on this unsatisfactory note. Four years ago, I mentioned this dream to a colleague who suggested that I ought to consult a dream therapist, which I subsequently did. After I described the dream, the therapist told me a stream of detail about myself and my life, to my amazement. The dream apparently indicated a search for psychological wholeness. Moving downwards in dreams always means going down to the subconscious. The dirty toilets symbolised the 'dirt' and ugliness that I had to face in my darker side in order to be integrated and achieve harmony between my external and internal realities.

Now here comes the fascinating part. After I received this insight, the dream occurred less frequently and the toilets became cleaner and cleaner until the night that I found a lavatory without any searching; it was on the same level as I already was, and I entered the first toilet to find it perfectly clean and ready to use. The whole transformation took about eighteen months, but it was the most liberating of experiences. I have had the dream only three or four times since I first found out what it meant. After I found the clean toilet, the dream stopped altogether. That means that my dream directly reflected the work I was doing on myself at the conscious level. When one is healed, the other disappears, as if in acknowledgement of the achievement.

Dreams are simply the flip side of waking reality. Psychoanalysts use them extensively to measure everything from trauma to psychological progress. Use dreams in whatever way interests you. In conjunction with an overall personal development plan, they are a valuable source of information and a vital clue to that elusive true identity you seek.

Present the woman you desire

7. If you believe that you are a mirror that reflects the people and events around you, others' reactions to you are a vital provider of direct information about the signals you are giving. People who complain that no one likes them are usually the ones who either give out negative vibes or those who are totally wrapped up in their own feelings and are unaware of what others may be experiencing. If you go to a party and sit in a corner with your head down, is it any wonder that no one speaks to you or you feel isolated and just want to go home? Not everyone can be outgoing and the life of the party, but they can, without exception, smile and be concerned for others. Shy people are often the most self-centred people. I can make this statement because I used to be shy myself. Only when I found that being self-conscious prevented me from doing so many things I wanted did I actively set out to change my behaviour.

So, look around and watch the way that people relate to you. It is said that we are most likely to like people who make it obvious that they like us, again a reflection of feelings. There is a direct correlation between the way you treat people with whom you come into contact and the way they treat you. Again, that puts the power right back into your own hands.

If you signal people that you are a particular type of person, they will act accordingly. First, you have to know yourself, establish your identity, and then be true to it. Life will not become totally trouble-free, but your attitude to conflict, relationships and yourself will change considerably. In turn, the substance of your days will alter. You will suddenly start to feel the power of your own destiny, instead of feeling like a helpless victim of fate, a bottle bobbing up and down on the sea of life. The evidence is really convincing when you look at how responsible you are in shaping the joy or misery of your daily life. Jot down any interesting interactions you encounter, looking for any recurring patterns. As with dreams, the pattern will emerge very sharply after a while. The common thread tells the story, not the random quirks.

The signs of silence

8. Ever since Desmond Morris wrote *The Naked Ape*, body language has been seriously studied as a tool of human communication. He showed us how much you reveal by your every movement, action and nuance of expression. It takes in not only walking and talking, but the way you hold your head, walk into a room, carry your body, eye contact or the lack of it, everything you feel about yourself and your relationship to the world around you shows. That is what it literally means— the language (communication) of the body, silent, non-verbal, but just as clear and potent.

Some linguists would argue that body language is a far more accurate gauge of a person's real attitudes and feelings than normal speech. For example, a woman may be smiling as she speaks to another woman sitting next to her, but if her body is twisted away from her companion, that position indicates there is some animosity or tension between them. Another sign is if she has her legs crossed in the direction pointing away from the other woman. Reading these signs in others is not difficult once you learn the basics, but for the purpose of gaining identity, your *own* body language needs to be the subject of scrutiny. The most revealing ones are those poses you catch yourself in when you are not thinking about it. Pay particular attention to the way you speak and position your body around people; you may get some surprises!

Remember that, consciously or unconsciously, people are picking up the signals you continuously give out. As was said in points two and four, relationships are largely built or destroyed on those thousands of silent signals that you subtly throw off. This isn't to suggest that you should manipulate your mannerisms like a marionette so as to give the impression you desire. Only robots should be programmed that way. As a human being, you are a veritable network of ever-changing behaviours and emotions, and that is what makes each person special and exciting.

Self-knowledge means self-help

9. Chapter Three talked extensively about the relationship between stress and the physical self. It showed the importance of learning to 'read' the body's signs and messages in order to prevent breakdown of normal functioning, just as you keep your car serviced to make sure it runs well. One of the best gauges for measuring well-being and general health is tension levels within the body. You know when you feel tired, the first place it shows up (apart from yawning) is in the physical structure of the body. You find yourself rubbing your neck or complaining of backache. That is a fairly immediate response and is usually alleviated by adequate rest. But remember that 'stored' tension can accumulate as the result of excessive stress over weeks, months, or even years. This stress is more emotional than physical. If it is caused by an unresolved emotional problem, then only resolution of the problem will really cancel the pain and feelings of discomfort.

Emotional pain sits like a heavy lump inside the 'gut' area of the body where the solar plexus is located. The solar plexus is the centre of the emotions, vulnerability and conflict and should be opened up each day in order that the passage in and out is unblocked. There is a form of therapy that uses breathing techniques to free the body of remembered distresses. There are many books available now on this subject, one of the best being Louise L. Hay's *You Can Heal Your Life,* a detailed study on the relationship between self-esteem and good health. At the back of the book, Hay lists many common ailments and the reason for their occurrence. There is much truth in her theories and beliefs. A lot of what is said is commonsense, for example: constipation is caused by holding on, not letting go of past grievances or painful experiences; sore knees indicate rigidity of thinking and inflexible attitudes; itchy skin is saying 'I want to move on', restlessness and impatience. There are suggested affirmations for each condition to break down the body's resistance to natural good health. In other words, so many of us are our own worst enemies!

Make note of tensions you feel when you experience them, who you are with and where you are—more vital clues for your identity kit. It is like being a collector. You learn to tell the gems from the worthless articles.

Follow through for the best you

After at least a month of studying these nine points in detail and noting down all the data, you will finish up with more material than you know what to do with, but it is in the sifting through and throwing out that you learn your most valuable lessons. Do not let it be a chore, or make the excuse that you do not have enough time to do the exercise. Have fun with it—it will be so useful if you make the effort. You will be amazed at some of the things you find out and the patterns you will see in your life. I hope you will let it help you by using the answers and insights you gain to guide you to a more honest, happy and healthful existence.

Marriage, a decade of change

Now that you know how to create and maintain successful relationships, a close look is needed at the workings of one of the most important human interactions. As we move into the twenty-first century, many regard marriage as an outmoded institution. Magazine articles abound with information and survey material weighing up the pros and cons of marriage as compared to living together or the single life. This discussion will be confined to a brief look at marriage in the 1990s: what the ingredients are for successful man/woman relationships, and why marriages fail. Marriage today is very different to the way it was even ten years ago, for a number of reasons.

Loss of the nuclear family

The nuclear family can consist of any variety of components, combinations and styles. Mother, father and children may still be the norm in people's minds and certainly in the realms of ideal fiction, but, statistically, families are more often made up of: single parents bringing up children; a woman living with a man who is not the children's father; two homosexuals raising a child, or communal groups involving several lots of adults and children sharing one dwelling. This change is not necessarily a bad thing. Certainly, children are being exposed to a wider appreciation of varying lifestyles and types of relationships.

A real choice

Many more women now work, which has caused a shift in family dynamics, making roles within the home harder to define. Men do not all go to work, and women are no longer always homemakers. Domestic responsibilities have to be viewed differently; they are not automatically the province of the female partner. Some men are choosing to stay at home and be the homemaker while their wives go out to a job and earn the family income. More and more single fathers are opting to bring up children full-time and are accomplishing this task successfully.

The most common arrangement is where both parents work and the children are at school, at a day-care centre or the family has home-help. I personally am pleased to see the breaking down of the stereotypical roles of yesteryear. The only people who are likely to feel threatened by the loss of set labels and accompanying expectations are those who are not comfortable with themselves and their true identities. Some people prefer to hide behind their imposed identities and enjoy the anonymity of titles, such as Mrs or Dr or Sergeant or Director, etc. We are all just people; chores in the home should be divided out according to taste and ability and regardless of gender.

The material family

The pace of life increases every year. Things and people keep moving faster and attitudes are accordingly shaped. Marriage, no less than other important human institutions, has altered to fit the expectations of the 1990s man and woman. For example, people tend to expect more and more from life in keeping with higher incomes, better technology and advanced education. There is much more pressure on the breadwinner(s) to provide additional material possessions and complex lifestyles. The second television must be in color, not just black-and-white; the children must have their own VCR and computer; domestic vacations are passé, only the Caribbean will do, and so on.

The stress of extra affluence and inevitably, greater appetite, is immeasurable. Speak to any financial counsellor, and they will supply horror statistics of credit card addiction, bankruptcies and emotional breakdown. All of these situations cannot be attributed to mismanagement and greed alone and you need to be aware of the traps. The harsh realities of life in the 1990s have spawned a whole range of marital difficulties, undreamed of in simpler times.

Seeking independence

Increased education and information regarding personal development and human relationships means that individuals are not as prepared to endure problems in a marriage. Everyone is looking for happiness and satisfaction. If partners are missing out on what they consider important, they are more ready to walk away, whereas the couples of previous generations were more inclined to believe in the permanency of marriage.

Increased awareness in women's rights also means that the interaction between men and women has largely changed. Some men feel castrated by the fact that they are not the sole breadwinners or the fact that women want the right to earn their own money and make their own decisions. This feeling can be avoided by honest communication. If men and women simply respect one another, there is no need for either party to feel rejected or repressed in any way. The old dependence has become redundant, except in cases where individuals choose to perpetuate the need for one partner to be seen as the dominant one.

If people are going to bother getting married at all, they should go into it wholeheartedly with positivity and trust. However, some modern couples prefer to regard marriage as a business partnership, to be entered into by mutual agreement with a clear understanding beforehand of the terms and conditions. Pre-marriage legal agreements are gaining popularity, especially in the United States, where community property laws in some states mean the equal sharing of combined wealth and income in the event of divorce. Some men and women within the married state like to keep their earnings separate. This exercise was relatively uncommon even a decade ago when either the man would keep all his wages, pay the bills, and dole out house-keeping money to his wife, or the wages would be handed over in their entirety to the wife who would attend to the family's financial needs. These are matters of personal preference. Obviously, what works is right, but this change is another indication of the variations that are now possible in marriages and de facto relationships.

The ease of moving on

The easement of divorce laws has almost single-handedly changed the face of married life in Western countries. Where the sheer weight of the legalities of marriage once conspired to keep even bitterly unhappy couples together, now people tend to take the attitude that they will stay as long as it works. It certainly keeps you on your proverbial toes and removes any chance of complacency you may once have experienced. It can no longer be assumed by an unfaithful man, for example, that his wife will automatically continue in the marriage. Nor can a woman regard a man as belonging to her. Some women taking this attitude and appearing in tatty dressing gowns at the breakfast table shortly after the trip down the aisle have had a most unpleasant shock when their husbands began eating breakfast at another woman's table! Fidelity is largely a matter of individual choice and morality, and never more so than in the late twentieth century.

These are the key reasons marriage is different for a lot of couples today. That is not to say that people no longer live their lives by traditional values and religious beliefs, but even these people must feel the impact of the many sociological evolutions that have taken place during the course of this century.

Recipe for successful marriage

The attitude of the two people entering into marriage is a vital factor to its success. For this reason, premarital counselling is a good idea. Some couples automatically go in for this when booking the church for the wedding ceremony. The minister or priest of their church will talk to the couple about the significance of the holy institution they are entering into and the religious aspects of the commitment.

What about all those people who do not hold religious convictions or those who wish to marry in a park or private home? Must they be denied the education that could mean the difference between success and failure in their marriage? Premarital counselling should be available freely to young people contemplating the joining of their lives. They should not have to arrange privately to see an adviser; it could become part and parcel of the whole process. When you think of the thousands of hours that are spent in preparing for the big day— the gown, attendants, reception, guest list, food, flowers and honeymoon—it is appalling that often so little thought is given to the emotional and psychological aspects of the commitment. A couple meet, fall in love, and decide to marry. Often they know little of each other beyond the trivial and superficial facts. Even such seemingly important details like jobs, income, future plans, desire for children and house preferences pale into insignificance when stacked up against the overwhelming statistics of marriage breakdown.

People should discuss beforehand such issues as staying individuals, the roles they would like to play within the marriage, mutual respect, allowing each other space for private interests and friends, how they like to spend and organise time, attitudes to money etc. These points may not seem very romantic, but people must realise that love affairs are romantic, marriage is serious business. One should not enter marriage with the view that it is easy to get out, or failure is assured. In short, 'prevention is better than cure'. Divorce can be utterly devastating and is so unnecessary if only people enter marriage with their eyes open instead of in a starry-eyed haze.

In some ways, marriage is like a business partnership. Each person has certain assets to contribute and an expectation of return. It is no use pretending otherwise—we all want something back. Self-delusion in this instance is a recipe for disaster. Why not be frank about this fact from the beginning? Go over your likes and dislikes together, with candour and in good humour. Some may disagree, but marriage is not a place for surprises. After the first flush of passion, there is a long time ahead to regret any lack of preparation and honesty.

Apart from preparation and talking things over beforehand, other important considerations are compatibility and psychological maturity. Women who believe that marriage will make them happy have a much more difficult adjustment into married life. Disillusionment is waiting just around the corner. The same type of situation applies to men.

The men who are most apt to indulge in adultery are those who did not 'sow their wild oats' before settling down. Women need wild oats too, but they generally appear to be ready to enter a monogamous relationship by age twenty-three or twenty-four while many men are only getting started then. They find a girl they like reasonably well, propose, and everything is rosy for the first two years or so.

As a man and woman journey through their lives joined in matrimony, each is apt to be experiencing a different stage, depending on each person's age and what has been done in the way of personal growth. Without communication and open discussion, no understanding can be reached. Before long, paths begin to diverge and lives that promised to cleave separate. The single most vital ingredient of a good marriage is effective communication. The word 'effective' is used because many couples communicate on the surface and think they are getting along very well. This state may carry them for a short time or even many years, but if and when the marriage travels into troubled waters, the bond and the ties that time has either forged or not forged will be tested. Only the strength of the relationship, built each day in hundreds of little ways, will carry couples through the crisis. Thus, couples need to spend quality time with each other every day, not just on weekends or holidays. Developing a 'tomorrow attitude', forever carrying over the things you want to do into the next day, is too easy. Today is never lived at all.

Separating job and marriage

If job and marriage are not separated, it is unfortunate for the individual and spells death to a married couple. Couples who work together have a particularly difficult challenge, but not one that cannot be overcome. There are some golden rules that prevent stress for people in this situation and also allow them to enjoy each other's company at all levels. A man and a woman may run a business together and spend most of their workdays in the same environment. During business hours, as far as possible, they should not act as spouses, but work-mates. Conversely, once they get home, the workday attitudes should be dissolved and their personal relationship reign supreme. The worst thing they can do is bring home any of their work worries or disagreements. If there is something they *must* discuss, it should be done quickly and then put aside. When roles overlap in a stressful or negative way, it affects a person's temperament and the relationships between people.

How do you make time?

Bearing in mind the crowded lives most people lead these days, this question is a valid consideration. Also, when there are children, their demands tend to overshadow everything else, especially at certain points in the day. There are highly sensitive times that are best avoided for any extra activity, such as meal times or bedtime for the children. One of the most vulnerable periods of the day appears to be the first hour or so that everyone meets up again after spending the day apart. Everyone is talking at once and wanting attention. A lot of men have expressed to me the difficulty of relating to their families when they first come home. They have been out in the workforce all day, they're exhausted and want to be allowed to unwind slowly and enjoy the paper or whatever. At precisely the same time, the wife wants a bit of relief from the ankle-biters she has had around her feet all day, so she resents his 'switching-off'. She wants some intelligent conversation, he wants to do anything but talk, the children are all trying to get their news in, and pandemonium reigns.

Sound familiar? Solution? Give in! Why fight it and create more stress for everyone? Make a pact that you will not even attempt to communicate at this chaotic time. You know your own schedule best so choose a suitable time when you and your spouse can be together uninterrupted, preferably after the children are all tucked in for the night. At first, this 'time-out' procedure may seem a bit strained, even false, but after a while you will wonder why you did not start it years ago.

Many couples may protest heartily that they communicate all the time, but when pinned down to subject matter will offer such topics as the children, holidays, money, relatives, home improvements. The real issues are swept under the carpet. It is hardly appropriate for married couples to engage in 'small talk' or worse still, for the atmosphere around them to resound with the loudness of their silence. Not that talking is the only or best way for couples to communicate. Just sitting together and enjoying some quiet time is very therapeutic; going for a walk together after dinner, an occasional evening out without the children, a surprise gift when least expected—that is the stuff of good marriages. If this were an ideal world filled with ideal people, a good marriage would be commonplace and easy; instead, it remains as one of the last bastions of faith that requires all your courage and determination for success.

Another important ingredient is having realistic expectations. In marriage, there is a real temptation to allow personalities to merge, to the detriment of both parties. Kahlil Gibran, in his book *The Prophet*, speaks of marriage thus:

Love one another, but make not a bond of love:
Let it rather be a moving sea between the shores of your
   souls.
Fill each other's cup but drink not from one cup.

Give one another of your bread but eat not from the same loaf.

Sing and dance together and be joyous, but let each one of you be alone.

Even as the strings of a lute are alone though they quiver with the same music.

Give your hearts, but not into each other's keeping.
For only the hand of Life can contain your hearts.
And stand together yet not too near together:
For the pillars of the temple stand apart,
And the oak tree and the cypress grow not in each other's shadow.

Marriage is a two-person team made up of individuals—it is one team with two separate people. Only very rare couples can be in each other's company constantly and not burn out. Cloying, possessive attitudes suffocate a relationship and starve the two people of dignity and personal freedom. Both parties need to be able to operate without external limitations. They should allow only the commitment of the heart to lead the way. One example that comes to mind is the case of ex-lovers or even platonic friends. It is inexplicable to me why some marriage partners object if their spouses want to see an old friend, male or female. It can only be attributed to insecurity, either in themselves or in the marriage. After all, a marriage is only as strong as its individual links.

Having clear ground rules is important so that no one gets hurt down the track. For instance, an obvious question would seem to be, 'If I were to be unfaithful to you, would that be the end of our marriage?' This type of misunderstanding can backfire horribly on people. Some women think they are being good wives by enduring treatment they cannot stomach, such as putting up with a husband who is into cross-dressing (wearing women's clothing), allowing her husband to use her for a punching bag every time he gets drunk, or engaging in wife-swapping at her husband's suggestion when it is the last thing she wants to do herself. Of course, self-delusion operates here as well, and often the marriage is badly shaken up by the time a woman discovers her true feelings and finds the courage to do something about it.

Finally, shared attitudes are vital to a good marriage, and a similar level of commitment. I recall a poster saying, 'Love isn't two people looking into each other's eyes; it's two people looking in the same direction.' If only one partner is really working at the relationship, the marriage has a limited chance of success.

There is a difference between a good marriage and a successful one. The former is one in which many desired elements are present, the two people involved are well-matched, and both are putting in an effort to keep the marriage working and happy. The latter is one in which possibly no desirable elements are present, only one partner gives a damn, but for some inexplicable reason, the relationship works for the people involved.

Why on earth does a woman stay with a man who mistreats her? Many reasons can be offered. In my experience, I have found that the woman unconsciously chose this precise man or type of man in order to fulfil a deep-seated need to be mistreated. The desire can stem from self-loathing or, more often, a background in which she was ill-treated by a parent or other adult. It is almost as if the subconscious mind seeks to relive the pain of the original rejection in the hope that this time, love will triumph instead of violence and hurt. Therefore, both are victims, despite the fact that a wife-beater is viewed in our society as a coward and a bully. This explanation may be an unpalatable notion, but if you are honest, you will recognise the need that arises in you at times to provoke dissension, to rock the boat when things are starting to get too comfortable, to destroy your own happiness out of fear and a lack of faith in the goodness of life.

Like a garden bed that is never watered, love shrivels up without attention. Keep your marriage fresh, never take it for granted. If it is happy ninety per cent of the time, you are one of the lucky ones. Nevertheless it is not luck that makes a good marriage, only your own ability to bring the things you want into your life by your own power and under your own steam. It's mostly hard work, but it can also bring immeasurable joy and reward you in a way that no other relationship can. Go for broke. No each-way bets, just lots of love and trust will win out in the end if the rest is there.

Key marital problems

The following are things that can cause problems or rifts in a marriage:

- boredom/staleness.
- stress/tension.
- sex.
- money.
- children.
- communication.
- cultural differences.
- individual psychology.
- religion.
- poor health.
- politics.
- poor lifestyle.
- alcohol/addictions.
- family/friends.
- guilt and retribution.
- infidelity.
- immaturity and lack of understanding and commitment.
- wrong signals.

Marriage breakdown is not only about separation and divorce. It can mean a parting of the ways *within* the relationship. The partners are no longer close; either there is no communication or it is of a poor quality, and there are constant tension and/or quarrels. There is no lonelier place than a double bed in which the occupiers don't touch, physically or emotionally. Symptoms of a marriage in trouble include sexual problems (see Chapter Seven); digs, put-downs, or irritability on the part of one or both partners; a pervading air of tension; a lack of unity in parenting, if children are involved; a distance between spouses, with a lack of demonstration of affection.

Think of it as two boxers in a ring. Husband and wife are relegated to their two corners, they enter the middle, dance around each other without really touching, trying to hurt, but mostly impotent. Then they return to their respective corners. This behaviour can go on for years. In the main, unhappy people do not break up because they lack the courage to make a new beginning, cannot find the right opportunity or motivation to make the break but, most often, because they do not wish to hurt the offspring of the marriage. Couples with serious problems should weigh up the alternatives. Children can be just as disadvantaged in a family where there is little love and much anger and quarrelling. Breaking up a family is not a light matter; both sides of the coin have to be examined to make the right decision.

What if things feel all wrong, but the couple still wants to try and patch up the marriage? In the initial stages, a simple solution might be all it takes, such as a short romantic holiday together or a bit of renewed courting on the part of either husband or wife. There is no reason why a woman cannot court a man with gifts and flowers, and this strategy works very well for bruised egos or neglected hearts. Time out can be quite effective; even a short separation cannot hurt if it means that each person is allowed the space and freedom to think things through and then come back, renewed and refreshed. If couples prefer to stay together and work it out, they should, as far as possible, talk *outside* the home in a neutral environment, do things together, and diffuse the situation by keeping everything in perspective and as unemotional as they can.

If the problems have become too deeply entrenched, however, marriage counselling may be necessary. A 'patch-up' job will not suffice in this case; the marriage will need a complete overhaul. Both partners need to be open and honest about changes they feel are needed and then a brand new commitment made. Some people like to officially renew their vows as a symbol of this fresh beginning, even to the point of repeating the wedding ceremony. Communication is important all the time, but never more so than after the warning signs have manifested themselves.

Unfortunately, so many couples drift on in misery until there is little left to salvage. Counselling will only work if both parties are keen to improve the marriage. Where there is a third party, the 'lover', involved the whole picture is less clear, but I have never known a case where a third person was able to intrude on a happy and close union; a sexual aberration, a one-night stand, perhaps, but not a love affair that breaks up the couple.

It is worth bearing in mind. Invariably couples with marriage problems don't communicate effectively, make time for each other, or listen to each other at any level.

Stress in marriage is mainly caused by a failure on the part of one or both people to interact favourably and in a loving manner. Selfishness, lack of consideration, stubbornness, intolerance—these in large enough doses will crush the love out of any two people. It is heartbreaking to see bright and fresh young hope suffocated by a simple lack of knowledge and education on what it takes to make a relationship work. You teach your children about algebra and science, how to cook, and to work with wood, but who teaches them how to love, communicate, and have self-respect? Ideally parents, but Louise L. Hay says in *You Can Heal Your Life* that we are all 'victims of victims' and many adults have only hatred and prejudice to pass on as their emotional legacy to their children. The stress of parenthood in the 1990s is considerable. For many of the same reasons cited earlier for the changes and differences in marriage today, family life has vastly altered in the last generation. With the onset of easier contraception, complex technology and increased freedom for women, fewer children are being born; the ones that are have been planned around the mortgage and the two cars; couples are opting to produce one or two children instead of larger families. Some are choosing not to have any offspring at all. A new vocabulary has even sprung up to describe these modern couples, such as DINKS (which stands for double income, no kids). The pressures that affect married couples apply doubly to families and are broadly classified under the headings of financial, emotional, and practical (see money management in Chapter Eight).

Mothers, God help them

So many stresses apply to women in their parenting role today. Outlined here are some of the common stress traps in mothering and being a parent.

The single mother

Women who bring up a child without the benefit of a father have a very difficult road to travel. There are those who would argue that a father is only a biological necessity, and that with the advent of test tube babies even the man himself has become redundant. His sperm, divorced from the sex act, is the only requirement to make new life. Whatever your beliefs, two parents are preferable to one, although women who serve the roles of both parents are admirable. Often, there is a good deal of undue stress on the mother and hangups later for the child. There is evidence for both arguments, but it suffices to say that a single mother is, in fact, doing two jobs, in addition to any she may have outside the home. Many single or divorced women who choose full-time mothering live on a pension or welfare entitlement, which means financial hardship as well as the inevitable loneliness of not having someone to share the burdens of every day. A recent West Australian study revealed that single mothers have four times the psychiatric distress of mothers in families with a man/woman partnership. Their most common negative feelings are unhappiness and depression.

The full-time mother

Full-time mothers are subject to a particular brand of stress, whether or not there is a husband. Women complain of isolation within the home, of not having the money to go anywhere and no vehicle, of boredom and loneliness due to being at home all day with demanding children. Even the most devoted mother can resent her family on days when a thousand things go wrong at once; the children are all screaming and cranky, and it seems as if everyone else in the world has a more interesting job than she.

Sadly, some mothers feel that way permanently about their lot in life. They drag around shopping centres, either slapping their children or ignoring them. Have you ever noticed how few mothers walk along, holding the hand of their child? More and more in recent years children run ahead and away from their parent(s), even quite small toddlers, while Mom (and/or Dad) walks blithely on, seemingly oblivious to the child's antics. If the child misbehaves, the parents, as often as not, ignore them and look away, almost as if to disassociate themselves from the scene. At the risk of setting back the cause of human rights a thousand years, perhaps parents ought to be licensed to ensure suitability for this most important of tasks. Prospective adoptive parents are grilled, yet natural parents can have as many children as they desire without any supervision whatsoever. If they harm their children, it is too late and the damage is done.

Too many reluctant parents

Once, a married couple automatically had children after a year or two. Procreating was seen as the main reason for getting married in the first place. Nowadays there are many alternatives and babies should be chosen, not just allowed to arrive as a natural consequence of sexual activity. People criticise women who wish to continue working after having children, particularly if it is soon afterwards, but it is far better to have a happy mother out at work than a miserable one at home (which is one of those issues married couples should consider before their wedding, as suggested earlier). In fact, the category of mother I personally admire the most is the one who holds down an outside job and then comes home to two or three children needing her time and attention. No wonder these women feel spread very thin at times.

Not enough hours in the evening

How does a woman resolve the conflict of her needs versus the needs of her children? For example, she has just come in after nine hours at the office or in her own business. All she can think about is a long soak in the tub and a relaxing read in bed. Within ten minutes of entering the house, such dreams are shattered. Her eldest child needs help with his maths homework, and Dad's out at a meeting. Does she refuse to help and feel guilty or give up her own wishes and feel resentful? Neither! Compromise, that good old standby, is the answer. She should tell her son that she will help him, but only after her twenty minutes in the bath because she is tired and needs to unwind before doing anything else. Reminding your children that you are also a person with limitations on your energy supplies and personal needs is always a good idea. They will respect you for your honesty. Being an eternal caterer is not healthy—it is unfair on you and your children because they are not going to have someone like you to run after them in adult life; therefore, you are teaching them false expectations.

To a large extent, everything said so far is about the

consequences of you parenting. In addition, every day you shape your children and their future by all that you say and do. You have an awesome responsibility and not one to be taken lightly. The papers are full of horror stories about the abuses suffered by children at the hands of their own parents, but even more frightening are the subtle fears and damaging hurts that scar so many young people. Teenage suicide is at an all-time high; the streets are littered with the debris of unhappy homes, the leftovers, makeovers, unloved and unwanted masses of wasted potential. There is no such thing as a perfect parent, but we owe our children our best efforts and our best love, while they owe us nothing because they had no say in whether or not they came into the world. Parents have all the power. With that power comes tremendous responsibility. Whole books have been written on the subject of parenting. Even with all the odds in your favour, it is still one of the most challenging and demanding of roles. If you have one or more factors against you, such as low income, a difficult marriage, or living in a poor neighbourhood, the stress account begins to pile up. Use the same techniques recommended for combating stress generally, as stress is stress, no matter what causes it. The same rules apply.

Give yourself enough time to do things of your own. Try to wear only one hat at a time; keep your roles separate. Set limits to your giving. Discipline is a necessary lesson for your children—you are not being hard when you say no to them as they need boundaries. Respect each individual member of the family; acknowledge their rights to speak and be heard, make decisions and disagree with you. Emphasise joy. Do not do your work, grumbling and grudgingly, but give what you choose to freely.

Using these basics, have no fear about your success as a parent or the future of your children. Whether the children are biologically yours, made in a laboratory, adopted, fostered, or stepchildren within the family, it makes no difference. At the risk of oversimplifying, all children need is to be loved, encouraged and helped to learn. Remember the overall message: stress is not about whether you are a parent or an executive, married or single; it is much more about who you are, how you spend your time and the way you think about your life.

Armed with that knowledge, parenting is no more difficult than any other role you have.

To summarise, choose your own roles, work on your inner identity and bring it forward, avoid the stress pitfalls and look closely at all the personal relationships in your life. Discard the meaningless or negative ones, but be grateful for everyone you meet as each person has something to teach you. Give thanks every day for *all* your relationships, even the ones you find difficult. Bless the people you 'dislike' the most. And remember to nurture your one sure lifelong relationship, the one with yourself.

AFFIRMATIONS

I am at peace with myself, my world and everyone around me.

I am in tune and in harmony with all life.

I am completely free of the past.

I no longer need to seek approval from anyone.

I welcome serenity into my life.

Chapter Six

The single life

T here is another alternative to married life for women: remaining single. Although not statistically as common or socially as acceptable, the single life is appealing to many women, especially with the advent of more and more job opportunities and women taking an equal role in today's business world.

Relationships are inevitable unless you choose to live a hermit's existence. How close those relationships are allowed to get is up to individual choice. Some women decide not to marry at all, some are never given the opportunity, and others do not remarry after a divorce or separation. This chapter will discuss the emotional pitfalls and stress traps for women who live alone and/or keep away from close personal relationships. Every woman who stays single or does not share her home with another person is not anti-social or unable to love, but there is no doubt that the type of lifestyle you select for yourself is indicative of your background, self-image and emotional state.

Are there any benefits to staying single? The obvious ones are: having total independence; not having to consider the wishes of another person or an immediate family; usually being better off financially; being freer and more mobile, e.g. travelling, moving house, changing jobs; and on a deeper level, a big benefit for some women is not running the risk of being hurt or losing a loved one. However, the old adage holds: 'The grass is always greener on the other side.' Single women often envy the love and security married women with families appear to have, and wives and mothers think that it would be wonderful to be free and independent, living the life of a single woman. The wise woman loves the life she has created for herself, and if for any reason she wants to make changes, she goes about it with optimism and confidence.

Always single

First a look at the woman who never marries. As stated earlier, society is somewhat uncomfortable about this particular role. Even if a woman is successful in business or her chosen career, there is a cloud hanging over her if she does not appear to want to join her life with a man's. The usual reasons for this decision may be: suspicion of men in general; an interest in women sexually; fear of intimacy or being hurt; low self-esteem, resulting in rejection of invitations, proposals, etc.

Mistrusting men

What would cause a woman to mistrust men? The most likely reason is a poor relationship with her father. If she felt ignored by him or if he beat her or in some other way abused her trust, she would be inclined to identify other relationships with males in the same light. Conversely, some women have such a close and loving relationship with their fathers that no man can ever compete or be 'good enough'.

The most tragic type of mistrust is the legacy of incest. Sexual abuse to a little girl can come from her father, brother, stepfather, foster parent, or other relative, male or female. Parents are regarded by children as protectors, and as such hold a sacred trust. The damage done by incest is not just physically harmful, but emotionally devastating and permanently scarring. Sufferers are often unable, in adult life, to relate to men sexually or in any other way. Even if they enter into a male/female relationship, they either cannot enjoy sex or find themselves unable to orgasm. More crucially, many women who have incest in their backgrounds report that they feel cut off emotionally, fearing to love a man because he might hurt and disappoint them in the same way as their fathers did.

The stress of living with such a sordid and painful memory causes many women to have low self-esteem, to feel somehow responsible for their father's bad behaviour, shameful and 'dirty'. Some women do not tell anyone, certainly not their families or close friends. They may enter into relationships, even marriage, without confiding their terrible secret, thus bringing the burden of the past into current alliances. If things start to go wrong, the issue has to be confronted head on, which can entail extensive counselling with therapists experienced in sex abuse cases. No such sufferer could walk away unscathed, no matter how strong or determined the woman.

Another case where a woman might be suspicious or nervous of men occurs when she has been badly hurt as a young girl in a romantic encounter. Everyone is particularly vulnerable in their first love affair or infatuation. If nothing more is involved than a teenage crush, you get over it eventually. However, if tender feelings are damaged by false promises or, once again, an abuse of trust, the disillusionment takes a lot longer to heal, and in some cases never does.

Homosexuality

Lesbians—women who form relationships with other women or, at least, are attracted to them sexually—usually do not marry. There are women who leave a male/female alliance and then, at some later date, become involved with members of their own sex in a romantic way. In either case, unless the two women 'marry', lesbians tend to remain single by choice.

Some women with homosexual tendencies marry males in order to have children or for respectability in the eyes of their communities. As social awareness of minorities grows and there is better tolerance of different lifestyles, women are able to stand up for who they are and be unashamed of their sexual preferences. The need to live 'in the closet' is lessening, although it is still a reality in many occupations and sectors of society.

Once, women who did not marry at all were regarded as undesirable or strange; now, it is seen as yet another blow for independence, and accepted along with equal pay for equal work, contraception, abortion on demand and women in government. These social changes sit uneasily on the shoulders of traditionalists and moralists but are the signs of the times we live in, when a woman can have a baby in or out of marriage, in or out of a uterus, in bed or underwater, with a man or alone. We may not always like these radical waves of transformation but we cannot seem to stem their tide any more than we can stop the sea. Therefore, many lesbian couples live together openly, more married than married heterosexuals in some cases, paying off mortgages and bringing up children, living in suburbs and doing ordinary things. These women do, in fact, have committed relationships as much as anyone else (see Chapter Seven for more on homosexuality).

'*I'm not worth it*'

The next two reasons for women remaining single are connected. Women who are afraid of intimacy and being hurt are usually deeply insecure; often, they have self-esteem problems and feel unworthy to be loved.

Female workaholics drive themselves mercilessly with hard work and ambition in order to feel fulfilled and worthwhile. All addiction stems from a need to be propped up, to boost self-confidence in a false, externalised way so that the means loses importance and only the need remains vital. If career is merely a substitute for love and family, it soon grows hollow. Staying single, if indeed a personal and conscious choice, should be a way of life, not a soulless, loveless existence. The key issue here is the need in some women to maintain absolute control over their own lives, never allowing anyone to get too close, preferring aloneness to vulnerability, sterility to sharing.

If a woman feels unattractive and uninteresting, she will give out the signals that affirm these images to all who see her. A woman's beauty can be obscured by a negative attitude or self-denying body language, and, by the same principle, a plain woman can dazzle everyone in a room by the brightness of her personality. Therefore, a woman who has never received a marriage proposal or had a serious boyfriend may not be ugly or dull, but simply unattainable. There are lots of ways to be unavailable, including being so painfully shy that no one attempts to speak to you.

So women can stay single by design, by choice, or by circumstance. There are cases, for example, where women stay at home to care for an aged parent or to contribute financially to a large family. This allows little opportunity for meeting members of the opposite sex. The same applies to women who work in one-sex occupations or who work irregular shifts and socialise very seldom. The examples abound, but these few set the scene for a discussion of what it means to be single and how to enhance the benefits while minimising the disadvantages. (Women who are widowed or divorced/separated have slightly different stories—they will be discussed later.)

Disadvantages of the single life

The obvious disadvantage lies in the fact of couple-worship in most modern societies. Despite the many social changes, traditional family life is still seen as desirable and a lifestyle to be cultivated. Therefore, being single carries a stigma and negative tag. I can remember hearing at school that Christian teaching considers spinsters/bachelors to be the least useful section of the community because they only live for themselves! Generally, male singles are looked upon with more indulgence and with a mixture of pity and envy by their married male friends! Women have to face a lot more of the pity and get a lot less indulgence and envy. It's back to labels and stereotypes again.

Public judgment is often harsh and inaccurate; how you are seen becomes more important than who you really are. That is why a strong sense of personal identity is so crucial. Even the choice of terminology tells a story—what a difference there is between the words 'spinster' and 'bachelor' in modern literature, in magazine articles, media usage and colloquial language. 'Spinster' suggests a tired old maid that no one wants, conjuring up images of plain features, paisley dresses and school-marm occupations. How far from the well-groomed executive women who spend their days in boardrooms and their nights in luxury apartments. Both extremes exist, but hardly any unmarried woman would answer to the name of spinster these days. But for bachelors, it's a whole different ball game. Men who never marry are seen as clever, a 'good catch' and simply having a fun time before they settle down, if they ever decide to. There never seems to be any suggestion that no one wants them, only that they have their pick of women and have not made up their minds or found one good enough.

Anyone who marries and divorces by, say, their twenties, will escape the questioning and doubting procedure that unmarried women have to endure if they have the audacity to reach thirty and still be 'available'. Is there still a perception that a woman cannot exist happily without a man? Just as a man can relieve sexual tension by masturbation, so can a woman. Thus, women do not have to marry simply to enjoy regular sex.

Choices

A woman asking men out on dates or making the first move sexually so she does not have to sit on a shelf waiting for men to pay attention to her is no longer socially taboo. Some women have low libidos and avoid relationships with men because they find sexual intimacy an undesirable feature in their lives. More and more, women are not *needing* to marry, but those who choose to, it seems, have fewer reasons and many more options than women did a generation ago. Options are another contributing factor to the high divorce rate of the 1980s. Once women stayed in unhappy marriages because they basically had nowhere else to go. There was not a range of welfare services to help women with violent husbands, those who could not manage financially, those who were hooked on Valium, or the ones bashing their babies. Now, everything is open to a woman who seriously wants to make changes (educational, emotional, psychological and professional). She can study or go back to work or start a business. It is a healthy movement overall, if only in that it allows talented women avenues of expression. Those who want to be full-time mothers can do so, despite some remaining areas of difficulty.

There are many obstacles still to overcome, but we have come a long way since Germaine Greer wrote *The Female Eunuch*. She and other feminists may disagree, but we cannot effect change in such a way as to be destructive. All movements tend to begin radically, then, as the leading lights age and mellow, reason is restored and followers are reminded that the wheels of progress grind slowly. How all this affects the argument of single versus married is that male/female relationships no longer need to be seen as a haven for either gender. Women do not have to marry in order to gain an identity or a social place in the world. Individuals can come together purely to form a team, a working partnership, where the members are equal and have different abilities and interests, but choose to share and join strengths.

The incidence of divorce is not the only gauge of success or failure in the old attitudes to marriage because many women stayed with their husbands despite serious problems. Relationships may very well be more honest these days. If people are unhappy or the marriage does not feel right, they say so straight out. In the same way, women who want to remain single can claim the same privileges as a man and even adopt a baby or have one biologically with a surrogate or a sperm donation. Imagining how much further the next decade will take us, in terms of female independence and male/female relationships, is very difficult.

This book speaks of 'women' under one umbrella heading, as one gender. Factors such as personality type, socioeconomic background and levels of intelligence will bring different responses from women in similar circumstances. This book attempts to offer perspectives and insights that will ring a bell with all women, despite these differences. We cannot all share the same experiences but, as women, we do have a commonality that binds us and bridges even the widest gap. For instance, I came from a middle-class background and was encouraged to make the most of myself from an early age. I had no plans to marry young and lived with the guy I ended up marrying for nearly six months before we were pressured into marriage by our respective families, in particular, mine. For a time I behaved as most new brides, subjugating my own needs and desires to those of my husband. Soon it became obvious that we were miles apart and could never stay happily married. The point is that my background, motivation and ambition carried me through those dark days of separation and scary new beginnings. Being single had no fear for me, and I was never interested in playing the 'singles game' as such. I sometimes used to wonder if there was something wrong with me because I did not want to rush out and find another man. I do not regard men as a meal ticket; the more women steer away from that image, the better off they will be. It is a false image at best and, at worst, it is degrading to both parties. Not that women who marry and are kept by their husbands are bludgers. Far from it—they earn their way just as much as if they were to go out to a job, but it is a question of attitude.

If a woman regards herself as the property of a man or believes that she needs him to survive, emotionally or financially, then she is selling herself very short indeed. Statistically, most women who are bashed by husbands, seek help from refuges, or have husbands who are alcoholics and compulsive gamblers, come from lower-class backgrounds. It would be too easy to say these women have not had the advantages of education and, therefore, lack the knowledge to stay out of unfortunate marriages and victim situations. Perhaps they start off naive and unsophisticated, wanting only the simple things and expecting fairytale splendour, but I have a lot of faith in the strength of Woman as a species. Those women who do not start off with book knowledge certainly become 'street-smart' in the trenches of suburban life. Later in the chapter it will be shown that many of these ladies are now coming out of marriages and other long-term relationships stronger and smarter, not cowed and afraid of life but ready for new challenges and fresh beginnings.

The singles scene

Another major disadvantage of being alone is having to grapple with the 'singles scene'. This scene has been the subject of many a B-grade movie and is a constant supplier of material for stand-up comics. Since the 1960s, when sexual and emotional matters took on a new face, when people were encouraged to reach out, touch others, smile a lot, have a happy day and love, love, love, human interactions have become freer and freer. So many ideas and behaviour that were once taboo are now openly discussed. Special bars and nightclubs had to be created to cater for all the men and women spilling out of marriages. Entrepreneurs saw the enormous market and the unlimited potential for moneymaking. So, in fact, the 'singles scene' is not just a lot of single, separated and divorced people randomly looking for entertainment. It is a highly organised entity that lives and breathes and defies you to take it on. Many people bypass it deliberately or out of fear. Some dabble in the various offerings of the scene, but never fully immerse themselves. Yet others plunge in bodily and make a full-time occupation out of it. This phenomenon will affect a large majority of single women at some stage, either before, without, during, or after marriage.

There are so many sociological and personal implications in the singles scene. Singles bars are voracious and deeply sad places—men and women complain endlessly about pubs and clubs that cater specifically for meeting and picking up available people. They are bleak and soulless; the regulars are cynical and on the prowl for only one thing—so the common cries continue. Men tend to say that the women are looking for husbands or, at least, a free night out; women say the men only want a one-night stand. Allowing for those singles who fit into these categories, the average person does not want anything of the kind. The question most asked is, 'Where can one go to meet sincere, decent people?'

Those singles over thirty-five have the hardest time in this area. First, as already stated several times, most people have been married at least once by their mid-thirties, so unmarried singles in this age group are difficult to find. Eliminating homosexuals and adulterous marrieds, you are left with separated and divorced people in the main, and many of these people are hurting from their last relationship.

One amazing thing about some social clubs is the level of conversation and topics of discussion; the last subject single people, out to have a good time, should want to talk about is the very one that engages their intense interest—you guessed it, their broken relationships. Can you imagine anything more depressing than a roomful of party-goers exchanging notes on how, when, and where they were let down and hurt by their ex-partners? There is an appropriate time for sharing of this nature, but it is not at a social occasion surrounded by strangers. What happens is the creation of a pervading mood of tension and bitterness. Coming out of a relationship is a delicate and tender business. Some people need professional help; all need understanding and, most of all, time to heal. Going over and over the betrayals and who was right and wrong is not the way to mend a broken heart. It in fact keeps reopening the wounds and ensures that the pain cannot be forgotten.

The most positive steps to take after a relationship break-up are these:

- be aware of what emotions to expect. Talk to a friend who has been through it, read up, or see a counsellor.
- deal with specific warning signals such as body tension, stress, or depression.
- work through the reasons for the break-up as unemotionally as possible under the circumstances.
- try to avoid laying blame or harping on the failings of yourself or your partner.

We are often our own worst enemies when it comes to matters of trust and new beginnings. At the risk of generalising, women seem to be more anxious to put the past behind them and move on, while men are often more devastated, particularly if the break-up was sudden or not their choice. Men will opt to stay in a difficult relationship rather than change partners out of laziness or out of a sense of futility. What they want is a wife, not a particular woman. Of course, this does not hold in all cases. When a woman walks out, it shocks her husband greatly and the reaction usually is: 'I never thought she'd really do it.' The trouble is that a man's pride does not always allow him to get to the root of the matter. He simply adopts a position of coldness and resentment.

The man you meet at a party who is the most cynical and unpleasant is quite likely to be the one who is hurting deeply inside. I used to run functions for singles at my counselling centre a few years ago, and one guy stays in my mind because he was so incredibly bitter that I could hardly endure to speak to him. I went up to him to engage in pleasant, cocktail-party conversation, only to be met with a tirade on the worthlessness of all women! I felt deeply offended by his remarks and tried, without success, to make light of them. Finally, I suggested that he brighten his conversation or go home because I did not want him depressing the female guests who were, after all, grappling with their own insecurities.

That is the most vital clue to remember in these situations. The person you are sounding off to may be hurting far worse than you, but disguising it better. It is not a question of game-playing, although it may sound like it; rather, it is a case of consideration and simple good manners. Talking about oneself endlessly at a social occasion is the height of rudeness and is guaranteed to push everyone to the furthest corner of the room, away from the offender.

Walking into a party or club unattended is extremely difficult for most women, particularly after a bruising divorce or messy separation when self-esteem is low and being single is a long-forgotten game, now played with new rules. It is like being a teenager again, going to a first dance, but with none of the innocent splendour of youth or the joyous expectation; instead, a trembling heart and a prayer to get through the evening unscarred.

Those people who dabble in the relationship game have a very real responsibility as singles are probably the most vulnerable and misunderstood of social classes. If they have never married, they are nervous and unsure in this setting (even the seemingly sophisticated ones); if they have emerged from a long-standing relationship and are learning to cope without a partner, they are defensive and guarded. So, to provide wholesome entertainment for groups of these people is a tall order; little wonder that the seedy operators are the ones who thrive. Singles are very hard to please—they are almost daring you to take them for a ride. Yet the most appalling stories are told of blatant rip-offs, such as people being charged hundreds of dollars for matchmaking only to hear a few months later that the company has closed down and left town. There is a distinct paradox in this discussion: singles are suspicious and untrusting, yet, because of their vulnerabilities, they are wide open to being cheated. The same lesson applies here as in other areas of life— never be desperate; maintain your dignity and self-respect in all transactions; be cautious without losing sight of life's possibilities.

Until the age of seventeen years there is usually little awareness of being single. Only after women are thrust into the world, leaving behind forever the relatively carefree days of childhood and school, is their awareness heightened about the pressures put upon people not attached to a partner. The late teens and early twenties usually mark carefree enjoyment, career building and developing a personality. During these years, society generally makes it 'okay' to remain unattached. Men can seem to stay fashionably single throughout their lives, but woe betide the woman who reaches thirty without at least one engagement. With the emergence of female equality in daily living, many women are choosing to stay single for the sakes of their careers. Perhaps these double standards regarding bachelorhood are finally disappearing. Nevertheless, being single gets harder for women and men as the years pass. You are conditioned to believe something is wrong with you if you cannot attract a member of the opposite gender and hold on to that person.

Another facet of playing the singles game is having a love affair with a man of a different age group. Hollywood is full of lovely ladies who engage in full-blown relationships with men much younger than themselves. Double standards in our society dictates that these relationships are worthy of comment and the focus of titillation, yet it's extremely commonplace for older men to form liaisons with younger women. In both cases, women sometimes worry about the effect of these relationships on their overall psychology. They question why they're with the younger or older man and torture themselves with hundreds of anxieties about the future. There's really no need because it's the two people themselves who have to make the relationship work, whatever their differences. They have as much or as little chance of success as any other couple.

The second time around

Arguably, the largest group of singles making up the customers of the singles bars and introduction agencies are men and women in their thirties and forties who have already experienced a marriage or a long-standing relationship. These 'second time arounders' are understandably a little bruised and tarnished emotionally and not quite as eager or unsuspecting or willing to give love unconditionally.

There is a transition period following any lifestyle change. Probably one of the most stressful situations anyone has to face is getting used to being alone again. If the break-up is abrupt or one-sided, or if the loss of a partner occurs through sudden death, recovery may literally take years. The next partner needs to be extremely patient and understanding.

Some personal identity seems to be lost by people married ten years or more. The breaking up of such a long-term relationship makes it easy to feel cut in two, no longer whole. Add to this the feeling that somehow you no longer belong, that your friends have stopped inviting you to double date or to dinner parties; you begin feeling like a misfit. The psychological toll can be extreme. The answer is to regain your sense of self-worth as soon as possible. A woman with a strong self-image will not allow a broken relationship to create doubts in her mind about personal value. After a reasonable time of mourning, she will release the disappointment and pain of the past. People with a poor self-image, however, will suffer much longer and deeper because they tend to blame themselves.

Bereavement

Losing a life-partner because of marriage breakdown is painful enough, but if one member of a relationship dies prematurely the shock and grief can be enormous. The word prematurely is used because humans tend to think (incorrectly, I believe) that we are all entitled to three score years and ten, which means that death is acceptable, though still unwelcome, in your seventies or eighties. Anyone who dies before that feels somewhat cheated, as do their families and close friends. Every day of life is a gift, complete unto itself and, therefore, precious, untarnished by the number of those days granted. In other words, death is part of the process of life, not its enemy. This may sound logical and reasonable on paper, but for a person who has just lost a loved one there is nothing but blinding pain, uncomforted by rational argument. Widowhood is certainly one of the saddest ways to be single. Personal choice is swept away and a woman is left to cope and survive, or know bitter defeat.

There are some grim similarities between death and divorce, particularly in the emotions that each evokes. These common stages of response to a relationship breakdown will show that they can be equally applied to the bereavement process:

1. Shock—the immediate, spontaneous result of the event.
2. Grief—sadness for the loss as well as yourself and the future.
3. Anger—feeling that you want to lash out at God, the whole world, even the person who died and left you.

4. Acceptance—once you've let out the pain and anger, you're ready to accept the reality of the situation without bitterness.
5. Resolution—ready for a new beginning. Hopefully, you have said goodbye to that relationship, both literally and emotionally and now can look to the future and a fresh start.

Elisabeth Kubler-Ross, a Swiss psychiatrist and author of *On Death and Dying*, has forced a look at the subject of death from a new perspective and she has not achieved popularity for it. Many people are afraid to have their misconceptions examined and dismissed. Social myths and taboos are jealously guarded and death has been one of the most ubiquitous images throughout time. Poets have personified it, there are countless nicknames for it, and the nightmares of generations are full of its supposed horror. As with so many other things in society, it's ignorance of the subject that creates the most fear. Enlightened teachers such as Kubler-Ross attempt to dispel the doom by casting light on your demons and forcing you to see their hollow faces. Her main argument is that while you are grieving and avoiding the subject, you're denying the dying person the gift of honesty and the once-only opportunity to say goodbye. Another of her important messages relates to the need to get the pain and grief out as soon as possible, e.g. her suggestion that hospitals provide 'crying rooms' so that bereaved families can immediately and privately let their feelings out instead of having to display polite behaviour and coping strategies when they're falling apart.

Bereavement counselling has increased in recent years to help people come to terms with their loss rather than shutting off their emotions and carrying on. Jennifer lost a baby through crib death (or Sudden Infant Death Syndrome) thirty years ago but had never come to terms with it. When consulting me on a totally different matter, a painful memory was triggered and thirty years of crying came flooding out. Jennifer was staggered at the strength of the sorrow after such a long time. Counsellors help you to confront the sadness of loss and to finally deal with the unresolved issues surrounding your loved one's death, for example, the emotions commonly experienced by grieving people, such as guilt, despair, futility, depression and anger.

How a woman deals with the loss of her husband, lover or

best friend will once again depend on the individual herself. Just as divorce brings a painful severance but also a chance for a new beginning, so can there be life after death. This is only possible after healing has taken place. Reactions can vary from reclusion to the other extreme of uncharacteristic, outrageous behaviour. Recognise these symptoms and be gentle with yourself. The sooner you join a support group or read some of the many books available on the subject or consult a counsellor, the sooner you can begin a new life. It's not heartless or pragmatic but rather an affirmation of the ongoing nature of life. If widowhood occurs early in life, a second marriage may be in the cards; if during the autumn years, it's more difficult for obvious reasons to make the adjustment and, often, more practical support is needed.

Loneliness

One of the major pitfalls of single life is the trap you can fall into of imagining that life is unbearably lonely without a partner or special person to be with. It's a mistake to look for someone to fall in love with. As soon as one relationship ends, so many people rush out to find a 'replacement', which is fairly illogical if you stop to think about it. Does this behaviour imply that anyone will do, as long as your bed is not full of space and your life is free of silent solitude? There is a world of difference between solitude and loneliness. The first is enjoyable and freely embraced; the second is unwanted and soul-destroying.

Loneliness conjures up an image of a sad, dejected figure who is extremely shy and quiet and relates poorly with people. Yet, every life is tinged with some amount of loneliness. You are born alone and you die alone. In between, you can make friends, form a family and attach yourself to a whole range of different people, but your life, and what you make of it, rests only with you. Many people fear loneliness so much that they stay in bad relationships just to avoid it. Aloneness is quite different and can be quite satisfying. Aloneness suggests solitude and peacefulness, something you need to some degree in your life. When that being alone becomes bitter and unwilling, it can cause a great deal of psychological pain. Of course, existing in every community are the stereotyped lonely people: the old man in the park; the wallflower at the dance, and the child sitting by herself in the playground.

Loneliness has been of psychological interest for many years; with it go a large number of myths. There is the idea that loneliness is only found in large cities, that people with families, with careers, cannot possibly be lonely. This idea has created the impression that, in order to escape loneliness, one needs to attach oneself as soon as possible to another person, have children and fulfil oneself through work, thus averting any psychological problems. More can be gained by not viewing loneliness in a negative way. Aloneness is always positive; loneliness can be positive or negative, depending upon one's attitude. Having a positive attitude will make a difference but will not totally prevent loneliness. Loneliness does not require being alone, only feeling isolated. One can feel lonely amongst a group of people. It depends on one's attitude to life and our attitudes are borne of life's daily lessons: the things we are told, the opinions of our peers, our experiences.

Men attach the image of their virility to how many dates they have in a week or if they have a beautiful family. The equivalent is true for a woman who sees loneliness in her life as directly relating to her attractiveness and femininity. Another sociological aspect is the ever-increasing complexity of the twentieth-century lifestyle. In the faster, louder world of the 1990s, silence is almost to be feared. Yet in Asia, people do not need the constant stimulus of radio, television, music, or conversation. Solitude is considered a joy, something refreshing and noble, in contrast to the noise of living, both internal and external. We, too, should be able to find enough interest within ourselves for the quieter pursuits of life that can be just as rewarding.

Loneliness can have a deep psychological effect as well as the social repercussions that affect everyone. The type of loneliness that turns into itself and becomes extreme introversion can eat away at a person until that person feels singled out, unable to find communication and happiness with anyone else. Although anyone can experience this feeling, some people spend their entire lives with this attitude.

Loneliness, then is a matter of degree, type and frequency. A static remark would be, 'I am lonely', when 'I feel lonely tonight' would do. There are also the various types of loneliness, such as being physically alone or feeling isolated. This feeling can occur within a family, in the bleak loneliness of an unhappy marriage, or in not belonging to a group; the list goes on. Frequency, of course, relates to how often one feels lonely. As the song says, 'Everyone gets the blues now and then.' Still, there is a difference between the 'blues', which means feeling slightly sad, and chronic depression, a state of mind that can develop into an ongoing problem.

How do you combat loneliness? If it is not merely a matter of keeping busy, being in the company of others, or enjoying the media, what is the essence of this social phenomenon? The first step is recognising that loneliness is part of everyday living and is present in everyone, to some degree. Then you must seek the nature of your individual loneliness: is it chronic, self-pity, laziness? Once you have been honest with yourself and reached the necessary answer, then you can know what to do.

The first suggestion is to stop pretending, stop feeling as if you must be out constantly enjoying yourself or pretending you are. An evening with no plans is an opportunity to suggest to friends that you get together. You don't always need to be invited out or feel unwanted because you have not been asked. Take the initiative, and consider that someone else may be as lonely as you are and glad of an invitation. Try not to let doubts and fears about your own popularity prevent you from reaching out to other people and offering the hand of friendship. One of the best cures for dwelling on your own problems is to think about other people's feelings. There is always someone lonelier than you.

You do not have to be happy or busy or popular all of the time. Once that hurdle is mastered, honesty with yourself is possible as is functioning at a more honest level with others. Communication is the key to the betterment of your relationships and towards better psychological health. Admitting vulnerability, expressing feelings and being unashamed of them immediately makes you a better communicator. Saying to someone, 'I feel lonely', may do far more to alleviate those feelings than saying, 'I feel terrific', 'I have lots of friends', or 'I go out every night', when you know it isn't true. The dichotomy of what appears to be true and what is true causes a great deal of confusion and even despair in the human psyche.

There are many practical ways to reduce loneliness for yourself and people around you. Here is a list of hints on ways to combat loneliness:

- remember loneliness is only bad if you allow it to be. Aloneness can be enoyable.
- do not rely on others to keep you entertained and happy. Develop your own interests.
- keep in mind that everyone in the world is lonely at some time, even the most famous and successful person.
- keep busy but don't do things just to fill up your time; find activities that really satisfy and fulfil you.
- do not pretend or play act about your feelings. Be willing to deal with people honestly even if it means putting yourself on the line. For example, do not pretend to be busy on a Saturday night because you are ashamed to admit you are sitting home alone. You may be surprised at a sudden invitation or an unexpected visitor.
- reach out to other people. Closing in on yourself only increases loneliness.
- do not waste your energies and time on wishful thinking or envying others who seem happy. Remember that appearances are not always the truth. If you were someone else, you may be much worse off. Enjoy being yourself.
- a bright, happy person is rarely lonely. True isolation comes from self-centredness and a lack of concern for others.
- remember it is possible to be lonely in a crowd. Only inner strength prevents loneliness, not noise and activity and riotous company.
- happiness is a condition, not a goal. Pleasure is fleeting, but contentedness with yourself lasts forever.
- being lonely for a time is better than staying in a relationship that makes you unhappy. That type of selling out is the worst kind of psychological death. Discover all of the wonderful things life has to offer that can be enjoyed alone or with friends: the arts, nature, a beautiful day.
- allow yourself to be depressed or discouraged sometimes. It is all part of the human condition. The effort of appearing

to be happy all of the time is too much of a strain. Your true friends will accept you, moods and all.

You do not have to be happy or popular all of the time. Once this realisation is made, it is possible to be much more honest with yourself and function on a more honest level with others. There are many ways to reduce temporary loneliness. Overall, it is your own attitude to your life that will determine how well you cope with loneliness. Start enjoying your own company. You may be surprised at how much fun you are!

Love on the rebound

Another trap for the unwary is 'love on the rebound'. Loneliness can cause us to be less clear-sighted than we might otherwise be—what passes for love may really be exploitation or a cheap imitation. Nightclubs are designed to create maximum illusion and minimum reality. When people complain that they cannot find true love in these places, they must ask themselves why they would expect to. They are places for meaningless fun (which has its role) and escapism and quick thrills, not deep conversation or getting to know people. Do not ask a racoon to be a mink and then get angry because he's not!

If you are feeling lonely or sad, try going for a walk in the fresh air, preferably near water. There is no cure like nature. This activity not only helps the blues, it is also uplifting in other ways. A fast fix will only leave you feeling more bleak and depressed than you already are—the last place to be when you are down is a club; that is a venue reserved for happy times, so frequent them on social occasions when you feel good and have something to add to the proceedings. The same attitude applies to food and drink. These are for joy, not camouflages for unhappiness. Choose what feels comfortable for you and do not get talked into activities that don't feel right.

Introduction agencies have their place, but check out the one you are thinking of joining before you pay out any money. The best reference is a satisfied customer so get a personal recommendation if possible. After you have decided to join and have registered, keep in regular contact with the company. Do not allow a lot of time to pass between phone calls or visits, as the biggest complaint against matchmaking organisations is that, after fees have been paid, little action results. Either no introductions are forthcoming at all, they are to bogus people, or the contact names given are totally unsuitable.

Divorce

Society's attitudes towards divorce have softened recently, mainly because this condition has touched so many lives across socioeconomic barriers. As stated previously, there are several similarities between divorce and death: both constitute endings, both are extremely painful and both require a period of mourning.

Getting adequate legal advice before beginning divorce proceedings is important, especially if you are the main instigator and if there are children and property involved. It is a rare couple that can handle the whole thing themselves without any disagreement, but, even in cases where both parties are conducive to an amicable settlement, all the facts should be clarified by separate solicitors for husband and wife.

Emotionally, professional help can be sought, and there are support groups that meet regularly to make the transition back to single life a little easier. After an initial period of introspection and healing, it is vital to 'get back up on the horse' by going out to meet people again, even if you do not feel ready to date. There are very definite rules governing acceptable behaviour in widowhood, but the mores regarding divorce are a lot more hazy. The 'gay divorcee' tag no longer fits as few women would rush out of a marriage and straight on to the social circuit. Hopefully, the dust is allowed to settle along with everything else that takes place before, during and after a divorce.

Ground rules should be established about the future relationship of the two ex-partners. Arrangements regarding children are usually settled by the courts, but informal plans often create problems, for example, the husband who feels it is his right to still drop around to the marital home unannounced or the wife who changes the husband's visitation arrangements without warning. This type of inconsiderate behaviour causes a great deal of bad feelings and is largely unnecessary. When two people have made children together, there can never be an absolute severance of their contact because they will always have those children in common, and for the sake of the offspring courteous and reliable agreements ought to be honoured.

Children are the innocent victims of a broken marriage. Their world is suddenly made insecure, but the blows can be lessened if both parents assure the children that they are blameless and unconditionally loved. A man and a woman divorce each other, but children can never be divorced from their parents.

Another factor to keep in mind is the choosing of another partner after divorce. It may be the last thing on your mind, but, once you start dating again, attractions happen and relationships form. Being clear on a few points is important before 'falling in love' and then saying it is too late. Everyone has a tendency to repeat their mistakes in life until they learn the appropriate lessons. Whatever it was that made your marriage unsuccessful needs to be understood and released into the past where it belongs. Many people do not take the time and trouble to do this exercise, carrying the unresolved problems into future alliances.

Earlier in the book it was purported that you choose people to become involved with who are able to fulfil a specific purpose for you. A quiet person may be attracted to an extrovert, a woman who felt unloved by her mother might continually choose the same type of personality in a mate in order to find the missed love, a woman whose father was an alcoholic might marry one so that she can grow to understand what made her father drink. These are largely unconscious decisions. If these examples sound a bit far-fetched, think about your own case and see if, in some degree, this theory has held true for you. For instance, divorced people who talk about their relationships or multiple marriages usually describe their partners as all being very different. When asked to consider again, they begin to see any number of similarities and it is usually in the areas that count most, emotional interaction rather than choice of toothpaste. Only when you know *why* you choose the people you do and why this particular type does not result in a happy union for you can you steer clear of repeating the mistake. With increasing self-love and knowledge, you will begin to feel attraction for those individuals who can and will fulfil your positive needs rather than your negative ones.

Remember that so many of your limitations are self-imposed and unnecessary. The sky is the limit, psychologically, and in every other way, once you accept yourself, put in a bit of work on gaining insight and more understanding and trust in life to open all the doors. A good affirmation to make daily is to say, 'I let go of all limitations in my life.' Release the negative excess baggage you carry in your mind first and then everything becomes easier to achieve.

The positives of being single

So much for all the difficult aspects of being single. What about the positive side? Time spent alone can be constructive, positive and even joyous. Whether it is for four months or four years, whether by choice or circumstance, you can enjoy time living alone as you develop personally and spiritually. You cannot find a suitable partner in life just by wishing, so why not enjoy the waiting? Join clubs, make friends, get out, develop your professional life, learn new skills and hobbies, read the great books, improve your physical fitness—the list of possibilities is endless.

The key to the entire exercise is caring enough about yourself to make yourself happy. Do not rely on anyone else to do it for you. It is a myth to believe anyone can make you happy. Others can only add to your happiness, provide the icing on the cake, but true happiness lies in inner peace and belief in yourself. The common belief is that self-love is an ego trip or self-centredness. In fact, the more you care about yourself, the more you have to give others. The best relationships begin with two individuals respecting themselves and coming to love and respect each other.

Remaining single is better than entering relationships uncommitted or for the wrong reasons. Know yourself and your own motives and believe in whatever choice you make for your marital state. Single, married, divorced, or looking, you are always only you. If you do not like what that means, all the rest is meaningless. The single life can be as productive and joyful as any other state of being, and being married is no guarantee of happiness and eternal satisfaction. In double bed or boardroom, the incidence of loneliness in your life is entirely reliant upon your perception of who you are and how you fit into your society, so do not expend energy worrying about whether you have a ring on your left hand or whether you are going to get that next promotion. Just concentrate on being the best person you already are and living each day to the fullest. Dreams are for lovers. We should all be lovers of life. Being single is great; enjoy every minute of it!

AFFIRMATIONS

I am a person who says yes to life.
Whatever I need comes to me in the right time/space sequence.
I receive my good from expected and unexpected sources.
All I need is always taken care of; I am safe.

Chapter Seven

Sexuality

What is sexuality really? Is it just the act of intercourse between male and female or does it take in the whole range of human activity that involves physical inter-action? Since the first breakthrough research, *The Kinsey Report*, and then the radical Masters and Johnson data, women have been awakened to the possibilities of a full and fulfilling sexual life beyond satisfying a male partner. To some extent this awakening is what is spoken of as the 'sexual revolution'. Opinions and behaviours freed up for both sexes, but the implications for women ran far deeper. Women began demanding an equal role in the bedroom, reflecting a wider search for identity that was happening out in the world arena. These demands put a great strain on man/woman relations as roles became confused and, in some cases, reversed.

Sex as a social phenomena has been examined since humans first began to organise thought, an ability that led to further searching and questioning. There have been many significant contributions, notably the *Kamasutra*, the theories of Freud and the *Playboy* empire. The *Kamasutra* taught us sexual positions, Freud told us why we feel guilty about sex, and *Playboy* said to hell with all that, just enjoy! Your personal philosophy of sexual behaviour will be determined by such factors as your upbringing, your parents' attitudes and your moral system. I would like to believe that all women are well and truly out of the closet on this issue, and you can finally take your rightful place, side by side with your partners, enjoying your body in intimate contact together. However, the number of women with sexual difficulties prove that this freedom is not enjoyed by the majority of women.

The many issues of sexuality will be explored here under four main headings: the concept of sexuality; sexuality in relationships; sexual problems; and general issues.

The concept of sexuality

With the social changes just mentioned, sex has undergone a massive transformation. Some people may still live by the old rules, but most have had to come to grips with changes in such matters as courting, sex before marriage, contraception, childbirth and divorce. Although general human issues, these cannot be separated from sex as such, because one set of behaviour creates consequences for the other.

The image of a man taking a woman by brute force, her loving it and having an orgasm the moment he enters her is simply no longer acceptable even as fiction. The trend towards realism in literature, film, theatre, dance and art reflects community desire for life to be less complicated in an ever more complex world. We live in a 'don't jive me' era, where anything that is false is rejected. That is not to say that people no longer need to fantasise or dream; perhaps we need to create magical worlds of imagination even more, but that is acceptable because everyone understands that it is make-believe.

Sexuality in relationships

Since the advent of AIDS as a negative force in our society, so many liberated views about sex have required revision. Advertising now deals with safe sex rather than free sex, and the public would rather know about condoms for a man to put on than lingerie to make him turn on. These external changes have made an impact on everyone even if they have resisted the influence. Not everyone is prepared to modify sexual behaviour, but being social animals we are affected inevitably by the attitudes and actions of those around us. The public view of women is one area that has undergone enormous alteration. The buxom, empty-headed, blonde beauty in a tight sweater still has a place in some male-orientated advertising, but with anti-discriminatory laws tightening up she had better change her clothes and get some other job skills before she finds herself redundant in today's marketplace. The view here is not that prostitutes, strippers and nude models degrade women by their choice of occupation. If we are going to talk about women's rights, they must include the right to choose what job to do and which assets to promote. We must be able to accept women without prejudice, in whatever way they choose to portray themselves. No matter what a woman's choice of occupation or lifestyle, it is her right to do what she believes is best. Acceptance—even celebration—of these differences is the key to equality in society. The best way to heal society is to get out there in the community and do things that prove women are the equal of men in every area. That is the way to end sexual exploitation of all kinds—rape, wife-beating, sexual harassment, unwanted pregnancy, and the tyranny of contraception.

The word 'sex' should be synonymous with love and tenderness and touching and sharing. Yes, there is such a thing as raw sex, but the word for that is lust. No value judgment is made here of this particular passion, realising that, in harmony with all the other emotions, it is natural and delightful. However, in isolation, it is troubling and strange. There are women who enjoy one-night stands and sex with strangers; this is a matter of personal choice and preference. Whatever your particular stance on this important subject, let's face it, sex is here to stay! It is part of life, creativity and the very essence of being. It also must be one of the most overrated, misunderstood and distorted of all human activities.

Although many people think they are so liberated in the 1990s, some people still have a problem talking freely about sex. It would be easier if sex was a 'take it or leave it' proposition, but as it engages everyone at some time in their lives, it continues to be a volatile issue. Sex has biological, emotional and psychological implications and is singularly the most powerful weapon against growing up unscarred and unscathed. It is also one of the worst creators of stress. Most puberty nightmares are connected to sexual matters. Sexual prowess, especially for men, is tied up with notions of ego, self-image and desirability. Everyone wants to be thought of as attractive, especially during the insecure teenage years. This desire puts a great deal of pressure on relationships because liking and loving are often translated into physical expressions only, when they need not be.

Children should be taught about sex at home as soon as they are old enough to understand. That discussion on the 'birds and the bees' should not be put off until it is 'absolutely necessary', such as when a girl gets her first period or a boy experiences a wet dream for the first time. Procrastination can be damaging to the future sex life of the child. A healthy attitude from the start can prevent a lot of heartache (and stress) later on. Rather than a formal talk, a more casual approach often works better. For instance, when a mother uses a tampon herself, it is the most natural thing in the world to explain to her daughter what it is, how to use it and its benefits. Unfortunately most people report that they learn about sex 'along the way'. What is the most concerning about haphazard sex education is the strong possibility of misinformation and serious omissions, such as the emotional aspects of sex. Some parents are reluctant to discuss sex openly with their children, for various reasons. Either they were brought up in families where sex was not spoken about freely, they themselves feel inadequate to the task, or they are too shy and embarrassed to broach the subject. Sex education is not only a matter of passing on information; it is also showing by example. The strongest argument for sex education taking place in the home is based on the statistical evidence that most human sexual activity occurs in domiciles of one kind or another.

If young people are not going to learn about sex directly from their parents, then there should be provision in school curricula for it to be taught in an unemotional, undramatic way. An ostrich attitude by parents is hardly constructive. They have a right to know what their children are being taught, but not to demand that students are kept unenlightened and unprepared for the real world. I remember the problems I had with some parents during my years as an English teacher. Novels like *Catch-22* (by Joseph Heller) would bring a howl of protest because of swear words and sex scenes. Do parents think that their children do not hear these words outside the pages of a book? Isn't it better that such matters are discussed in the presence of a responsible and caring teacher than in the schoolyard? Wouldn't it be much worse for their ignorance to spill out into their social life, manifest in crude sex in the back seat of a car, or result in an unwanted pregnancy? Sex is natural and good; only the abuse of its beauty is destructive and harmful. Pass on to your children not only the legacy of your material wealth, but also that which is much more valuable, the wealth of your experience and your knowledge.

Any sex education course in a school context must be relevant and up-to-date. When I was in high school, a nervous priest would come in once a week to tell us about the 'perils of the flesh'. We all thought it was highly amusing and learned nothing in these classes except the unsuitability of the teacher. How must the poor man have felt facing thirty teenage girls, armed only with an antiquated book, a set of clichéd responses and a face made red by our impertinent questions? If you wish your children to be responsible, caring and balanced citizens of the future, you must supply the tools of learning today, in *all* areas of endeavour.

Peer pressure causes many a teenage girl to go against her moral standards and personal beliefs and indulge in sexual activities before she's ready. Whether thirteen or thirty, 'the first time' is usually disappointing because of all the false hype that has surrounded sex since Hollywood was born, 'Hollywood' being a place and a dream. Everyone has unrealistic expectations about 'sex'. Those who think it will be magical the first time end up asking, 'Is that all there is?' Those who dread the first experience find that it is not so much horrible as tedious, which the actual physiology and geography of sex undoubtedly is without love or passion. For centuries, women have gritted their teeth and prayed for it to be over or stifled their yawns and obvious boredom at their husband's fondlings. My mother thought that having babies with a man meant only lying in the same bed as he, and nature would do the rest. She got a rude shock on her wedding night! She was twenty and totally inexperienced as girls often were in her days.

Liberation without understanding is just as bad, if not worse.

Girls know that virginity is not so highly prized today. Still, self-respect can never be devalued by the passage of time nor the world's jaded sophistication. Even in these enlightened times, girls still whisper and marvel about sex in their pubescent imaginations. What is it really like, they wonder. Although immensely interested in the physical minutiae of the sex act, they are usually more immersed in the romantic aspects than the biological ones. They cannot fail to be aware of the many changes going on in their blossoming bodies, and hormonal transformations demand recognition. There are periods to deal with and unnamed urges, infatuations and heartache. Innocence is appealing as long as it does not cause unnecessary pain.

The second reason for the disappointment of the first time is the inexperience of one or both partners. This occasion normally occurs for young men and women in their late teens, and neither is likely to have had many encounters before. Even if it is the first time for one and not the other, it is still quite likely to be a case of the 'blind leading the blind'. If this situation is not corrected before entering a permanent relationship, cute naiveté can sour into marriage-threatening frigidity in women and in males, premature ejaculation, or impotence.

The first time can also occur late in life. As with the singles scene generally, it appears to be more difficult for over thirty-fives to make the transition from virgin to lover. Whatever the age at which you have your first experience, do not despair if skyrockets fail to fire off in your mind and multiple orgasms are elusive. You may not have a climax at all. For some women, it does not happen until a relationship is established and comfortable trust replaces uncertain excitement. There need not be impatience and urgency in these matters; do not fall for media hype and society's many myths about sex. You have your whole life to practise!

Many first times are with members of the same sex, in other words, homosexual experiences. The reason is easy to understand: those adolescents who attend one-gender schools, particularly residential, are presented with many opportunities to experiment. At puberty emotions run strong, and girls easily develop crushes on their schoolmates or teachers. Sometimes, apparently sexual encounters are more likely to be expressions of passionate feeling of an emotional nature. Teenage girls tend to be very affectionate towards one another in general, touching each other freely, linking arms and holding hands. Overreaction by adults can actually encourage further closeness. So, again, a quiet discussion about these vital friendships is infinitely more advisable than a lot of warnings, ultimatums and threats. A thirteen- or fourteen-year-old girl cares far more what her friends think of her than her parents. That is just a fact of life; so if you, as a mother, force your daughter to make choices, you will probably be the one to lose.

Whether it is simple touching or a full-blown sexual experience, a homosexual beginning does not guarantee a life choice in this regard. Young children of the same sex will touch each other's genitals without thought and think nothing of it until grown-ups begin screaming about 'filth' and 'sin'. Innocence does not name a thing dirty. As such sexual events occur without intent, so do they desist, if left alone. Teach your children, then trust your children. There is really nothing else.

If a daughter does have to break the news to her family that she is 'gay', there is usually a negative reaction, even from the most tolerant and understanding of parents. With some parents it is the moral considerations; with many, it is the notion of social disapproval, the thought of their daughter living on the fringes of society, and the loss of their own future expectations of wedding, grandchildren and 'happy-ever-after'.

There are many sociological arguments regarding homosexuality; everyone, it seems, has a theory as to why it occurs, whose fault it is and whether it should be accepted or abhorred. Some girls know by the age of puberty that they are interested in members of their own gender in a sexual way, beyond friendship. Others seem to fall into lesbian relationships almost by chance. Women who love other women are looking for an emotional attachment that they believe they cannot get from men. Some have a revulsion for the penis and find men unappealing. The brouhaha about homosexuality is unnecessary unless it offends your moral system. Even then, no one says that you have to try it yourself or socialise with gays (who tend to either stay in the closet and blend in with the rest of society or live in their own circles, mixing with other gays). Gays are just ordinary people. What they do sexually is no more bizarre and way-out than their heterosexual counterparts. What a woman does in the privacy of her own home is between herself and her conscience, not a matter for public scrutiny. The most outwardly respectable person could be indulging in a ripe and torrid sex life that no one is aware of, so you should be wary of judging situations from overt evidence only.

Homophobics have found a fertile release for their hatred in recent years, because AIDS is thought to have originally generated from the activities of homosexual males, especially in relation to anal intercourse. Heterosexual couples also indulge in this form of sex, but now it is considered risky for both parties and discouraged by the experts unless condoms are used.

One-night stands are frowned upon as a further means of spreading AIDS. No amount of fear will totally eradicate this option from the spectrum of sexual behaviour. Young or old, married or single, experienced or not, there are appealing features in the one-night stand for all these groups. Some obvious ones are: the excitement of a new and different sexual partner, experimentation in early sexual experiences; the pleasure of uncommitted sex; and the fact that impotent men report that they can often perform with a prostitute or casual partner because there is an absence of anxiety and performance pressure.

The whole point of a one-night stand is that it should only last one night. Films like *Fatal Attraction* raise this very issue. Can you as an emotional human being just have sex and then walk away without another thought for that exchange? Millions of people around the world would testify that you can. Again, it is not everyone's cup of tea. None of us are as casual about sex as we like to make out. It is a vulnerable and sensitive area of interaction, and no one wants to be assessed, compared, or rejected. One-night stands would be all right if both parties were completely honest about their intentions or lack of them! Certainly, they are a common feature of the gay scene. One of the main concerns of the wider community is the fact that homosexual males can interchange partners hundreds of times in a twelve-month period. Even so, it is just too easy to blame one section of society for all our frailties and fears. Look at what created the fear in the first place, the fear of loneliness, of rejection, of being unloved. When these are eradicated, perhaps solutions for AIDS and other social ills can be found.

One-night stands may well become an anachronism some day, as outdated as doing the twist or congregating in snack bars. To repeat (yet again!) stress breeds more stress, immunity to disease is decreased and so, by persecuting gays, is not society adding to the incidence of illness and death? It is a reasonable proposal by virtue of its simple logic.

Some wives find themselves in an extremely difficult position when they discover or are told their husbands are homosexual. Some gay men marry because they want the respectability of marriage and children, family life and so forth. After a certain period of time, even years, they are once again drawn to an alternative lifestyle. It may begin innocently enough with the occasional drop-in to a gay pub or club, but it is a short jump from that tentative beginning to forming an alliance with a male. Whether it is a casual encounter or a blossoming love affair, it creates terrible conflict for a man who loves his family and knows he is putting his straight life at risk. Moreover, he has no assurance that he is not taking home a variety of health risks. Adultery forces a person into a 'Walter Mitty' existence with little of the fun and fantasy; a bisexual male ends up living the worst kind of double act. When inevitably the truth comes out, some women say it is easier to deal with a male rival than another female while others say that the whole situation revolts them beyond words and they want nothing more to do with their husbands. It surely must be one of the most stressful experiences any woman can endure. How she handles it will depend on the strength of her marriage, her own level of development and what she wants to do in the future.

Friendship between a gay man and a heterosexual woman is said to be one of the best mixes possible because neither wants more from the other. There is no game playing, and the usual stereotyped male/female behaviours are not present to intrude upon the affection between the two people. There is a lesson here for all interactions, regardless of gender. If we could all just love honestly and not waste so much energy on sexual games, the world would be a better place for everyone and much easier to function in.

This is the perfect point at which to turn the attention to sexuality in heterosexual relationships specifically. Sex can cause a lot of stress in relationships, particularly marriage. As was seen in Chapter Five, marital problems tend to show up first in the bedroom. Why does this happen, and what can be done? The best way to answer that question is to look at why sex in marriage is different to sex in other relationships or in casual affairs.

The normal assumption is that married couples inevitably have sex. In fact, some stay together, but agree not to share connubial activity once the bliss has gone. Celibacy is a real option for some individuals and couples today because of all the sexual problems, especially health risks. An English couple recently published a book about sexless marriage and all its benefits. People in love usually want to reach out and touch each other in a physical expression, but it has to be accepted that sexual ardour *does* wane after the first year or two of marriage and there are many types and levels of love. No sex is probably better than bad sex, so as couples grow apart, they may very well choose to continue the marriage without sharing a bed or sharing a bed without the sexual intimacy. One song says that 'love and marriage go together like a horse and a carriage', but it appears that sex and marriage do not. There is a lot of sexual activity in the world that has nothing to do with marriage and marriages in which sex plays no part. For the purpose of this section the subject will be the 'average' marriage, which often means sex approximately three times a week.

Sex in marriage is different to sex in other relationships for a number of reasons:

- there is a definite and committed relationship involved. There is less preamble because of the nature of marriage. Both parties feel they have a right to each other, which is why it is so easy for spouses to take the sex act for granted and either get lazy or stop enjoying it.
- sex in marriage is usually accompanied by a good deal of domestic stress. Life in the suburbs can be a harrowing experience for the uninitiated, with its usual round of children's noises, dogs barking and early Sunday morning mowers. It is difficult to be romantic in the face of drudgery and routine. Daily stress can take its toll on the most auspicious of beginnings. Married couples take to bed with them thoughts not of sweet nothings but unpaid bills,

unwashed dishes and unresolved quarrels. Also, the children may interrupt at any moment.

■ much stronger need for communication, to avoid boredom and staleness. Married couples have to work at sex much more, while in pre-, extra- or postmarital affairs, it is lighthearted and fun.

Why does sex turn sour in a marriage? Isolated here are six possible causes:

1. Some women still suffer from male dominance in the bedroom.
2. There is not enough preparation for marriage, either educationally or emotionally.
3. Poor sexual attitudes, usually learned from childhood and/or parents.
4. Failure to recognise the important link between success of sexual interaction and the relationship itself.
5. Loss of sex drive due to biological reasons: low libido in women and sexual dysfunction in men.
6. Insensitive attitude or behaviour on the part of the husband, such as not allowing enough time for arousal of his wife or taking the trouble to ask what she likes in bed. A woman's sexuality is far more subtle than a man's and, therefore, requires a different approach.

The key to good sex in marriage is acceptance of yourself and then your partner—the good old 'give and take'. You do not need to sacrifice your individual rights, needs, and tastes on the altar of marriage, or surrender your identity in exchange for a wedding ring. Yet, marriage cannot survive without love and tenderness. Everyone walks up the aisle with a stranger. Somewhere between the gaiety of the wedding day and the daily realities of married life, a kernel of happiness lies waiting for you to nurture it and give it the best of yourself. Then it will reward you thousandfold. Sex is one of nature's greatest gifts and, perhaps in marriage, lies the potential for the most fulfilling enjoyment of it.

One of the most difficult situations occurs when one partner is keener on sex than the other. This can be simply a matter of a difference in libido levels or it may run deeper than that. The most common reasons for refusal are: ill-health; the personal psychology of the less interested partner; poor communication; stresses; quarrelling, and infidelity. Men and women have to realise that they do not only bring their present selves into any relationship but also all of their past experiences, unresolved hurts, hang-ups and disappointments.

Incest plays a large part in the reluctance of some girls to engage in normal sexual relations with men. Some abuse victims are so damaged by these experiences that they never recover; relationships at any level are impossible for them.

Another common reason for a lack of sexual interest is low self-esteem. If a woman thinks she has an ugly body or that she is grossly overweight, she cannot be expected to give herself to her husband in an open and unreserved way. Sex is one of the most vulnerable areas of human interaction. You are unmasked totally, naked emotionally as well as literally. If there is any game-playing, power roles or posturing, tension will bristle in the air and make easy loving unattainable.

Biological variations are a major factor in sexual activity (when it takes place and how frequently) in a marriage. A woman's periods, the incidence of PMS, if she is pregnant or going through menopause—all of these factors will affect her libido and performance. Many husbands have complained that their wives turn right off sex after childbirth, and some have even pointed to this time as being the juncture at which their marriage began to go downhill. According to the experts, the reasons for this turn-off are: hormonal changes in the woman directly linked to childbirth; postnatal depression or, at least, adjustment to a new and very demanding lifestyle; the total absorption of the mother in the baby, and the substitution of baby for husband in tactile closeness and touching interaction. Husbands can feel pushed out, isolated, almost strangers to their own families. A woman dealing with a small and self-centred infant all day has little of herself to give in the evening. Sleep becomes a much greater need than sex or even time with her husband. A wise couple plans for these changes and challenges and talks about them *before* the event.

Recent research shows the significance of the 'distraction' principle in sexual problems, particularly lack of interest and impotence. When you are unduly fatigued, stressed, or busy, you become 'distracted' from normal sexual urges and activity.

Even if you continue to perform, you find it difficult to concentrate. You may have your mind on other matters and thus operate mechanically on the sexual level. It is often the body's way of reminding you that you are overloading again and need to recharge and reorganise your system of priorities. You cannot perform equally well in all areas of life without a plan or at least sufficient self-love to ensure harmony and balance.

The key point to keep in mind is that sex cannot be considered apart from other human emotions. If both partners are suffering from burnout and have essentially lost interest in the marriage, sex becomes hollow, a dance between strangers without rhythm, love, or meaning.

One unfortunate factor that can develop in these situations is a classic form of role-playing. Patterns become established after the first crucial months of marriage and, commonly, each partner takes a posture at polar ends of most issues. They become extreme advocates, eager exponents of opposing behaviour and attitudes. If one talks a lot, the other becomes quiet. If one is keen on sex, the other starts to make excuses to get out of it. If one is tidy, the other slops around. This behaviour is most unfortunate in sexual matters because the final product entails one partner doing all the initiating, 'making all the moves', which leads inevitably to resentment. The keen one resents the reluctant one for being unloving. The reluctant one feels constantly pressured and put-upon when, in reality, both people just want to be loved.

Try to get away from all the stereotyping that generates such common beliefs as 'men only want sex' and 'women can live without sex'. True or false, such generalisations dehumanise you because they take away your individual impulses and relegate you to a herd mentality. If spouses begin to believe implicitly in their roles, little room for change and growth within the marriage is afforded. When sex is good in a marriage there is no need to talk about it, but when it is out of balance in one way or another it assumes larger-than-life proportions. It is, in reality, merely a heightened form of human communication, one of the most beautiful expressions available to you. Just as all communication is not speaking, all sex is not intercourse.

173

There are many ways to make love. When there are problems in the bedroom, sometimes one of the best remedies is to stop trying for awhile. Give each other a massage instead. Sexual partners are not giving themselves the best chance at a good sex life if they fall into bed dead tired after a long day and then make what passes for love in a hasty and unsatisfying manner. Dr Michael Clarke, in his book, *Sexual Joy in Marriage*, speaks of the 'twenty-three and a half hour foreplay.' In other words, every moment of the day leads up to the half hour of intercourse. It can entail a special look, a light touch, a smile across the room that says 'Let's make love tonight'. It is worth the trouble to make special arrangements to ensure uninterrupted privacy, perhaps going to bed a little earlier, making love in the morning, or escaping for the occasional weekend alone together. You should also feel relaxed and peaceful before any physical contact takes place, so it may be advisable to lie still for a moment and not invade your partner's personal space the moment you get into bed. There are polite and pleasurable ways to go about these things. Just as there are rules of conversation, such as allowing others to speak and listening with attention, it is important to listen with your heart to your partner's sexual preferences and be receptive to mood changes or any hesitancies. Take care of the little things and the bigger ones will be fine. If necessary, work on general improvement of communication skills and your sexual interaction, in or out of a marriage, has to improve.

Infidelity

The issue of sexual infidelity remains one of the most testing in modern relationships. Like incest, it is not only the sexual aspect that requires examination; the emotional ones are important as well, particularly in regard to trust. Some marriages are crushed by adultery and others, believe it or not, are enhanced by it. The individual attitudes of the two partners and indeed, the third party, will ultimately govern the outcome of the affair.

Statistically it happens more often that the husband is the unfaithful one and the woman the 'victim'. There are undoubtedly perennial womanisers who chase extra-marital sex, regardless of how good their home-life is.

Many men and women fall into unlooked-for relationships

and often find it difficult to extricate themselves when the novelty has worn off. After all, it is the married lover who eventually wants out. The interloper is the party most likely to be dispensable. If this seems like a bleak view, it is nevertheless a realistic one. Anyone entering into a relationship with a married person has to know deep inside that there is no future. In some cases, wives and husbands are left for lovers, but the marriage was probably faulty to start with or no third party could have intruded.

Nowadays, as modern couples search for ways in which to have more honest and durable marriages, 'open' relationships are often mooted. Monogamy is seen as obsolete, based on the argument that no single person can satisfy all your various needs. So, it is better to say from the start that both parties are free to seek pleasures outside the marriage union. If the notion of marriage itself in the 1990s is idealistic, open marriage is hundreds of times more so because it calls for more than usual maturity from the spouses; it also asks a generosity of spirit, an absence of jealousy or possessive feelings of any kind and an inactive imagination. Couples who engage in extramarital sex had better be sure they can wear the consequences, the unanswered questions, the self-doubts.

The saddest aspect of this is the high incidence of self-delusion, the 'I'm cool, I can handle it' attitude. Be sure that you talk these matters over very carefully as a couple before one or both is unfaithful because it is not the sort of thing that can be taken back.

Most infidelity occurs with one partner being left in the dark and finding out by accident or if the unfaithful party 'confesses'. Needless to say, this knowledge comes as a tremendous shock and is extremely hurtful. In France, the courts look on murder for reasons of adultery as a 'crime of passion' and are more lenient than they would be in other cases of homicide; it is considered that the killer is entitled to be 'out of his/her mind' at finding the one they love loving someone else. Many people say they could not forgive their spouses if they were unfaithful— absolutely, with no possibility of changing their minds. As with so many human experiences, you cannot truly know how you will react until you are placed in that position.

Infidelity brings shock, humiliation and feelings of betrayal from which men and women have to recover. After her husband's affair, Mary sought counselling and although she felt better, she could not put out of her mind the thought of her husband's affair with the other woman, who was known to her and now an object of loathing. She refused my suggestion to seek the woman out and confront her with the anger and hatred that were crippling her. This meeting could have had a cathartic effect on both women, lancing, once and for all, the poisonous wound of betrayed love. Mary did not leave her husband, but refused to resume married life with him, banishing both of them to a sterile imitation of marriage.

Some women opt for this choice, to stay with erring husbands, only to torment them with their weaknesses and treacherous behaviour ad infinitum, never again gifting them with trust or sexual favours. Of course, that trusting is the hardest exercise of all after such a blow as infidelity, often lagging far behind forgiveness and even making up. If a woman can forgive a man or a man a woman, sincerely with no reservations, their marriage can be much stronger for it. Never again will they look at each other in quite the same way, perhaps the love light might have dimmed, but there can be a lot more honesty and a new beginning.

Broadly, the reasons for infidelity are likely to be one or more of the following:

■ search for excitement and/or novelty;
■ lack of sexual satisfaction in the current relationship;
■ emotional immaturity;
■ general and specific stress, and
■ incompatibility in sexual desire.

Infidelity need not spell death to a healthy marriage; if the marriage is already in trouble, the other person will essentially be used as a catalyst to focus attention on the problem area which may or may not be sex. If you choose to learn from the experience instead of engaging in the very self-indulgent pastime of blame-laying, you can benefit. Those people with moral systems that proclude the continuance of a relationship after infidelity must make this very personal decision in the dark night of the soul. People who find it impossible to forgive had better have a pretty clean slate themselves, as no one is perfect.

Contraception

One issue which must not be neglected in this section is that of contraception. With the current emphasis on condoms, most people know more than they want to about the need for hygienic sex and prevention of unwanted babies. The Catholic Church still holds its ground on this important family matter. Any artificial means used to avoid conception is regarded as a sin. However, the average couple finds it necessary to engage in family planning so that they do not bring children into the world that they cannot afford or care for. With the food shortages and economic conditions of many countries, an organised contraception programme is seen as the only viable solution to overpopulation. A sensible attitude to prevention of pregnancy is far more responsible than having unwanted babies, abortion, or being forced to face the trauma of adoption.

The three most commonly used methods of contraception in America are the pill, the condom and the diaphragm. Women can also have their tubes tied and men can undergo vasectomy. Recently, a male contraceptive pill was developed and is showing good results. It may become a widespread alternative to the other things available at present. It also may eventually be possible for men to be injected with the hormone once every three to six months with minimal side effects. The main enemy of contraception is ignorance. People harbour all sorts of misconceptions (excuse the pun) about it without knowing or researching the facts.

Some have it drummed into them at any early age that sex is only for procreation and the glorification of God. Why on earth would God in His infinite knowledge give us such a beautiful expression of love if He didn't mean us to enjoy it? God could have created life without any human intervention whatsoever, but He chose to give us the gift of sex. How and why have we abused and distorted it so grossly over the centuries? There has been debasement by overindulgence, but ascetics and religious zealots have also played a part by denying the beauty of sex and only emphasising its temptations. Are there not worse crimes than those of sex? Isn't it worse to kill than to be gay, or to be unkind rather than a prostitute? Those who denounce sex should realise that they are actually promoting it by their protestations, seen in the case of the movie *The Last Temptation*

177

of Christ. Whether the film was good or bad is not important, but it was an artistic expression and had a right to see the light of day. Are we going to go back to burning books because we disagree with their contents? Sex is seen as a threat by many people, at best a thing to be endured or a scourge to be overcome. This legacy was inherited from the Victorian era, and many of the myths are as yet unexploded.

Sexual problems

Non-orgasmic woman and male sexual dysfunction are two common sexual difficulties. Although this book is for women, impotence and premature ejaculation affects females as much as it does males, albeit differently, and therefore cannot be excluded as a vital issue.

Why is a woman unable to enjoy sex fully and reach the normal and enjoyable climax that nature intended? What about the woman who loves her man and desperately wants to give herself completely, but somehow cannot? Possible hang-ups have already been discussed, so here the emphasis will be on *how* this inability manifests itself and what can be done about it.

Some women tighten up before anything even happens, and so cannot enjoy any aspect of sex whatsoever. Even touching and fondling is repugnant or unpleasurable. More commonly, non-orgasmic women are fully involved, get close every time, but just cannot quite reach orgasm. John and Michele were experiencing this problem. They were very cheerful and good-humoured, not depressed or strained. Michele had no difficulty in being aroused, but when it came to the point of climax she said she felt 'blocked'. They discussed various possibilities with me. As John was giving and patient, the inability to orgasm was more likely to be a childhood inheritance rather than a product of the marriage. For that reason, I worked with Michele individually and not with the couple together.

One major consideration is the difference between clitoral and vaginal arousal. Women are rare who can climax from either stimulation and have no preference. Most females favour one or the other and in some cases are unable to achieve orgasm without that form of interaction. Those women who masturbated as young girls and began at a fairly early age, say ten years, would be inclined to enjoy clitoral arousal and reach orgasm quite easily if caressed there. On the other hand, some women cannot even get fully aroused unless there is vaginal contact, either by penis entry, the use of a vibrator, or finger stimulation. Therefore, to enjoy sex a woman needs to be in touch with her own body and to be in tune with her likes and preferences.

Different positions should also be tried. Many women, for example, report that they reach orgasm more easily and quickly if on top of the male rather than underneath him. This position allows deeper penetration and the woman can control the rhythm and speed. Obviously, patience on the part of the male is crucial, especially if the woman is experiencing any special reluctance or difficulty. The worst thing a man can do is pressure or nag. Women who are working on their own orgasm say that they dread their partner's inevitable question after intercourse, 'Well, did it happen?' They feel as if they are somehow being tested.

So the main areas that may need attention in the non-orgasmic woman are: personal history, upbringing and sex education; overall relationship with their partner; experience level of the husband; experimenting with different positions and techniques; self-esteem and knowledge of your own desires and physical needs; awareness of the different ways to orgasm; the partner's understanding and patience; and professional intervention, if necessary.

For the male with a sexual dysfunction, the condition inevitably affects his relationship(s) and his self-perception. He usually ends up with two problems—the one he started with and the anxiety he builds up. Therefore the first thing a man experiencing the problems of premature ejaculation or impotence needs to do is to stop worrying about it. The woman should try to make her partner feel as comfortable as possible about the situation. If they are in an ongoing relationship, she needs to be patient and not make him feel badly if he cannot 'perform'.

Impotence
The main causes of impotence can be summed as these three: physical/medical; emotional/psychological; and hormonal.

The first and last can be ruled out by a simple blood test. Sexual dysfunction used to be thought of as generated by stress or a psychological block. In fact, the cause can be a physical disorder, such as hormonal imbalance, low testosterone, or the taking of certain drugs like Beta blockers for a heart condition. General lifestyle and such factors as diet also play a part, and smoking is thought to cause impotence. It appears sometimes that the problem has a psychic nature. Stress may very well cause sexual dysfunction in the first place, but then also becomes a consequence of it. So, an understanding of the whole subject is desirable to avoid unnecessary worry and further dysfunction due to anxiety. A high proportion of impotent men have low penile blood pressure, which usually decreases with age. Old sporting injuries can also cause impotence. Many sufferers complain of back trouble and insomnia. The point really is to check out all the options and then narrow down the likely solutions. There are penile dysfunction centres in most major cities. Once a male has conquered his reluctance to consult a therapist for such a personal problem, help is near at hand; often the 'cure' is not as embarrassing or difficult as imagined.

Then there are the psychological reasons for impotence. Matthew suffered from the condition as an eighteen-year-old. His problem was initiated by a thoughtless remark about his penis by a girl who saw him nude. So, anxiety can be the cause and the result. If a man is by nature an 'anxious', nervous person (as opposed to a 'worrier'), possibly a perfectionist, he will want to excel in everything and that includes sexual performance.

Impotence sufferers are often the first child in the family which is interesting in light of the remarks about this earlier in the book. The more intense his desire to succeed, the more his body will inform him that he is not a machine that can be turned on and off at will. Surrounding conditions have to be conducive to sexual closeness and performance. The very word 'performance' is misleading in that it implies a need to do well, as with a professional stage artist, who must not disappoint the audience. The flaw in this view is that when it comes to emotional matters, people are not programmable and are, particularly in the bedroom, vulnerable and easily bruised.

Remember that the seed of anxiety grows in the mind. Work on relaxation techniques and, most importantly, positive thinking. Be a person who says yes to life, not maybe or I can't. If you are aware that you are having anxiety attacks prior to sex, try deep breathing exercises or even something as simple as a long, hot bath. Spas are wonderful because they relax the body and the mind. If sexual activity can begin in the tub, all the better. The more natural the execution of the sexual process is, the less stressful it will be. Sex is more than physical performance so relax, go with your natural feelings, and let things just happen.

Men have a lot of social pressure on them in regard to sexual behaviour. The image is of males being able to have sex at the drop of a hat, without consideration of feelings or individual needs. There are no sacred rules that say they have to be in control all the time. Women are now prepared to take a more assertive role in male/female relations, and that assertiveness extends to the bedroom. Two people have sex or make love *together*; a man does not 'do it' to a woman, unless she's lazy or unaware.

Single men tend to find impotence so humiliating that they avoid sex and even dating altogether. Their self-esteem erodes; they become more introspective while the problem continues to worsen. Married men have to confront the condition more openly because being in an ongoing relationship, sex cannot be avoided indefinitely without questions and recriminations. Either way, avoidance is not the answer unless it is done as a recommended therapy which can be very effective, especially if other forms of lovemaking are substituted.

These are some common myths about impotence: it only happens in old age; it's all in the mind; nothing can be done about it; real men don't suffer from it; if you do not talk about it, it will go away.

Premature ejaculation

Premature ejaculation is also a major problem for many men and their women. It's probably the sexual dysfunction that affects relationships the most because it results in a lot of unsatisfied, frustrated women and angry, guilty men. The men who suffer from it seem to be ones who began masturbating at an early age and therefore, fixed a pattern of quick climax for themselves. If they marry late or have their first experience of intercourse later than usual, that will be a complicating factor. Not having a lot of experience with women generally will make it worse, and not having sex very often will bring the climax forward even more. In a nutshell, do not allow yourself to get frustrated and then overanxious or it will be all over before it begins.

The following strategies are proven as being effective ones to try:

- sex more often;
- sex with someone you do not care personally about helps, if you are not already in a relationship. For instance, some sufferers have been helped by seeing a prostitute regularly for a period of time;
- changing position—it's apparently easier to maintain erection if you are under a woman as there is less movement for the man;
- spontaneous sex is good as there is no time to get anxious! First thing in the morning or during the night is particularly beneficial.
- various techniques offered by therapists to 'teach' the penis to slow up, to take its time and maintain control. The best known of these is the 'squeeze' technique, where the penis is held and the tip squeezed each time orgasm is close. This trains the penis to behave differently, as sexual activity is simply learned behaviour even though it comes naturally to all of us if we do not allow ourselves to get uptight about it.

General issues

The general issues cover sexual harassment of women, incest and rape; not pleasant subjects, but essential to any discussion of stress in modern society. The nature of pornography and the arguments for and against it will also be looked at briefly.

Sexual harassment

Complaints of this form of sexual posturing and exploitation come rarely from males. Is it because men would not complain or it is another indication of society's double standards? Is the assumption that women do not want to be treated as sex objects, hence the objection to being sexually hassled in the office? Do male bosses or co-workers still believe that women, by their very existence, invite seduction and sexual innuendo?

The questions are complex, but the bottom line is that cases of sexual harassment in the workplace continue to increase, and women are becoming more verbal about it because they now have more credibility. Most countries carry anti-discrimination laws that cover sexual harassment. Believing that it could be stamped out altogether and that women can be regarded as equal fellow workers, worthy of respect, would be nice. Men hold on to the view that women secretly like being 'bothered' at work and that they would feel hurt if men did not take special notice of them. The women who need that kind of reinforcement are few, but those that *do* exist set the cause back by their expectations.

Carol works in an all-male office and recently found that she had to take an assertive stand on a particular issue. After months of putting up with remarks about her hair, make-up, clothes, and general appearance, she finally told the guys to back off and keep their comments to themselves. Would they, after all, notice each other's hairstyles and clothes in such minute detail and feel the need to voice a loud opinion on each item? It may seem to be a big fuss over a small matter, but it represents the kind of battle that women have to fight every day, while men take their rightful place in the workforce for granted. Women who complain about the unwanted attentions of their male co-workers are usually accused of 'leading them on', or being a 'tease'. There is also the threat of being sacked.

An employer has so much power in these situations that a woman can feel helpless to hang on to her job and her self-respect at the same time. One case involved a fifteen-year-old girl who was told by her boss, a delicatessen owner, in no uncertain terms that if she did not 'put up and shut up' she could find another job. Employers tend to believe that in today's job climate, young girls will do anything to hang on to their positions. Those who do give in to their boss's wishes usually say nothing and hope that he will tire of them. Looking on from the outside and shaking your heads in disgust is easy, but the blame lies less with individual men and women than with society's tolerance for these situations. The picture of the busty blonde sitting on her boss's lap and awkwardly balancing her dictation pad is a cliché of sexual humour and no one thinks twice about it. An unusual case was one of a driving instructor who kept touching and fondling a female student while she was learning to drive! Teacher/student relations come under scrutiny from time to time—'An A for a lay', as the saying goes. So the problem is not confined to office Romeos, but more cases seem to surface about this group than any others.

A wise and mature woman enjoys being admired and thought attractive, but not to the exclusion of her other attributes. Cases of sexual harassment are very difficult to prove and often come down to 'his word against hers'. Perhaps the quickest and most effective way to handle it is to stand firm and simply tell the offender to stop. It may have only been a half-hearted try in the first place, and a firm refusal may be all it takes to put the guy off. 'Harassment' does not only mean overt requests for sex, but can incorporate subtle hints, unwanted touching, or looks and gestures. Remember that you don't have to put up with it or live with the stress that this predicament wroughts. A recent newspaper article lists these as the common effects of sexual harassment: anger, embarrassment, depression, aches and pains, nausea, insomnia, and damage to work performance.

Incest

This terrible form of sexual abuse has been mentioned in earlier parts of the book, but it deserves its own section. Until very few years ago it was a silent crime, characterised by a voiceless victim. The children rarely complained, those who did were not believed and most people pretended that it did not exist. Like so many other taboo subjects, incest has been brought out into the open and examined in all its horror and complexity.

The main paradox is that the victim is being hurt and taken advantage of by someone they love. Thus a dreadful conflict is set into place. Take the case of a father and daughter. The thinking is, if Daddy is doing this to me, it must be all right. A promise of silence is usually evoked—'This will just be between you and Daddy, our little secret, a special thing that we do. We do not want anyone to know about it.' So, the child is caught in a conspiracy of love, a web of intrigue in which she is the victim. On the one hand she appears to be helpless, under her father's domination, but, in effect, she holds his life in her hands and is wielding a lot of subtle power that her father hopes she will not use against him. He is literally banking on her love. Experts have offered the theory that some men cannot relate to their children emotionally and so they reach out sexually because that is the only communication at their disposal. This may sound like a very kind interpretation, but there have seen cases of incest in which this is precisely what has happened. The men are usually not very intelligent and begin harmlessly enough kissing and fondling their daughters or sons, but they either become sexually aroused and are too weak to stop or they feel such a rush of love that they want to get closer and closer until the whole thing gets out of hand.

Statistics indicate that incest is on the increase. This type of sexual abuse is usually chronic, that is to say it happens on a regular basis over a period of weeks, months or even years. Ninety per cent of these cases are estimated to remain undiscovered, or if they are reported, the child's story is rejected.

One of the saddest stories tells of the long-term sexual association between a father and his daughter. The girl, Rebecca said she was twenty-five. Her father had been having intimate relations with her since she was a teenager but Rebecca felt powerless to stop him because of the fear of disclosure. Through extended correspondence with me, she found the courage to stop her father and move out of the house, towards not only freedom but a whole new life. Of course, she would need professional counselling to exorcise all the pain and anger, but at least she had made a start.

Many girls say nothing because they believe their mothers have no idea of what is happening. They cannot bear the thought of hurting them and breaking up the family. In reality, a lot of mothers *do* suspect that something is not right, but are too afraid to investigate for fear of finding out the truth. This inaction does not make them bad mothers, but merely vulnerable human beings. It is difficult to believe that a mother could allow her child to suffer for even one second when she could stop it, but to have to question your choice of mate in such a stark and frightening way must be exceedingly hard. These women blame themselves; they wonder if it is because they don't satisfy their husband in bed. Are they imagining the whole thing? Are they jealous of their own daughters? How could they marry a man who would do these things? And so the self-torture continues. Meanwhile, time passes and a mother prays she is wrong; everything in her wants to believe she is mistaken. When the truth is revealed, some mothers lash out at the child, hungry to lay some blame that will make their husband less of a fiend. Others cast out their husbands and harden their hearts against pleas of innocence or innocent motives. It is a tragic family crisis and no one has the right to judge any of the participants unless they have lived through the devastation of incest themselves.

Experts emphasise the need for mother/daughter bonding and mothers are encouraged to seek advice from the appropriate authorities as soon as they have even an inkling that incest could be taking place.

The stress on every family member is immeasurable and the long-term effects are many and varied. One obvious one is the incidence of incest in the backgrounds of prostitutes. If a sufferer is determined to leave home, they may have no other means of earning money but to turn to crime and working on the streets. Youth workers say that their usual advice to teenagers to return home to their parents may be the worst move in these cases. This major community problem is not one that can be swept under the carpet any longer.

Rape

There is a lot of literature and information available about the best ways for women to prevent rape and what to do if they are a victim. As this book is about stress, it is more appropriate to talk about the effects and how one can overcome the feelings of guilt and worthlessness that often accompany rape. It would be facile to say that there is no need for a woman to accept any blame after a sexual attack. That truth is obvious, but the human mind is not always logical. Sometimes, you are blinded by anger, pain and humiliation. Rape takes away a woman's very individuality, her power of choice and her natural human rights.

Guilt follows rape for the same reason that a bereaved wife or lover or child blames herself for the death of the loved one, looking for reasons to berate and find fault and hate, seeking anything that will ease the pain of loss for even one second. Letting pain go after a rape is more difficult because there is another person involved, someone who has violated you and numbed your mind with fury and hatred. Some sections of the community still believe that rape victims ask for it by accepting rides from strangers, hitchhiking and being out alone at night. Women's groups argue that females should not have to modify their activities and behaviour to accommodate the potentially dangerous situations lurking in the shadows of night. Anyway, most rapes take place indoors where the attacker is known to the victim.

Of course, no one should take unnecessary chances. For instance, after an outing late at night, it is wise to ask a friend to accompany you to your car and wait until you drive off. Such small precautions can make all the difference. Again, community awareness has heightened in recent years, and women at least have been informed about what to do. If they do not wish to heed the advice there is nothing that can be done to help them, apart from picking up the pieces after the event. Prevention is preferable to cure any day. Minimising certain activities may reduce some freedom, but it can save lives and a lot of trauma for survivors. Understanding the nature of rape is also helpful. Psychologists generally agree that it is an act of violence and not a sexual act, as one would imagine. The rapist is usually a man who is unsure of himself sexually. Perhaps he is impotent in normal circumstances and only feels like a 'man' when he empowers a woman and forces his will upon her. In the United States, rape within marriage is acknowledged as a crime in some states. In other words, a woman can refuse a man his conjugal rights. If he forces sex on her, she can charge him with rape.

Reactions to rape are commonly these: emotional shock; disbelief; embarrassment; shame; depression; feelings of powerlessness; disorientation; denial; fear; anxiety; and anger. The onus is not on women to actively prevent rape, but to be aware of the possibility and to take *reasonable* precautions.

Pornography

This issue is one that seems to have no middle ground. People usually feel strongly about it one way or the other, without necessarily knowing much about the subject. Few people are neutral. So what is it really? Just 'dirty' pictures, sex movies, and the like? There are varying degrees of pornographic material. The bottom line is that the rights of the individual should be protected, and the dollar not allowed to be the only yardstick by which a photo or magazine or film is judged. There are two sets of rights to be considered, those of the participant and those of the viewer.

Adults should have the freedom of choice as to the literature and photography and social entertainment they wish to enjoy; that is a fundamental human right in free countries, the proviso being that another individual or group is not hurt in the process. That eliminates the legitimacy of child pornography immediately because nobody under the age of sixteen years can be expected to know the consequences of their actions when they grant permission for explicit photos or movies to be taken. They are being exploited one hundred per cent. This form of 'entertainment' cannot be justified.

Putting this form of pornography aside, the link between sexually explicit material and the element of fantasy is particularly interesting. For instance, has pornography a place in the sex lives of a married couple, as a tool for additional pleasure? The word additional is used because if it is the primary source of enjoyment for one or both partners, the relationship probably needs some work. One speaker at a conference said recently that if one or more of the two persons engaged in lovemaking is mentally fantasising, he or she is being unfaithful because they have introduced a third party into the bed; if either is thinking, they have left the lovemaking process. That would sound fairly radical to the average person, but it has a point. The nature of fantasy is interwoven into the human experience and cannot be totally eliminated from our daily activities. Sex and pornography are focuses for the fantasy life of many people. If a sexy video or adult publication is enjoyed by a couple out of a sense of fun and sexual adventure, that is their business and can only enhance their pleasure in each other. However anything that becomes obsessive and addictive is out of balance and, therefore, not healthy. Very often, the obsessive behaviour is masking a deeper problem. Rob lost his father, with whom he had never been close. Despite a good job and a loving girl-friend, he suffered from an obsessive need to spend all his time in sex shops, looking at pornographic material. The reason behind Rob's behaviour was, in fact, not related to sex at all, but connected to the bereavement process that he was undergoing without recognition. He felt a lot of unresolved guilt over his father's death and the urge to look at pornographic books was only an expression of his emptiness and pain. Addictions, as you will recall, are essentially just a focus for whatever is actually bothering you.

Guilt is a very destructive force in our lives; many self-destructive people have the need for guilt. It can distort their views of things. If a man was brought up by overly religious or strict parents, he may regard sex as a furtive thing to be enjoyed in secret, so that sex becomes connected in the mind with guilt and punishment, being 'bad'. A variety of antisocial behaviour can result, such as obscene phone calls, 'flashing', even child molestation. Remove the guilt and you very often remove the desire. Feeling bad is in fact the kick, and when that is missing the fun is taken out of it.

A good test for this problem is to gauge the way you feel after any activity. When you lose your temper, is it a cleansing process that makes you feel fresh and satisfied or are you wracked with guilt? After viewing a 'blue movie', do you feel happy or sick inside? Look at your motives and ask yourself why you would want to do something that makes you unhappy. Ask yourself if your chosen activity is enhancing the quality of your life or reducing you as a person. Imagining worlds of experience beyond what you have actually known is fun, but do not let it become a destructive, dark force in your life. That last statement could be true of all sexual behaviour. Sex is not a mindless, purely physical function—it involves the mind, the emotions, the intellect, not just the genitalia. To enjoy sex fully you need to think, act and feel sexy. Only then can you truly be sexually and sensually fulfilled.

AFFIRMATIONS

I live totally without fear, doubt and worry.
I release all need for anger, resentment and blame.
I accept my good, knowing that all my needs and desires are being fulfilled.
I am a radiant being, filled with light and love.

Chapter Eight

Work

In Chapters One and Two it was seen that work provides one of the main sources of stress, if you let it. Chapter Four, taught you how work can and should be undertaken with love. This chapter, will look at work itself, its many faces and complexities and specifically these areas: work and career; self-employment; money; workaholics; unemployment; career changes; and study skills.

Work and career

Work and career are not synonyms for each other. The majority of people work to earn the money to feed themselves, pay their bills and keep a roof over their heads. Women who aspire to have 'careers' are usually those who have been encouraged by parents or who show such obvious potential that they have been able to undertake tertiary education and go on with their studies. The days when a girl in the family would be stopped from continuing at school because she was 'only going to get married and have children, anyway' are hopefully over. Even if a young woman does marry early, her education can never be said to be wasted. Isn't she going to be responsible for training young minds as a mother? There are women in their forties and fifties who were forced to go out into the workforce at fourteen or fifteen when they would have preferred to stay on at school.

They have deep regrets over that situation, even after all these years, and in some cases still resent the parent(s) who prevented them from learning more and developing a career for the future.

Once, women entered the world work arena at a much later stage as their role was traditionally assumed to be exclusively linked to mothering and catering. Much depends on the upbringing of the individual, such matters as ambition, intelligence, quality of schooling and attitude of parents. There have been bright, motivated young women who have emerged from working-class homes, seemingly against all odds, and women with all of the advantages and encouragement who have wasted their talents and years of training by drifting or not studying or refusing to take work seriously. It is a personal choice, but it is possible for you to make a lot of fundamental mistakes with your children. You can crush their creative impulses and then force them into activities in which they have no interest whatsoever. It is said that parents want to live out their frustrated ambitions through their offspring. If Dad always wanted to be a pop singer, he may be inclined to insist his son or daughter take singing lessons even though the child cannot sing a note! While it is easy to understand, it is highly unfair to the young people who have dreams and talents of their own. The most loving parents are the ones who encourage their children to be individuals and discover their hidden potential, support them in whatever direction they choose, even if it clashes with personal preference. Some girls even today only want to get married and have babies. That's a worthy ambition, but with the world in its current condition nothing can be taken for granted for the future. Women cannot marry and assume with certainty that they will never have to work again.

Apart from the contingency of necessity, work is linked to concepts of self-esteem and personal pride. Not all jobs can be glamorous or wonderful and even those that appear to be have an element of tedium and mundaneness about them. What about the endless hours of rehearsals to bring a ballet or musical performance to perfection? Pilots have an awesome responsibility riding with them on every flight, and lawyers literally take their clients' lives into court, not to mention the mountains of research they have to undertake in preparation.

There is always the choice between regarding work as an evil necessity and trying to enjoy the many hours that are spent in the workplace each day. Of course, attitudes of bosses and fellow workers will contribute to the overall satisfacton of employees.

Pleasant work with reasonable conditions and income is what everybody wants and unions and workers' associations strive to get on behalf of their members. However, attitude is the main indicator of personal joy, not what people around you do. You only get what you put in. Those who are overly concerned with their rights and getting everything they can out of their employers are cutting off their noses to spite their faces. As in marriage it should be a team effort, and give-and-take works best. If you are not ever prepared to stay back to finish work or change your shift at the last minute, you can hardly expect the company to let you have time off when you need it. The concept of working to bells, timetables and clocks is hard to tolerate, and a highly regimented job where individual initiative counts for little or nothing will not bring out the best in workers.

Self-employment

I can remember a woman saying to me some years ago that any woman of intelligence would always end up working for herself. At the time I thought it an odd remark, but have since understood what she meant. I have been self-employed for five years, and although it has been the toughest time of my working life, it has also been the most interesting, rewarding and fulfilling. So many women around the world are going into business for themselves. I would like to share my experiences with you as I think I am a fairly typical example. My mistakes will be the same as those of many of you who have tried something similar. My triumphs will be understood by all who have learned the hard way how to keep going when the odds seem stacked against them and the road ahead appears impossibly difficult.

I never planned to 'go into business' when I began working as a counsellor. I thought it was just a matter of hanging up my shingle and people would beat a path to my door. Instead, I found that getting a qualification was only the beginning and that I had to learn about marketing, advertising, writing business plans, financial management, dealing with bank managers and handling staff as well as matters of insurance and taxation. The list seemed endless. I will not bore you with the details of my various mistakes and lessons, but I will give you an outline of the different stages I went through to reach where I am today. An occupational consultant recently summed it up for me very neatly. She said that the self-employed person goes through these three states: lethargy, impatience and fear. I found that to be exactly true. Lethargy set in when I first found that my 'business' was not at all what I expected. Having worked as a teacher for thirteen years, I associated hard work with the wages I received. In the same way, I believed that I only had to be industrious and professional to earn the same lifestyle I had always enjoyed, but diligence is only one piece of the small business person's weaponry against bankruptcy. I found that, to be successful, I had to become a 'Jill of all trades', versatile and flexible. None of those extra hats sat very well with me, so something in my psyche opted out. Motivation peeled off me in sheets and was replaced by frustration, disillusionment and bitterness.

This stage lasted for the first six months. Then I gradually began to fight back. I started to think creatively, to search for ways to diversify and let people know that I existed. Sometimes I think I went too far because, about nine months after I first began counselling, I was asked to write an advice column for a major local paper. Little did I realise at that time how many other doors would open. As the column grew in readership and popularity, I became a minor celebrity and was approached to speak at various functions and for all sorts of organisations. With my teaching experience and being by nature a communicator, speaking was a natural flow on from my other activities. My opinion was of interest to media bodies, and I became a regular on television and radio programmes. Of course, this enhanced my business interests and provided the visibility that I needed to become established.

For a while everything was easier and more enjoyable. I went from counselling at home to joining a group of other professionals in an office building. When I look back that was the most satisfying time and venue for me as a counsellor.

I had a vision of opening a centre that would be accessible to clients, not only for counselling and crisis intervention but for social get-togethers and drop-in facilities. Unfortunately, I had more dream than substance. The first six months after establishing the place proved to be an absolute nightmare. Talk about stress! I was a walking cliché of a stressed person, with all the classic symptoms. I hated being a 'boss' and found that I had little aptitude for it. My experiences have supplied the fodder for many a humorous speech to business groups about the pitfalls of inexperience, but it was not too funny at the time. As a result I became ineffective in other departments of my life. Financially and emotionally, that period was a disaster for me. It took a trip to another state to wake me up to the real issues. I had attracted the wrong people as employees and that was adding to an already difficult situation. So, upon my return, I let everyone go and streamlined the whole operation, doing everything myself for the next six months with just a part-time assistant. As soon as the lease ran out, I gladly left the building and the project. It was certainly not a time I would like to relive, but it taught me some invaluable lessons.

The best thing that happened to me during my time at the centre was the appearance on my doorstep one day of a gnome-like Chinese man who told me he wanted to publish a book written by me. That is how my first book (*Stress, a Handbook for Women*) came into existence, and I shall be forever grateful because that invitation arrived at a time when my self-esteem and confidence was at a very low ebb. Once again I had come to a major turning point in my life which would be the beginning of many new things for me. The book was subsequently published in the next year. It opened up yet more doors, more people to meet, more roads to travel. As always, there were also lessons to be learned. The publisher was from overseas, so a lot of the marketing of the book was left to me. I had to knock on doors and invite myself on to talk shows and radio programmes, write press releases and contact bookshops. At first, it was exciting, then it became tedious. Finally I resented the time and effort I was putting in as I only had my standard author's royalty to gain. With hindsight I see how short-sighted my view was then. The first book gained me prestige, led to the writing of this second book, has given me the confidence to try many other projects and I learned the finer points of being a 'book importer'.

Getting out and selling the gospel according to Charmaine Saunders has been rather unpalatable as I have always felt horn-blowing should be undertaken by another person. Yet the marketing and networking skills I gained along the way have been most illuminating. For those of you who may be unfamiliar with the term, 'networking' simply means building up a network of business contacts with whom one can enjoy a reciprocal exchange of information, support and financial benefit. Since I gave up the centre, I have worked from a medical and para-medical clinic on a sessional basis which means that I pay as I go without being tied to leases and having responsibility for staff and bills. This situation gave me the freedom to work from home more often, to set my own schedule without pressures and to work creatively because there is no stress! In turn, other areas of my life have improved, and I am happier and more at peace than I have ever been.

My story highlights several facets of business life that are traps for the novice, in particular these: knowing one's own strengths and weaknesses *before* starting; doing your homework thoroughly when starting a new venture; working within the financial and personal limitations that are present; deciding on the best type of business premises that suits your style of operation; not equating your 'worth' with what is in the bank or the way you are treated by bank managers; constantly exercising your powers of positive thinking and mind control as confidence and self-esteem are directly linked to success and failure rates; and talking to experienced business people, asking for help freely as you need it. You can't possibly be expected to know anything when you start out; cut your losses as soon as you realise that a venture is wrong for you and do not be afraid to admit mistakes as you are always stronger for them.

Money

I deliberately discussed money to a minimum in telling my story as this aspect of business and, indeed, general life is too inportant to mention incidentally. There is not very much to add in terms of money management for the wage-earner that a thousand books carrying financial advice do not already contain. It basically comes down to spending less than you have at your disposal. The surplus can be saved with a banking institution for future needs or invested to gain higher interest and better income. Credit is fine as long as it is controlled and the money is forthcoming at a later date to pay for the goods being bought now.

When I was working on salary I never experienced one moment of financial anxiety. I knew what to expect each week and I kept within my budget. I always had everything I needed and more, and there was a small amount of savings in my bank account. What has been so maddening for me in the last five and a half years is the fact that when you are self-employed, you have to constantly create income. Nothing is certain. It takes a special kind of courage to live from week to week in such insecurity. That is why the stages mentioned before go from lethargy to impatience to fear. Impatience starts up when all your best efforts seem to end in dust, when there is no money available no matter how hard you try, and when you are continually harassed by creditors who treat you with little respect because you are no longer a person of financial substance. One's ego takes a pretty severe battering under all that.

Society judges us on all those external realities spoken of in Chapter Five, such factors as where you live and what you own. So when you own nothing, you presumably are nothing. That is where the test of what you really think of yourself comes in. For a long while, I fell right into this obvious trap and thought less of myself because I could not achieve a *financial* success; the harder I tried, the worse it seemed to get. I kept borrowing more money just to keep going and the only reason I did not crash, as so many do, is that I had a lot of help along the way and I never lost sight of my overall vision. Remember what was said before about ignoring the hurdles and keeping your eyes fixed on the goal? Well, this is a classic example of it.

Money itself is a problem for many people, whether self-employed or on a salary. There are three main areas of difficulty: not earning enough or managing it poorly; having a poverty consciousness and lack of deservability (see Chapter Nine on how attitude of mind is linked to the physical realities of your life); and being obsessed with money to the point where *having* it becomes the goal, rather than earning it and using it in a balanced way. There is nothing intrinsically bad or good about money. It is a commodity and thereby governed, to a large extent, by the user. Ever since the barter system gave way to units of currency, people have been affected by 'money', killed for it, manipulated, schemed and even loved for it. Money provides the essentials for living and according to how much of it is owned, lifestyle is determined. The essential principle of economics is distribution, so if you feel that you are not getting your fair share set about achieving a more equable flow-through in your favour.

The worst thing you can do is to get emotional about money or the lack of it. Yet it is one of the main causes for marriage breakdown, as poverty brings out a meanness in people that they will use against the one they think is responsible. Husbands say wives are extravagant; wives say husbands should earn more, and so the circle goes round.

Money is not the 'root of all evil', but many evils have been perpetrated in its name and for love of it. Greed is the sin, not money. There is nothing wrong with desiring money, but it is still true to say that the best things in life are free. When your heart is light and you feel good inside your skin, watching a sunset or lying on a stretch of lawn with the sun on your face, no one anywhere can be wealthier than you. Those pleasures are available to all who choose to enjoy them.

Apart from material possessions, you also need emotional and spiritual nourishment every day; the secret to happiness is to achieve a balance in these. Neither worshipping nor scorning money is necessary or healthy. Money scorners believe that there is something unsavoury about money, forgetting that it is a totally neutral item. Money worshippers endow the notes with much more than buying power, investing themselves in the acquisition of wealth and revelling in the status and position that comes with it. A wealthy and successful person should be judged on how they utilise their assets, remembering also that money is a currency—it is intended to keep moving, not to be hoarded and clung to.

Men and women of great wealth constantly pit their strength and intelligence against the odds, not in a reckless or foolhardy way but with knowledge and good sense. That is how they make their millions, not by working hard and counting out the pennies each payday and following a rigid and unimaginative budget. Like diets, budgets are good only if they are designed for the individual and by the individual. Standard budgets are useless except for use as a guideline.

One basic tip for self-employed people is that it is most sensible to pay oneself first. What tends to happen otherwise is that all the money earned goes out to pay others and the owner/operator is left with a pittance for their own expenses. This not only creates a financial difficulty, but is very bad for morale. When you are working hard all day, every day, and there is not a decent remuneration in exchange, self-esteem is affected.

From lethargy impatience grows, and then fear sets in. The fear is usually related to such things as not being able to pay bills, having to deal with irate creditors and, finally, the fear of bankruptcy and losing everything. This is a very real fear, not just borne of fatigue and struggle but based on frightening statistics and the constant battle with making ends meet. Just as business plans should be written and all practical details thoroughly researched when a venture is begun, so should the financial requirements be very clear. How much capital to put in, what office facilities and staff can be afforded, how much money can reasonably be borrowed and so forth. Women are latter-day millionaires and financiers in the world arena, but in the second half of the last decade have appeared in more and more boardrooms and executive offices in their own right, rather than as helpmates or assistants to men.

One of the main barriers to money for a lot of men and women is the feeling of guilt associated in some quarters with great wealth. Those who are born into moneyed families or even middle-class circumstances tend to take it more for granted. Money is just there to be used and enjoyed. When it runs out, there will always be a further supply. If a woman was brought up in a family where money was always short, she will have it ingrained in her mind that every cent must be accounted for, never wasted and she must appreciate everything she has. This type of background prepares a woman for frugality and limited expectations all her life. If she wants to change her station and broaden her social horizons she will have to work on her belief systems and thought patterns before she can live differently. Neither extreme is desirable. Whichever side you tip towards, you can return the balance by examining your motives and position on this money issue.

Workaholics

The very influential consideration of motivation cannot be overlooked. Once again, upbringing and family priorities will be a significant factor. If learning is not given an important place in the home, it is unlikely that children will have much interest in study or achieving high grades. The reverse can also apply, where very high standards are expected of children. When these children leave home, it is possible that they will continue the pressure on themselves by driving themselves too hard and having a 'perfection' complex. That is, of course, what leads to workaholism, which is no different to being an alcoholic or suffering any other addiction. You are never really 'cured', but can control the symptoms once you are aware of your weakness and have the desire to change. What are these signs of workaholism? In a nutshell, living for work. It gets to the point where everything in your life takes a secondary place to it. When you are not physically working, you are thinking about it. When you are working, you take on far too much at one time. Recapping what was said in the first three chapters, work stress is one of the most insidious forms and can appear in many guises: overwork or obsession with work is only one. Workaholism has as one of its more unpleasant features a strong element of guilt. No matter how hard the workaholic slogs at her chosen tasks, she always feels dissatisfied. Does this sound familiar, in light of the discussion on addiction?

Remember the key point: the source of the addiction is not vital, but the source of the need is. So, why do people need to punish themselves through work? Usually because they learned at a young age that work is socially acceptable and an easy way to win approval. The first child position exaggerates this need for acceptance and praise. Many male executives drive themselves for years without ever stopping to ask why. One day, they fall down dead from a heart attack or are severely incapacitated after a stroke, usually with not the slightest warning. The lucky ones get a second chance to live differently, modify diet, exercise more regularly and reduce stress. (Males are cited in particular because statistics show a much higher incidence of heart trouble and cardiovascular disease among men in a certain age bracket.) The trick is to make the necessary changes *before* the onset of illness, as emphasised in Chapter Three. Workaholics overfill their plate and allow their entire self-perception to be bound up with how much work is achieved daily and how well it is done. The saddest part is the number of hours devoted to this one aspect of life, neglecting personal pleasures, time spent with friends, hobbies, relaxation pastimes and more.

Time management will be looked at in Chapter Nine, even though it is most relevant to a healthy and happy work life. It should be considered as a key stress management technique, which it surely is. As mentioned, guilt plays a role too. Workaholics dread taking time off; holidays are anathema. One way to cure workaholism is to adopt a philosophy of stopping to smell the roses. Examine your lifestyle if you are a working woman (and most women are!) and be brutally honest about the changes you want to make. Remember women who stay home with children can also suffer from this syndrome. They work so hard and long that they become like machines set on automatic, unthinking, unfeeling, just mechanically doing what is expected of them. Women who carry two jobs, such as nurse/wife, secretary/mother, architect/wife/mother have to organise their time especially well and nurture themselves sufficiently to avoid the stress pitfalls.

As long as women have the attitude that looking after themselves is mollycoddling, little progress can be made in this area of educating the 1990s' woman. Wendy, who has her own business, gives herself every Wednesday off but admits that she cannot possibly spend it doing frivolous, fun things as there are always so many jobs in the home waiting for her attention. What she is really saying is that she works the full five days, but on Wednesdays, she changes her venue. The modern woman has so many different hats to wear that it is easy to get confused. There are seemingly more chores than hours to do them. Some women opt out and choose negative solutions, such as Valium addiction, or they turn into 'superwomen' and attempt to juggle one hundred tasks a day without thought to stress burnout. They get on that same deathly treadmill as businessmen even though they may suffer fewer heart problems than their male counterparts.

Many of the tips given in earlier chapters are applicable here, like using your intuitive processes to make decisions for yourself. If you are in a work situation that you hate, change it to one that allows you more flexibility and freedom. Instead of wishing and longing, do something concrete to create a new lifestyle for yourself—in this way you will find that you are always discovering and learning. Every day should be an adventure. You can stay safe and secure, but you will miss a whole lot of stimulation and excitement. The trick is to be prepared to track blind for a time, walk in the dark and be unafraid in the face of considerable uncertainty. If you can do that, the rewards are great.

More will be said on specific strategies of stress management and areas of personal development in the next chapters. Enjoying *all* that life has to offer and not expending energy on the opinions of others or self-defeating behaviour is wonderful.

Work-related illnesses abound in society and range from chronic influenza to RSI (repetitive strain injury) to backache. As with other forms of stress, prevention of the problem is more desirable than trying to fix it after it has developed. Executive stress has been the subject of much research in recent years, depression, tension headache and high blood pressure being the main indicators of trouble. Many managers and people in authority feel unrewarded for their efforts, have ambivalence about their true roles and feel ill-equipped for the demands of their positions. There is often also conflict between their working and domestic lives. You have to exercise your choices. Some women are not in a position to readily make changes, for instance, if they are supporting mothers or have limited education and skills. Opportunities have to be created and transformations are possible, but they take a little longer in some cases. Many technical colleges and universities now offer special courses for women wishing to return to the workforce, looking at such issues as self-esteem, transition from home to work, the workplace itself, how to choose suitable employment and how to prepare oneself for work, job applications and so on.

Unemployment

What does it mean to be out of work? How do you go about seeking work when the time is right? How do you make career choices and changes? Being chronically out of work is a sad fact of life for many people in modern society. The most disillusioning aspect is that young, bright, enthusiastic men and women come out of school with all their energy and youth to offer, only to turn into bitter, idle and potentially dangerous individuals. The decline of work attitudes and prospects can be seen quite clearly historically. Before technology, everyone worked in towns and villages at whatever they felt equipped to do; cottage industries ensured that women and children were also contributors and roles were very definite and defined. In early modern history, the armed forces used up a lot of male labour, and women basically clung to the obvious occupations of teaching, domestic service, nursing and secretarial work.

In decades past there was no talk of unemployment, only what you wanted to do with your life. The law of averages dictates that most young people will still prefer to go into 'disposable' jobs, easy to come by and easy to leave. The point now is that there are not any to obtain in the first place. The argument goes that young people cannot enter the workforce because they have no ready skills and no experience, but how will they ever acquire these without the opportunities? One way to go would be to provide, at both public and private levels, paid training for school drop-outs so that they can learn with pride and self-respect, instead of just being recipients of hand-outs and carrying the unenviable label of 'leach' or 'parasite'. There are limited schemes of this nature. Still, much more could be done in an effort to offer positive solutions to youth unemployment, which is a worldwide problem.

There is a veritable subculture in existence that has sprung up in the last two decades. These people form the group known in our communities as the 'unemployed'. It is bad enough to be out of work, to have to cope with poverty, boredom and low self-esteem, but add to it the ignorance of the public who find it easier to make blanket judgments than to look beyond the surface for answers. The links between unemployment and crime are well established. Society may not owe its citizens a living, but it has an obligation to create opportunities and educate young people about the usage of their talents. With the right equipment, the unemployed can turn their desolation and emptiness into useful and fulfilling productivity.

Apart from the young, there are two major categories of the unemployed: those who spend their lives drifting from job to job, never consolidating their assets, chopping and changing so that their résumé looks like a travelogue rather than a professional record; and those who spend a large percentage of their adult working lives in one job and then find themselves retrenched from the company at an age when they are no longer desirable to other employers. In the first case, there is likely to be a personality disorder that can be corrected with professional counselling. In the second, the psychological effects can be devastating to the person concerned. A man or woman who has the responsibility for the support of dependants is literally put into a desperate situation, and even without that added pressure, losing one's job after thirty or forty years of faithful service puts a major dent in the ego and pride. No one likes to feel redundant and disposable, and that is already the lot of too many of the older generation.

The main emotions associated with unemployment are: low self-esteem; guilt; feelings of futility; lack of confidence; depression; boredom; defeatist attitudes; lethargy; and negative thinking. More alternatives to the nine-to-five job have to be found. Many women with home commitments now share jobs with others. That is a good example of creative approaches to the rising problem of less work/more demand. Other viable ideas are a shorter working week and permanent, part-time jobs.

What can an unemployed person do if she wants to make a positive change in her life? Set one goal a day and achieve it, no matter how small. Work on self-esteem as this is a most vulnerable area. Keep occupied at whatever interests you, even if it's unpaid. Offer yourself for voluntary work as it will keep you positive and can often lead to paid employment. Make a list of your skills and personal assets and read it daily. Scour newspapers and magazines for opportunities; follow up the ones that interest you without waiting for advertised positions to appear. Spend some part of your budget and time on grooming, buying or making career-orientated clothes and attending courses and seminars. Have a professional résumé made up that emphasises your positive qualities. Stay positive and upbeat. Avoid self-pity and taking the easy way out. Find things you love to do and do them, regardless of whether anyone will pay you to do it initially. You may discover hidden talents.

The worst aspect of unemployment is the negative labelling that accompanies being out of work. Without a job identity, there is no ready personal identity to attribute and most people are too socially lazy to investigate further. That is no help to the unemployed person who has all the same feelings and needs as her working counterpart. Refuse to wear the label that says those stereotyped and negative things about you. Simply change your wording in describing your condition. 'I'm between jobs' or 'I'm currently looking for work' would be better phraseology than 'I'm not working'. If people insist on associating you with what you do, make it interesting; accentuate the positive and eliminate the negative, as the saying goes.

A four-part discussion/sharing course I have devised can be used in groups or by unemployed individuals to take a fresh look at their situation.

EMPLOYMENT HO! WORKSHOP

Week 1 Reasons for not working; society and personal attitudes; peer and family pressure; obvious and not so obvious problems associated with being unemployed.

Week 2 Psychology of being unemployed; loss of self-esteem; boredom; lack of direction and goal setting; guilt.

Week 3 Alternatives to the work ethic; practical suggestions; doing nothing for personal growth and self-realisation; spending and not killing time.

Week 4 Review and summary. Extension of selected topics.

Two other useful tips are to keep learning and to maintain a winning personality. Keep yourself informed about a variety of things and consciously update your skills and qualifications as far as possible. By doing this, you make yourself an attractive job prospect. This is not an era when you can take anything for granted and be smug and complacent about your position in life. When seeking employment, it is important to be as flexible as possible while still maintaining ambitions and personal goals. The other key ingredient is confidence. It exudes from you when you have it and shows in everything you do, from the way you speak to the way you enter a room. Deciding early in the piece whether you are a person who says yes to life or one who is happy just to cruise along and accept life's dregs is advantageous.

There are many methods to finding employment, but really only two basic approaches: the practical requirements, and attitudes and motivation. First, consider carefully and realistically your own skills and talents. Stretch your imagination a bit and look beyond the obvious. Once you have narrowed it down to about six potential job areas, begin scouring the papers, marking off anything and everything that is a possibility. Register with your local employment centre and collect your welfare benefit with pride, knowing that it is a temporary source of aid. Send your résumé to companies that offer services in an area that interests you. Kate walked into an office, asked to see the manager and then informed him that the company needed her! She, in effect, created her own job and then sold the company on the idea. This bold approach will not always work. Still, if you are impressive enough, the manager will remember you when a vacancy *does* crop up. They will applaud your ingenuity and initiative and, hopefully, file your application for future reference.

Advertised jobs call for three possible responses: a written application, a phone enquiry or a call-in personally. The latter is probably the most difficult, as you find when you arrive that you are directly competing with all the other applicants who are nervously arriving at the same time. Displaying your best qualities under those conditions is difficult. Phoning requires the least commitment as you can decide whether or not you want to go any further after a quick conversation. The employer can also eliminate you just as quickly; therefore, you have to get to the point very smartly. Do not babble on with a lot of irrelevant details. Ask intelligent questions; give a brief statement about your suitability for the position. The person on the other end of the line has only your voice and speech to go by. It is a one chance situation, so you cannot afford mistakes. You will only be asked in for an interview if you succeed in convincing this person that you are a likely candidate for the job and you have the right mixture of enthusiasm and motivation.

Written applications are the least nerve-racking because you can take your time and think through what you really want to say. Conversely, the employer will expect a higher quality of presentation. A simple letter will not do these days—most companies expect and get a detailed résumé with references listed. If you have a professional résumé made up you need only write a cover letter with it, as the résumé will include all other important information.

Once you get to the personal interview, there are a number of factors to take into account, the most important of these being: the way you are dressed; your manner and your speech; your knowledge of the company and the specific job you are applying for; the way you answer questions put to you; and your confidence level. You cannot expect anyone to employ you if you are not confident about your own abilities. After the interview, staying confident and positive while you are waiting for the 'verdict' is even more important. If you are not successful, do not immediately take it personally. There could be any number of good reasons why the job went to someone else; it may have nothing to do with your inadequacy or unsuitability.

Keep applying. If you become discouraged every time you fail to get a job you try for, you will just give up trying. A lot of people who struggle for months or years to find a job finish up with the perfect one because they didn't allow a sense of futility to overcome them. They battled on: good self-esteem again, tracking blind again. Watching for that light at the end of the tunnel rather than concentrating on the darkness.

Career changes

What about those who are forced to retrain or rethink their career goals at a late stage in life or those who, by choice, want to change jobs? This road is not an easy one to travel and requires careful planning. Consult a career adviser, not to assess your aptitude for counselling, but just to study all the different angles and possibilities involved in changing your career. The best gauge of whether a particular occupation is right for you is to ask yourself: would you do it even if you were not going to be paid? Decide what you want to do with your days, what excites you, what is your wildest fantasy. From a creative and, ultimately, financial point of view, you are most likely to be successful at work that uplifts and stretches you.

Here are some exercises you can do to assess your current ambitions and make adjustments as needed:

1. List five qualities you like about yourself.
2. Briefly describe your current career situation and how you feel about it. Include the negative and positive aspects.
3. Where would you like to be in five years' time?

Do this four-step process in learning how to achieve career satisfaction:

1. Get to know yourself.
2. Learn what you have to offer others.
3. Know what you want.
4. Find out how to get it.

The things you expect for yourself will determine what you actually accomplish as your dominant thoughts are always expressed in your life. Negative, limited beliefs erode your motivation and self-trust. First, identify your limiting beliefs about work. Make a list of all the ones you hold about yourself and your work. Then, go back through your list and write new positive beliefs for each item on your list. Ask yourself the following questions to determine where you are in your career development. Is your current position enhancing your personal and career development? Are your talents and skills being fully utilised? Is your personality compatible with your current position? How do you feel in your body right now? Can you realistically assess your current marketable skills? What is the one unique characteristic that you have to offer in your current work situation? Do you have a professionally presented résumé? Have you had four years' experience with your current employer or one year of experience repeated four times? Make a list of the actions you are committed to undertaking to maximise your career potential.

The biggest hurdle you will face in either seeking work in the first place, looking for work after retrenchment, returning to work after a long period out of the workforce, or making a major career change is a lack of self-confidence. Women who have spent literally years in the company of children with no adult stimulation and out of the work mainstream find the thought of returning to a paid job an extremely daunting prospect. If they can get over the initial 'I can't' mentality, they could surprise themselves. Skills long forgotten come flooding back, and they begin to enjoy using their intelligence again. A period of adjustment is necessary; it is wise not to hurry the process or expect too much at once.

Study skills

The same applies to study skills. Some women opt to return to college or university rather than go straight back to work. Campuses are a whole new world and very frightening to a woman who has been in total control of her own environment for a decade or more. Part-time study requires a special kind of commitment. Let me pass on the tips I learned after many years of study, beginning with a general look at what it is to study, how to avoid stress in this area and how to do well.

Successful study is made up of three parts: efficient study habits, keeping stress under control and effective exam technique/general performance. Whether you are fifteen or fifty, a student of engineering or literature, you have to start with a plan. Begin with the number of hours you have available each week for study itself, excluding time taken up attending classes, lectures and tutorials work. Divide that time up according to the number of assignments you have to deliver each week. For example, if you have to hand in two 2000-word essays every week, set aside, say, two afternoons or evenings for the writing. Research and planning of the essays will come into study time as such. The remaining hours are what you realistically have to work with. Remember to allow for periods of leisure, proper meals and sufficient sleep. One of the first mistakes that students commonly make is going at their books without any system, attacking assignments in a frenzied, overtired, stressed way, defeated before they begin.

Everything that has been said about stress in general and work in particular applies to study. Without a sense of balance nerves are stretched to a breaking point and, eventually, seams crack open and people come apart. The secret is to allow time for each part of your life in reasonable proportions. That way, things are done well with the least pressure on the individual.

Study should be done in a quiet, uninterrupted environment as far as possible. Remove outside stresses and distractions. If you are rested and at peace and you are happy with your regimen in general, you will perform much better. A recent research study on students showed that human beings work more intelligently and efficiently when they are just a little colder than comfortable. If it is a very hot day, wait until evening or even study at night and catch up on your sleep the next day.

Do not plan to work in long stretches, but in one-hour blocks with plenty of breaks. This stopping and starting will not disrupt your concentration as you might imagine, especially if the ten or twenty minutes you stop for are spent calmly with a restful hot drink, a light snooze, some breathing exercises, or stretching. For creativity to flow, you have to acknowledge its existence within you. That means no anxiety, no negative thinking, just open channels between you and your natural power, the life-force inside that can take you to unimagined heights. If it feels right to continue for two hours or more, that's okay; just make it a rule not to push on when you are tired or know that you have exceeded your limit for that study period. If I had observed these rules I would never have become a workaholic and would have achieved the same academic success without hurting myself so much in the process.

As exams approach, check the overview as well as the detail of what you have studied in preparation. Always set yourself small goals, and then enjoy a reward such as the occasional evening off or a favourite television programme you would not otherwise have time to see. If study is just an endless grind, something in you will resist; you will either achieve poorly, give up altogether, get stress burnout, and/or develop an illness. If you do not plan out your day, it is very easy to have an overlap where everything banks up on you and becomes overwhelming instead of workable. In summary, set small goals and work in units of time for stress management and an effective study programme.

Map out a study plan that suits you personally. Watch out for body signals during periods of study. Keep your goals realistic. If you are currently studying, do not procrastinate. Make a plan of action today and stick to it. No matter how poor you think your methods have been to date, it's never too late to make a fresh start. Positive energy can bring positive results. Use the support systems that are available to you—teachers, friends. Do not be afraid to ask. Your personal motivation comes from the desire to succeed—that is all it takes, plus hard work.

The following are suggested study exercises:

1. Isolate any feature of your study programme that you do not think is working effectively. Be clear on why it does not work.
2. What has been the most stressful event in your personal life during the past seven days? Try to resolve it and then put it out of your mind.
3. Where in your body do you feel tense? Did the tension come through the incorrect use of any part of your body, such as sitting for too long at the desk in the wrong position? When in the past did you experience a similar feeling and were the circumstances the same?
4. Write affirmations to yourself about what you desire to achieve before, during and after the exams.

There are certain golden rules to observe when the dreaded exam day dawns. Of course, the first thing is not to dread it! It is like the stress of performance that has been spoken about. Convince yourself that you can do something and do it well, even if it scares the blazes out of you. You see how it comes back to self-knowledge again. Discipline requires the most effort; capitalise on your strengths (these might be things like a good memory or an ability for thinking sharply) and work on your weaker areas. Be especially aware of your diet on the day before the exam because certain foods affect you differently and you want to be at your best. Avoid heavy foods or anything extreme, like very sweet, salty, or spicy foods. Make sure you have seven or eight hours sleep the night before. One absolute no-no is to 'cram' just before the exam. Students should try to not even open a book the morning of the exam as anything read at that late stage could confuse you and interfere with your equilibrium.

In the exam itself, there is a right way and a wrong way to go about attacking the questions posed to you. Take some deep breaths just before you read the paper. While the group is being given its instructions seems like a good time. Read the paper right through without stopping to worry over any undesirable questions. There will be time enough to sort out your thoughts once you have made your choice. Most exams allow for some choice on which questions to answer. Once you have skimmed the paper, quickly mark off the ones you want to tackle, then go back more slowly and make brief notes in the margin or above your answer on the test paper. Letting the examiner see your notes is not a bad idea. That will not only indicate that you are a thorough and organised student; any points you have not covered in your answer will at least be noted, even if marks cannot be allotted for those points.

Answer the questions in the order of your preference. In other words, start with the ones that deal with your area of greatest knowledge. Answer *all* the required questions. Do not leave any out because of lack of time or knowledge. You will irritate the marker if you are asked to do five parts to the exam and you leave out one or two. Examiners are only people, after all, prone to fatigue, hunger and annoyance as much as anyone. Make a good impression on the little things and the bigger ones will take care of themselves. A lot of students feel it is a waste of precious time to plan the answers in an exam, but again, plunging in without prior thought will, in fact, waste far more time. Suppose you have a mental block in the middle of an answer. If you have written out a plan in note form, you simply have to glance at the list to be off again.

Make sure that you give sufficient time to each question. Divide the allowed time equally between the number of questions you are required to do, for example, six questions in three hours would mean a half-hour per question. Do not spend an hour on the first one, then get into a frenzy over the other five. Work steadily through. It is better to have time left that you can use to read back over your answers and add a bit here and there as appropriate. Shut out everything around you; do not watch your fellow students. If they appear to be working faster or more slowly than you, you may get distracted unnecessarily. Everyone works at their own pace; it does not pay to make comparisons. If you get a panic attack in the middle of the exam, take two or three deep breaths and then quietly continue. Be careful not to let precious minutes slide by while you daydream or stare out a window. The other reason to attempt all answers even if you think you know nothing at all about one or two of them is that, as you are battling with the latter questions, a thought could come back that you had forgotten. Three lines of an answer might gain you one mark, but a blank page can only earn a zero.

Once the exam is over, put it out of your mind. Let off some steam. Banish fear and doubt and most of all, negative thoughts. There is no need to be insecure if you have followed the suggestions of this section. All the worrying in the world will not change the outcome of the exam result anyway, so relax and know that you have done your best. If by any chance you have not done well, there are always more exams and more chances. You will cope, whatever.

The most vulnerable periods of stress are the days leading up to final exams and the time when results begin to be posted. The pressure of success expectations and fear of failure can lead to breakdowns and even suicide. In countries where education has to be paid for and thousands of dollars are involved, there's more to poor exam results than just personal disappointment. Some campuses make available crisis hotlines for intervention of precisely these problems. Many mental health clinics offer phone lines that take calls twenty-four hours a day on every type of human dilemma, so utilise the sources of help that are open to you as well as college counsellors who understand the stress of study and exams. Don't hide inside your own fears and imagine the worst. No matter how much you think you'll disappoint your parents, your husband or your friends, stand by your achievements and your failures. Tomorrow is always a new day.

Part-time study is a specialised form and must be handled in its own special way. Try these strategies:

■ attend all classes—do not let your energies flag;

- complete all assignments and put them in on time whenever possible; they have a habit of snowballing if you get behind with even one—time management is even more vital when studying part time;
- take courses that you are really interested in as stamina lasts longer when you are enthusiastic;
- if at all possible, match your job to your study programme as they can work hand-in-glove and make life easier for you all round. For example, I was teaching English and studying for a higher degree in English at the same time.

There is probably more written about stress in teachers and students than any other sector of the community. Remember— awareness then a plan of action. There is no magic wand either for stress management or to make you a successful worker. That only comes from you as a person. Believe in what you want for yourself and in your ability to create magic in your life. The next chapter will teach you how to do precisely that.

AFFIRMATIONS

Everything I touch is a success.

I move into the winning circle.

I'm doing work I love and I'm richly rewarded, creatively and financially.

I'm an open channel for divine ideas to flow through.

My income increases every day whether I'm working, sleeping or playing.

Chapter Nine

Making it work

S peaking of such matters as self-esteem, personal development, positive thinking and life-skills may seem strange
at this stage because essentially the *whole* book is based
on these very issues. This section of the book has been deliberately
left until the end in order to pull together all the strands of
the various topics examined. Although everything in Chapter
Nine has been mentioned before, a specific discussion is needed.
In a way, this chapter will serve as a summary of the whole
book, and it is one you will possibly find yourself dipping into
more often than any other. Specifically, the following will be
discussed: identity; self-love; goal setting; positive thinking;
forming beliefs; mind power; spiritual guides; your limits;
creative visualisation; destructive emotions; helpful emotions;
success; time management; choices; risks; organisation; and
assertiveness.

Identity

As was seen in Chapter Four, personal development is
inextricably linked to concepts of identity and role. If you are
working through the book from beginning to end you may
be keeping an 'Identity Strategies' diary, already seeing the
benefits and learning a lot about yourself in the process.
Remember that the more knowledge you accumulate about

yourself, the more comfortable and at peace you will feel. You would not expect to speak French without tuition or be able to type without lessons; life-skills are far more complex and challenging, yet people are thrown into life with little preparation. Therefore, it is necessary to be patient with yourself; allow time for learning and mistakes; stay positive, and work to a plan that is right for you. The identity strategies help you to focus in on specific areas of interaction and the daily opportunities that arise which are useful aids to increased self-awareness.

Self-love

The exercise where you write a list of the qualities you like about yourself and a list of those you don't offers an accurate measure of your level of self-esteem at the present time. Most people end up with a short list for the first and a rather long list for the second. Is this an indication of false modesty, an inability to recognise fine personal qualities, or simply poor self-image? You decide the answer based on your own result.

Goal setting

Making a list of the ten things you most want in your life today clarifies your own goal-making system. Out of the ten items, it is unusual for people to feel they have achieved more than three or four. That tells me human beings generally are not adept at getting what they want in life. Those points you have listed but not attained are now your new goals, possibly ones you've just discovered.

Goals are inescapably tied to motivation. The former cannot be achieved without liberal doses of the latter. The 'how to' part has already been looked at extensively throughout the book, so this discussion will be confined to the subject of goal setting and achieving.

Keep goals simple, and reward yourself for each one you reach. Have short- and long-term goals that you are working on at the same time. Work in small, achievable units. See the end result, not the hurdles in between. Allow for setbacks and delays, but never consider giving up.

Positive thinking

Goals also need the fuel of 'positive thinking', a phenomenon that was a catchphrase born out of the heady, loving days of the 1960s and, therefore, suspect to a generation of harder, more realistic people. It sounds like an umbrella term for all of life's ills. There are some people who may use it as a panacea, but when fully understood, it can have a much wider application. What it *doesn't* mean, and this is the first myth about positive thinking, is that a practitioner of this philosophy has to be happy and smile all the time. That would not only be unrealistic, it would also be undesirable. Light and shade is part of the human condition, and as long as an overall balance is maintained, emotional fluctuations are acceptable.

The second myth is that, with positive thinking, all of life's problems can be eradicated. 'Problems' will always exist; it is part of living, but as with everything else attitude is paramount. Problems can either be seen as difficulties or challenges. The choice is yours. When you are tired and feeling discouraged, little hurdles can seem like insurmountable obstacles. That is when you need to remember back to the strategies for combating depression: go with it; don't analyse; keep it in perspective. The same applies here. Deal with your troubles in units; don't allow today's problem to become tomorrow's nightmare or your whole world to turn black because one thing went wrong today.

As with stress, you can use the adrenalin burst from unexpected adversity to spur you on to creative solutions. The energy you would normally expend on shouting or crying can be harnessed for a more fruitful purpose. Obviously, there are personal tragedies that cannot be dealt with in this fashion, but you will still be better equipped to cope overall if you have practised this way of life. Positive thinking may not ease the pain of a child's death or lighten your burden if you have no food to eat or money to pay bills, but what you will learn from this book is that you are the captain of your own ship and, therefore, have a choice over the events you bring into your life. This notion is not a popular one because it removes the comfort of predestination. Without fate and/or God to blame, people feel threatened by the awesome burden of responsibility. Yet others prefer to believe that all of life is an accident, one long, random event. That is an esoteric and basically unintelligent argument. No one side can produce infallible proof of the existence, or otherwise, of a Creator, a universal existence, or the human soul. However, commonsense tells us that life cannot be merely a chance encounter for mortal beings who inhabit a planet called Earth and then cease to exist. You know without being told that your life contains more than just physical realities.

Forming beliefs

Those who resolutely deny their spirituality lead shallow lives at best and empty, unhappy ones at worst. These things are not said by way of judgment but as a foundation for many of the ideas discussed in the present and next chapter. Some of them will be foreign to you. I was brought up in a strict, Catholic family with traditional beliefs and values. Not the type to rebel or question, I accepted the doctrines of the church totally. Something inside me embraced the concepts and practices. I truly loved God, Mary, the saints and the angels. I said my prayers every day, studied my catechisms, went to confession with my trivial sins, and attended mass as often as I could. All this was done in a spirit of pure, childlike faith; I felt close to God and happy in my innocent way. There were some things that I found puzzling and as far as I could understand, unacceptable. For instance, I never could comprehend any church proclaiming itself as the only instrument of the true faith. To me, all religions simply represent different paths to one's own inner beauty and spiritual perfection. I cannot tolerate self-righteousness in any form, and if we look at the Bible Jesus was none too fond of it himself. Yet, so many people seem to believe the path to Heaven lies paved, not with good deeds, but with Bible quotations; the more you know, the more you will be rewarded. It is not terribly likely, is it? A Christian is, by definition, one who follows Christ, and He never judged people or puffed Himself up or condemned those who did not think as He did. I am explaining my feelings on these matters because I hope that, whatever your own personal beliefs, you can suspend them long enough to consider other points of view.

I have always been interested in 'mystical' matters, not in

a gullible or fanatical way, but out of natural curiosity. Most people are interested, if they allow themselves to admit it. Being a natural seeker, I tend not to take things at surface value; I prefer to make a study of it myself and come to my own conclusions, which is what I have suggested you do with every concept that has been presented in this book. Only then will it be real for you, just as a word has no meaning until it is used and enjoyed. I remember teaching an English class the word 'lugubrious'. They adored the sound and became very playful with it. Everything and everyone was 'lugubrious' for the next week, until the novelty wore off. The meaning of the word was unimportant and would not form part of their personal lexicon until such time as they truly understood its sense and practised using it correctly.

I apply that same principle of learning to psychological matters, and thus, as I set out on my own inward journey, I always did my homework and discarded what did not feel right for me. Take the subject of reincarnation. This topic creates ambivalence in many of us. It sounds so logical and simple that we have multiple lives to live, that each life is a lesson in itself, which leads on to other existences. In fact, it is so simple that for years I felt unable to embrace its truth. Many of the attitudes that I describe in myself have changed in the past eighteen months so bear with me, walk with me along the strange and wonderful path that has led me to this day and this sharing.

For example, now I would accept much more on trust, allowing my intuition to guide me. In the case of reincarnation, I do accept its validity, not because I can offer proof positive or even give you a rational explanation but because I have proven it for myself; that is what is important.

I can only tell you how I came to my inner convictions and leave you to make your own judgment. Reincarnation is just one example. I studied astrology, numerology, tarot, palm-reading and other things for years, purely for my own interest. One area I have steered clear of altogether is dabbling in spirits and seances or ouija boards, and I have no curiosity whatsoever about the dark arts or witchcraft. I only want to dabble in practices that bring me into the light, although I accept the existence of evil in the world.

Basically, there are two types of people in the world: those who live within a narrow perimeter of experience and like it that way and those who are constantly seeking more knowledge, hungry for new facts and information.

I fall into the second category, so I grasp every opportunity that comes along to add to what I already know. I am the kind of person who has a jumble of useless facts stored in my brain, very valuable for games of trivia and quiz nights, but little else! There are some things that interest me more than others obviously, but, in general, I love to get my teeth into a new challenge. This is the spirit in which I read up on metaphysical matters, picking and choosing the credible from the noncredible.

I also have a tendency to not let myself off the hook too easily. For instance, I felt that believing in reincarnation would make life so much easier so I deliberately gave myself a hard time over it. I wanted to believe that we earn our own life experiences, that there is reason and justice in existence, that a tortured dog may perhaps have been a wicked rat. How wonderful and fair everything would seem, and how easy it would be to fall into such a soft trap. Only with understanding and time did I come to know the beauty of truth and the futility of scepticism.

Reincarnation is not about punishment for bad deeds, which is what I understood 'karma' to mean, but rather the learning of lessons. It was best explained to me thus: it is like going to school; with every lifetime, certain lessons have to be grasped and tests taken. If this does not happen, the lifetime has to be lived again, just like repeating a year at school. There are all sorts of subconscious choices and reasons that lead us to these lessons. We repeat interactions with key people in our lives as well. The relationship may not be the same. Your mother in one lifetime may pop up as your best friend in another. I don't pretend to understand all the details and concepts, but I am happy to learn as I go.

Mind power

When something is right and its time has come, no struggle for success is necessary. A wish or a plan can be in your mind for years. You berate yourself for procrastination and then one day, in a flash that very thing happens, without you lifting a finger. Who did it? That is the same type of question as who or what beats your heart? What makes the grass grow? The answers you have at your disposal only supply some of the story.

Timing is vital. Trying to force events in our lives only serves to push them further out of reach. The question of control has been mentioned before, but more will be said in this chapter because not needing to control is a giant step forward in personal development.

Is it possible that the energy of your thoughts and wishes is sufficient to make the substance of your reality? Philosophers can argue this point ad infinitum, but most metaphysical beliefs are based on the concept of mind power. This latter term is another one that is constantly misused and, therefore, rife with myth and misunderstanding. A more correct term may be 'spirit power', because the brain is capable of a good deal of fallacy while your true power lies within the subconscious workings of the psyche, the soul. What you 'think' has a direct relationship to your feelings, actions, behaviour and interactions. Those around you provide little more than mirror images. If you do not like what you see outside you, around you, you only have to look inwards. The more you open yourself up to the magic, the more good things happen.

Here is a personal example. For years, I thought it would be fun and useful to learn the computer, but a lack of confidence held me back as did a lack of funds. I had built up a belief that I was not the computer type. When it came time for me to work on this book, again the computer issue was raised. A friend of mine bought one from a relative who is in the trade and said I could use it for as long as I need. Another friend bought me an ergonomic chair because I have a bad back and was concerned about sitting for long periods at the keyboard. Without a conscious decision on my part, my writing equipment was set up before me; it all just fell into place. You can think of cases in your own experience where something you needed or wished you had simply materialised in one form or another, often when you least expected. If you honestly have never known this to happen, try opening up the channels of power within you by faith. Even if you do not believe in spiritual realities, believe in the power of good and the marvel of life. Drink in the sheer energy that surrounds you at every moment and the intense peace that resides inside you, the golden light that shines even in the darkest place. Anything is possible and your only restrictions are the self-imposed limitations of your negative thinking. The word 'magic' is often associated with the occult and the dark arts, but it only means the life-force and all that it can create.

What can you do to combat negativity? Take decisive action and, as always, be practical. Wishful thinking is less destructive than negative thinking, but it will not get you what you want either. Try making a list of the negative areas in your perception, such as lifestyle habits you would rather discard and relationships you hang on to for the wrong reasons. Next to each item on the list write a positive action you could take to replace the negative or unproductive one. Every time you are aware of a negative thought, chide yourself gently and consciously replace it with a positive slant. Try replacing 'Mary doesn't like me' with 'I'm going to make an effort to get to know Mary better so that she won't always act so coldly towards me.' Do away with all ideas of self-criticism and control; keep reminding yourself that you are learning a new way to live. It takes time and patience.

Charlotte left a teaching job in the country and returned to the city with no definite prospects. She rented a friend's house and decided that she would like to buy an inexpensive house on a minimum deposit as her cash reserves were low. She was offered a low-paying job in a school library and decided to take it as a stop-gap. Charlotte used to walk along the river and admire the beautiful homes that lined the esplanade, saying to herself that one day she would live there too. Little did she realise how close that day was.

A real-estate agent Charlotte knew in the area slipped a card under her door and on the back was written the address of a house for sale two streets away, very close to the river. She imagined a rundown, weatherboard cottage because the agent knew her price range. The next day, she duly drove to the address, but, as it was late, it was difficult to make out the numbers. When she found what appeared to be the right address, it turned out to be a large, rather grand-looking house with a sweeping lawn, impressive pillars, jutting balcony and wide steps leading up to the front door. It had to be the wrong number, Charlotte decided, and assumed the agent had made a mistake. Upon investigation the next day she was assured that it was the right house; the price was $10 000 more than she wanted to pay, but she could not resist a closer look. An inspection was arranged for the next day, and Charlotte fell in love! After the usual points had been checked, she made an offer close to the asking price.

Although she had no deposit and no real capacity to pay back the loan, somehow it just felt right. Charlotte went with her instinct. The very next day the principal of the school called her into his office, informed her that one of the teachers had suffered a mild stroke and, as his classes were in her subject area, would she like to take over his job? In an instant, her salary had jumped about $12 000 per annum, and she could now comfortably afford the house. Her belief in miracles had won the day!

If you tried to manipulate a situation like that knowingly, it would not come off, but trust yourself to find the means to have what you so desire. The less you dare, the less you have and what you *do* have may erode away in a sea of frustration and self-doubt. Not a very pretty picture, and yet, how many of you reading this book right now share this scenario and believe you have no choice? Hopefully these stories have given you a clearer vision of what true positive thinking can be.

Spiritual guides

One unusual and interesting spiritual adventure I had was to visit a psychic artist who drew for me a picture of my principal spirit guide. She does a similar job to the 'guardian angel' of my childhood days. What does it matter what name you give these helpers as long as your faith allows you to see the bright face of their love? I had already met 'her' (spirits are essentially androgynous) through my own efforts a few months earlier, so imagine my surprise at seeing her turn up on the canvas of a stranger's drawing board. The night I 'met' her was eerie indeed. For many years, friends had advised me to meditate because of my tendency to get tense, stressed, and be overactive.

Like many people, I thought that there was something a little suspect about meditation. Surely it was not a suitable preoccupation for intelligent individuals? All that chanting and waving in the breeze made me want to giggle. Perhaps again I feared something in meditation, not wishing to reach too far into myself, afraid of the unknown quality of my own essence.

As part of the spiritual journey I embarked upon I did begin to practise meditation and found it to be a cleansing, joyful and peaceful activity. Being somewhat restless in composure, I always thought I would find it hard to concentrate sufficiently and become relaxed enough to get the benefits of inner peace and tranquillity. Once I actually began, I never looked back and have enjoyed it ever since.

During meditation I first encountered Marie, my spirit guide. It was like a scene from a horror movie complete with storm, sound effects and flickering candles. I had waited until I was alone in the house (foolish me!) and then decided to create some atmosphere if I was going to attempt the exercise at all. I had read about guides and wanted to communicate personally if it was possible. I had a few things on my mind and expressed those aloud. Then I meditated and went silent to allow whatever messages that were forthcoming to filter through. I began to have a sense of a very tall, robed figure dressed in dark clothes. It is not correct to say that I heard or saw anything; it was more like a feeling of certainty without reason. Distinct messages began to come to me by way of a monologue occurring in my mind. I listened intently. By the way, I was only afraid until I got going and then all fear dissolved and I felt safe and loved.

A question came to me, 'Would you like to see me?' Like a child, I answered spontaneously, 'I'm not that brave!' When it was over, I felt warm and happy and more confident than ever about keeping in touch with this robed spirit who has loved me through eternity and stays close by to guide me in this lifetime.

Those of you who have encountered these ideas already will think nothing of my story, but for many of you I will be speaking of totally foreign things. All you have to do is open your mind and heart as I did, and you can enjoy the same peace and help. It is certainly the best stress destroyer I know, but I offer you many others because not everyone is prepared to try spiritual solutions or if so, the more conventional types are usually chosen. There is a saying, 'When the pupil is ready, the teacher will appear.' Most of what I am telling you about now would have been totally incomprehensible to me not too long ago, so stay with me.

My perceptions were confirmed when I went to the psychic artist, not knowing what to expect but full of excited anticipation. I was ushered into a small room with an easel at one end and a comfortable chair in the other. I settled in, and shortly after the artist began I started to feel an unmistakable peace descend upon the room. It was exactly like being cradled in loving arms. (I'm trying to reproduce these various events as accurately as possible, with little embellishment and addition.) The artist began to draw. As she had her back to me, I could only see the sweeping movements of her arms as they worked across the canvas. A face began to emerge in crayon, the face of a young Chinese man, a coolie, with a broad open face and loose, thin hair that trailed over his forehead in sweaty strands. The artist spoke softly of the spirits that were making their presence felt. The picture began to change in front of my very eyes, as if against the will of its creator; another image was literally pushing its way through. At the same time, the artist was speaking of a friend I had spent two lifetimes with, a nun named Marie who was and is my friend. Her face became clear on the drawing, superimposed upon the previous visage, as if she had emerged as a more potent force in my subconscious life than her predecessor on the canvas.

The most amazing part was still to come. She was dressed in dark robes, a nun's habit, and one fact was unmistakable. She was in that lifetime a very tall woman; in truth, she was my night visitor of several months before. Here she was again, bright and clear. I did get to see her, after all. I am about ready to ask, 'Believe it or not?' The answer is not important because these matters stretch not our intellect, but our faith and our capacity to believe in the tremendous possibilities of existence.

We are not insignificant specks in the universe, as scientists delight in telling us we are. We are truly magnificent beings, capable of all manner of wonderful things, and it is sickening to know how the joy is crushed out of so many people by distorted truths and unloving attitudes. There is one absolute truth: the beauty of life, and nothing I have yet experienced has changed my mind about that. There are those who would make fun of this conviction, mistaking the capacity for joy for woolly-headedness and sentimentality.

It may be easier to think like the cynics and the uncaring, but you should try to get close to the innocent simplicity of your childhood and put away the adult paraphernalia that keeps you from your true essence. You have to find your own truth in your own way. More will be said in Chapter Ten on meditation and many other stress management techniques that require much less suspension of belief than those I've discussed here.

Your limits

The main thing is not to be afraid of new ideas. If you have done basic work on yourself, such as has been suggested in earlier parts of this book, you are now ready to explore further. How far you go is limited only by the extent of your thinking. Everybody labels themselves according to what they have been told they are and by their personal belief systems. You may believe yourself to be hopeless, physically unfit, no good at accents, at mechanical things, at singing, but have you ever really tried? How many more things could you achieve if you remove all such restrictions on your thinking? What talents might you unearth?

The less you try to control and the more relaxed you become about life, the better things will work out. You will see how wide the net can spread when you are a true positive thinker. When you dream of how your life could be, be specific. Instead of 'Wouldn't it be nice if—', substitute concrete and detailed desires. Dare to dream big and believe it will really happen. Too many people feel unworthy to have their wishes come true, particularly women because they are brought up largely in a spirit of sacrifice, of caring for others first.

The two philosophies of new age principles that I find most appealing are: thankfulness and deservability. The way of life that it teaches is that it is okay to make mistakes, it's important to value yourself and, best of all, miracles can happen. If you are interested in learning more about this doctrine, there are any number of books around; there are also tapes and even a whole new style of music to enjoy. In fact, it is hoped that you will follow up ideas that have been introduced in this book by further reading, attending a variety of courses and talking to open-minded people. Start your own group and meet with other women who want to learn and grow. When you begin, it will take up quite a lot of time. Still, once you decide what you want from it you can develop a programme that is exactly right for you.

Creative visualisation

Most people will have heard of creative visualisation. It is one of the most effective and enjoyable exercises in mind power; it is also a form of meditation and, again, positive thinking. If you are not familiar with it, this is how it works: picture something in your mind that you want to bring into your life. It might be a very practical item like a better house or a car; it can also be something totally far-fetched such as flying in a spaceship or winning a million dollars. The important factor is that it must seem completely real and believable to you at the moment of imagining. Take the example of a woman who dreams of being an executive with a large organisation. If she thinks of this position in a vague and cloudy fashion, there is little likelihood of it ever really happening. Creative visualisation allows her to be transported into the world of her ambitions so that, in her mind, she is an important official of the company; either one she is already connected to or any other she chooses. That thought alone will not make it happen. She will need to be there in her mind. Using all her senses she can visualise a typical moment in her office. What will her desk be like? How will she be dressed? How will the room look? What will she actually be doing? If you want a fur coat, feel yourself wrapped inside it. A Mercedes? Picture yourself behind the wheel.

Another key factor is to be in the moment with your dream incarnate; it must be happening in the present. Your body and soul are always in the present; only your mind takes you back into the past which is gone, and tomorrow which is not yet yours to have. So know that what you are wishing for now may materialise in the future, but is already yours today. If you do not readily grasp that concept, think about it for a while as it is a particularly complex one.

The last necessary element is faith. Without faith, creative visualisation is just a fun exercise; with it, all things are possible. If it sounds unlikely, try it for yourself and see. It is certainly a lot more productive than spending your energy on 'If only' and negative thoughts such as 'Nothing good ever happens to me.'

Destructive emotions

Emotions such as regret and envy require just as much, if not more, effort than positive thinking and creativity, and are no fun at all! Regret is wasteful because you cannot call anything back once it is done. You can only forgive yourself for your lack of wisdom at the time of the mistake. Looking back at thirty-eight to an action you took at twenty-three and hating yourself for it is pointless. You acted with the knowledge you had at twenty-three and should not be judged by thirty-eight-year-old standards. Envy is also futile as it suggests that another person has a better life than you. By what criteria can you judge that? More money? Better house? Better job? How do you know they are happy? Are you prepared to swap and find out? Comparing yourself to others is guaranteed to make you unhappy, because one way or another, you cannot win.

Helpful emotions

Try thankfulness. Give thanks every day for all your gifts and blessings. On even the bleakest day, you'll be able to think of things you can give thanks for, such as a flower blossoming on your rose bush or the fact that the sun came out long enough to dry your washing. If you are a religious person, thank God; otherwise, thank the universe or life or yourself. The feeling behind it is what matters. Once you begin thinking like that, you will do it automatically and stop focusing on your problems. Being grateful out of subservience or guilt is quite another matter and not to be recommended. Take the attitude that you ought to like your dinner because millions in the world are starving. That point always seems so illogical. No wonder children who are told this find it difficult to accept. Isn't it much better to send love and donations when you can, to help in a practical way, than to give in a spirit of duty? The thankfulness spoken of here is quite different. It stems from a sense of the abundance of life. As with love, it is a case of the more you have, the more you have to give.

Living with a creed of forgiveness for others and yourself is also important. Each night before you sleep, let go of the day you just lived. If someone hurt you, forgive them and put away all anger. If you did the hurting, resolve to make amends. If this is not possible, say you lost your temper with a stranger in the street, then apologise in your heart and send that person love. Forgive yourself and put it all in the past. The next day you will awaken to a new day and a new beginning, instead of carrying all of yesterday's pain and anger around with you. Think how all the yesterdays accumulate. No wonder people are bowed down by the time they are old—so many grudges merged into regret and resentment; so much wasted time.

Creative energy does not only apply to the arts, as many people seem to think. You can choose to live your whole life creatively, which really only means that you are open to all possibilities and your own potential. How do you know that you could not write or paint or make pottery? It only depends on your degree of desire. Non-singers can be taught to sing; those who think themselves unmusical can learn to play the piano in a few short weeks; there are courses to help people get in touch with the artistic abilities lying undiscovered inside them. Once you have unlocked that part of your mind that tells you 'I can't', the rest should flow easily. Have the courage to try it.

Creativity flows from you in whatever form you choose when you allow it. Feel with the music or the words or the paint. Look beyond the imperfection to the purity of the expression. The more in tune with yourself you are, the better everything goes in your life—your relationships, your work, your ability to problem-solve and cope with difficulties that arise, your health, success ratio, ability to earn money, anything else you desire. You may have heard the old expression, 'Get out of your own way.' That is exactly what needs to happen if you are to be free, because so often people limit themselves unnecessarily. Pick some thoughts or attitudes that may be holding you back and devise strategies to introduce change.

Success

Take the concept of success. What is your personal definition of 'success'? You know what society judges you on, but what do you believe? Do you think you are a success or capable of being one? What decides this?

In an ideal world, success would be measured by the degree of effort put into a project. In the real world, productivity is everything, concrete results and tangible evidence are often measured in dollars and cents. Therefore, it is vital that you have a clear view of your own goals and praise yourself when you attain them. Don't wait for others to pat you on the back. Smile inwardly at the cake you just baked or the cupboards you cleaned out for the first time in six months. As you would encourage and compliment a friend, so can you love and honour your own work. Set your own standards and follow the rhythm of your personal energy. Acknowledge the power you have and then rejoice in it. You don't have to hand it over to your spirit guides or the universe or anything else. That would be defeating the whole purpose. It is a fine line between not trying to control everything that happens to you and around you, while at the same time, trusting life to take care of you. Watch the miracles of nature, the birds, the seasons of things—it all just happens naturally. In fact, it's usually human intervention that causes the most chaos and destruction.

It is the same when you are surrounded by sea, sky, trees, birds, grass, earth. These things heal you, wash away the fatigue, the disillusionment, the pain of living out of balance. There cannot be a purer or more pleasurable way to combat or reduce stress. If you do not live near any green areas, stand out on your balcony or simply open a window and breathe in some fresh air, pollution and all. A day in the country will do more to bring down your blood pressure than all the drugs, cigarettes and coffee in the world. Yet so many never choose to look beyond the obvious remedies, preferring harmful solutions or ones that, at best, offer a temporary improvement. Just doing something different from your normal routine is wonderful for alleviating stress. One person's remedy was to check into a luxury hotel for a night when he was feeling tired and stressed, lie in bed, call room service and completely indulge herself. After twenty-

four hours, it felt as if she had enjoyed a three-week holiday—
an interesting strategy for busy people.

Time management

As mentioned in Chapter One, a great cause of stress is poor
time management. Why? It is simple. When you are very busy,
things have a habit of piling up on you. For example, if you
neglect a certain job it grows and grows, finally to horrific
proportions, which causes you to put it off even more. It becomes
a vicious circle, and you either never tackle the task at all or
it ends up taking you ten times as long to complete. Rule One,
then, of time management is to keep abreast of ongoing tasks.
Then there is fitting the time you have to the chores at hand.
Economy and efficiency apply just as much to time as to financial
resources. Making three trips to the store in one day is wasteful
of time and energy—that is where lists are so useful. Do
everything in one hit instead of in dribs and drabs. Imagine
doing your housework in unplanned bits. It would take all week
to clean the whole house. Wouldn't you rather do it thoroughly
once a week or for two hours each morning, leaving the rest
of the week to spend on more creative pursuits? It is the same
principle as discussed regarding study habits. The time spent
on planning and organising will be more than made up by
the efficiency with which you will do the job.

Set yourself a strict order of priorities. If you just plunge
into a jumble of jobs without thought or plan, you will soon
find yourself in a muddle. Just as you need short- and long-
term goals, any list or diary notations you make should be
organised under headings of 'today', 'immediate', 'this week'.
Do not overload each day with more than you can realistically
manage as frustrating yourself is not the easy road to success.

Work to your own energy level. Whether you believe it's your
stars, your biorhythms, or the meal you ate the night before,
your capacity to work effectively will vary from day to day.
On some days you can go for ten hours or more straight with
little effort; on others, three hours are a strain. Do not compare
yourelf with others—'keeping up with the Joneses' is exhausting
and unsatisfying in the long run. Saving up and buying that
small boat you've always wanted is much more exciting than

going into debt for a huge launch that you can ill-afford. How much pleasure is it going to give you when you have to sweat over the bills each month? Keep saying to yourself that *you* are what counts and the trappings are icing, little more. What you look like, what you own, what people think of you is so much dust to the wind. What you are inside and what you contribute to a frail and needy world is your real legacy. Each person can make a difference. All you have to do is care enough and believe in your ability.

Choices

Much of daily life is about choices. There are small decisions to be made constantly and then, from time to time, you come to a major crossroad. It's frightening, and you feel alone and vulnerable, yet the choice you make can affect your life for decades to come. Trust in your instincts; ask for guidance, and then go forward confidently. You may never be sure if you made the right decision, and if you look back over your life, you will clearly see the various turning points that you reached and how your life changed as a result of those paths you chose. This poem says it all:

THE ROAD NOT TAKEN

Two roads diverged in a yellow wood.

And sorry I could not travel both.

And be one traveller, long I stood
And looked down one as far as I could
To where it bent in the undergrowth;

Then took the other, as just as fair,
And having perhaps the better claim,
Because it was grassy and wanted wear;
Though as for that the passing there
Had worn them really about the same,

And both that morning equally lay
In leaves no step had trodden black.
Oh, I kept the first for another day!

Yet knowing how way leads on to way,
I doubted if I should ever come back.

I shall be telling this with a sigh
Somewhere ages and ages hence:
Two roads diverge in a wood, and I—
I took the one less travelled by,
And that has made all the difference.

Risks

Risks are a necessary part of life because they affirm that you
believe in yourself and in life. Every time you feel cornered
or threatened, you have a choice. Give up or find a creative
solution. Remember fear is a fantasy. It is only real if you allow
it to be so. Once again, the following poem speaks for itself:

RISK TAKING IS FREE

To laugh is to risk appearing the fool,
Too weep is to risk appearing sentimental,
To reach out to another is to risk involvement,
To expose feelings is to risk exposing your true self,
To place your ideas, your dreams, before the crowd, is to risk
   their loss,
To love is to risk not being loved in return,
To live is to risk dying,
To hope is to risk despair,
To try is to risk failure,
But risk must be taken, because the greatest hazard in life is
   to risk nothing,
The person who risks nothing, does nothing, has nothing and
   is nothing,
He may avoid suffering and sorrow, but he simply cannot learn,
   feel, change, grow, love and live,
Chained by his certitudes, he is a slave, he has forfeited his
   freedom,
Only the person who risks is free.

Organisation

The final point about personal management is to organise the
things you need to get the job done: the physical workspace,

the writing area, the equipment you are using, necessary supplies, the immediate tasks in front of you, the other things in your life before you sit down to begin work and anything else you need. Something as silly as running out of staples could throw you into a spin in the middle of a job; not being able to put your hands quickly on a file you need; having constant interruptions because you forgot to turn the phone answering machine on or feed the children their lunch before you started.

Assertiveness

The final section of this chapter is about something you hear a lot of these days, but as with positive thinking, it is often misunderstood. It is assertiveness. Historically, women have tended to lack assertiveness in their personal, social and professional lives. When they did begin to emerge from kitchens, maternity wards and from behind typewriters, the cry went up that women were turning tough, imitating men and becoming aggressive. That may have been necessary in the early days of women's liberation, but so much progress has been made by the female gender in many countries of the world that the revolution can afford to quieten down and adopt more dulcet tones.

The old adage, 'You catch more flies with honey than with vinegar' holds true. Assertiveness is not raucous, rough, or raunchy. It is truth quietly spoken and comes from a deep sense of self-confidence. You truly cannot be assertive unless you think well of yourself. It builds slowly, but when it is ready it rushes out in a torrent, like a dam waiting a hundred years to burst its banks. The quietest, shyest, most unassuming woman is usually the very one that will stand up the tallest and replace her small, unnoticed voice with strength and determination. At first this new-found authority sits very uncomfortably on her, like an ill-fitting dress. The people around her give her a hard time; they feel threatened by her new mantle and waste no time in trying to bring her back to where she was. That is perhaps the most difficult part of personal growth—the fact that progress is hindered by the disapproval of those who mean the most to you. Most women experience their first encounter with the beginnings of assertiveness during the thirties syndrome, spoken of in Chapter Four. Once gained, this new skill brings a wonderful freedom and a different way to live.

Women should be educated to be open and strong and independent from the time they leave school instead of having to learn the hard way. Mind you, the young ones today are much more forthright about their rights and what they expect from life. As long as this expectation is not handled in a demanding or unreasonable way, then it's a good movement. When the young say that adults have left them an unworthy world, beyond repair, so why should they care, they're copping out. Who but the young can the world look to for reform and betterment? It is true that adults have all the authority and power, but the young have vision and energy. If these can be directed into positive change rather than negative pursuits such as drug-taking and violence, what a grand world might be fashioned.

Once you have worked on your identity as the first step in your personal development programme, your self-esteem grows. Then you are ready to set goals and make some real changes in your life. Assertiveness is not possible unless you clearly know what you want. A simple example of assertiveness is to speak up in a queue if your place in line is usurped by another person. It may seem like a small thing to insist on being served first, but for the average person it is extremely difficult and takes practice. The first time you try it, your heart will pound and your throat will go dry. Hopefully, the assistant will accede to your request without a fuss, but once you are confident enough it won't matter for you'll firmly stand your ground no matter what.

There is no turning back once you start on this path. Remember the analogy of life being like a train journey; well, there will be many times when you feel like jumping right off! The option is always there to take your marbles and go home, but persistence wins the day. If you can bounce back from a time of crisis, you will somehow find the courage to fight on. Then, as you incorporate more and more of your lessons into everyday life, there is less struggle and more joy. Victorian ethics teach you that life should be hard, so you obediently strive to make it that way. When you stop believing that problems are inevitable, they begin to dissolve before your very eyes.

Remember that confidence is a skill to be learned like any

other. Some people may be more naturally vocal or outgoing, but everyone needs focus and direction or their lives are just so much scattered energy. Decision-making is directly linked to the level of confidence from which you are operating. You cannot make brave, strong choices if you are afraid or prey to negative thinking. Do not give in to fear, doubt and worry which are your greatest enemies.

Everything that has been suggested in this chapter is POSITIVE. You decide. Find your own truth and don't be afraid to explore and expand. You have been offered a range of tools and ideas to achieve the improvements that have been discussed in detail. In the final chapter, a complete range of stress management techniques will be listed, some that have been mentioned earlier and others that are further suggestions. Some are minor and some will change your life. It is a smorgasbord, a feast of ideas for you to choose from. Start now on the last leg of your journey, a voyage of discovery and new beginnings.

AFFIRMATIONS

My way is made smooth and easy every day.
I completely trust my unconscious, creative self.
I accept the abundance of the universe now.
I am a magnet for divine prosperity.
I deserve the best and I accept the best now.

Chapter Ten

Putting it all together

I n the nine preceding chapters, the chief causes of stress in modern woman have been outlined and there has been offered a variety of techniques and strategies for you to follow. The goal is to achieve a more balanced and fulfilled lifestyle. Underlying all the ideas and suggestions has been the philosophy that the better you feel about yourself, the less negativity you will allow into your life, and that includes stress. So this book has looked at you, the whole woman, shared some personal stories with you and included as many examples and case studies as possible.

Now, let's turn to another aspect of stress management. In this last chapter, the aim is to achieve three things: to list common stress-inducing problems faced by many women today; to look at common remedies and give an in-brief view of their benefits or drawbacks; and to examine other stress-reducing activities that have not been discussed elsewhere in the book, or not to the same extent.

Driving

One of the most stressful aspects of city living is the proverbial traffic jam, or even just driving in normal conditions among the noise, pollution and delays of modern transportation. The most calm, rational person can turn into a screaming maniac behind the wheel of a car. Have you noticed how people's personalities change? Women have always been discriminated against as drivers; before they ever get their licences and first cars, it is already assumed that they are incompetent, careless and unsure. Yet female drivers are just as capable, if a little less confident as, just as in other areas of life, women have to work harder to be respected for what they do. To generalise, women's weakness behind the wheel is in being hesitant and erratic. Men, on the other hand, err on the side of recklessness and speeding. Regardless of gender, everyone can improve their performance on the road, in particular in respect to consideration for fellow drivers and correct procedure.

A lot of people set off for their destination without due thought to the route they intend to take. Also, drivers in general place their vehicles poorly as they are manoeuvring through traffic or stopping at intersections and lights. (There is a strong similarity between this and one's approach to life. You can either charge forward carelessly, ignoring everyone else's needs or take a more studied and balanced attitude.) Increased safety and pleasure on the roads would be of benefit to all who travel them.

You cannot do much to eliminate the stress of being out there among the tooting, stopping, starting and less-than-perfect drivers who endanger your life, but there are positive measures you can adopt, even in a car, to enhance your life. The simplest and most obvious is to listen to some soothing music on the radio or cassette. Loud, raw music is distracting and unnerving and not recommended as a driving companion. Having a comfortable seat is essential for stress reduction, especially if you spend a lot of time in the car each day. As part of your overall time management, use productively all those wasted hours waiting in traffic by running motivational or personal development tapes. Say your daily affirmations to yourself or out loud. Do some simple flexing exercises or deep breathing instead of shouting at the driver in the next car or pressing down on the horn.

Noise pollution

This one follows directly on from the problem of traffic, but is more general. There are some people with a high tolerance for noise and confusion and others who cannot work unless there is total silence. You will know as you are reading this section which category you fall into. If you like colour, variety and noise, then, for the best chance at happiness, you ought to surround yourself with those components. You would be ill-suited to life in a backwater town, with a quiet husband, and darning socks all day!

Women do not give enough thought to lifestyle when they marry. You are not just marrying a man, but a way of life. Consider if it will suit you after the first flush of romance is over. So, the secret of living comfortably is to seek out an area that you can best afford that offers the sort of lifestyle you want and need. If there are unforeseen stresses, then engage the techniques that you learned in this book and work on eliminating, as far as possible, the sources of discomfort. There is always a positive solution to a problem if you care to look beyond the obvious reaction.

Pollution involves a range of components that poison the environment, including noise. Talk of the greenhouse effect worries people and yet there are many practical remedies that you can adopt to counteract this phenomenon. It is distressing that the negative side of things seems to appeal more when there are so many positive and possible solutions. Governments are very good at offering remedies after the fact instead of spending money on prevention and educational programmes. If you are not happy with the state of your world, do something about it. Lobby your local representative. Start a protest group and research conditions in your area. Write to the newspapers. Claim back the earth that belongs to us all.

Arthritis, asthma, cancer

These three are grouped together because they are widespread diseases in the community and cause stress to the sufferers as well as their families. Disease and illness in connection with stress was looked at extensively in Chapter Three. Here, the concern is more about stress as a result of illness rather than as a cause. There are many other complaints of equal gravity that cause stress, but these three samples indicate the problem. Arthritis is painful and crippling and not only confined to the aged. Asthma is extremely common, debilitating, and due to its chronic nature, a constant burden to sufferers. It can also be life-threatening.

Cancer is one of the greatest killers known to modern society. Theories abound as to its nature, cause and cure. Cancer is linked in the main to poor diet, poor sleep patterns, excessive stress and smoking. Any one of these factors in isolation will probably not induce the disease, but if two or more are significant in a lifestyle the person concerned is not taking a precautionary stance in regard to her own health and well-being.

Cancer is not only a painful and wasting disease. It sometimes ravages the body over a period of years; it is one of the cruelest and most ruthless, exacting in its claim and relentless in its pursuit. Doctors say today that cancer is not automatically a death sentence and certainly there are now many alternative remedies that can recede the march of disease upon the sufferer, even if not offering a complete cure. However, for those mortally ill with cancer, death can be a welcome release.

Racism

All the 'isms' can be sources of stress if you let them. They represent varying points of view and philosophies. Racism has been chosen because it is widespread in the world today, causing violence, hatred and even war. Be clear on the term: to be aware of someone's race is normal human behaviour; to judge a person on that race constitutes racism. Australians are often accused of being particularly racist and, certainly, there are factions within the country that hate Asians, 'pommies', 'yanks', or all migrants; in other words, anyone who is not a white Australian is suspect. Aborigines are often treated as second class citizens, even though the land was originally theirs. Yet, in other countries, this same racial suspicion emerges from people of other nationalities. It is said that the French look down on anyone who cannot speak their language, regarding such an omission as uncivilised. Whether the reaction is positive or negative, an Australian abroad is always worthy of comment.

Racism is due to people's predilection for labelling one another. Here is an example. I was born in England, brought up in Hong Kong, and have lived in Australia since I was twelve years old. Here in my adopted country I am still regarded as 'English'. When I was in England many years ago, I was hailed as that most fascinating of creatures, an Australian abroad. I have always felt like a citizen of the world and not of any particular country. As aware as you may be and try as you might not to make judgments about people, there are bound to be times when you find yourself thinking thoughts that could be described as 'racist'.

In my teaching days, name-calling of the racial type was never allowed in my classrooms, even if no malice was intended. Italians, Greeks and Vietnamese may laugh when teased in this way, but Australians certainly would not like it if the behaviour was reciprocated. Having newcomers to your country is like welcoming visitors into your home. The host's job is to be polite and reassuring even in cases where some personal distaste or dislike is involved. Migrants have brought a wealth of culture, enterprise and new ideas into Australia. Your energies can be better spent than in writing racist slogans on walls and billboards. Children are never naturally racist. This particular 'ism' has to be taught, so be careful of what you say in front of your offspring lest they pick up your prejudices and rigid views. It is always amazing how loosely people talk in general. Suppose you are in a crowd and are overheard by a passer-by of a certain race denigrating the members of that race. Imagine how hurt that person would feel. You may have only been sounding off in a spirit of fun, but you have taken away someone's dignity and joy for no good reason. As mentioned earlier, humour is often used to cover up when people have been cruel or insensitive.

There is also the old argument that you must hate those races who were enemies in wars of the past. Without wishing to offend the valiant men and women who fought and died in the world wars, Korea or Vietnam, I must say that type of attitude represents the worst kind of clinging on to the past. What do the Japanese or Germans living today have to do with those who engaged in those altercations? Where is the sense in perpetuating hatred? Surely our role should be to ensure that there are no more wars. Is the man killed in battle not somebody's brother, son, or husband? Is he not loved and cherished as much as your own brother, son, or husband? Is he in fact not yourself with a different face and a different skin? The next time you see someone who looks or acts differently and you are inclined to mock, laugh, or stare, remember this thought.

Community concerns

Other things that worry the average woman today are the threat of AIDS, nuclear warfare and the growing incidence of crime. In the case of AIDS, all you can do is ensure that you take reasonable precautions in your own sexual activity, that you do nothing to endanger another's safety or health and that you keep yourself as aware as possible of trends and developments in this field of human concern. Worry is *useless*. It cannot be said often enough. It does not change anything and creates a double problem. The same applies to nuclear war. As an individual citizen, you can only make your concerns known to the lawmakers in your own country. Being paranoid and waiting for America or Russia to push the red button and destroy your world is negating of life. Call for disarmament by all means, but allow that politics run on slow wheels. Major change does not take place overnight, and you must live every day until you die. Those who live constantly in fear are already dead, although they continue to breathe.

As to violence and crime, these are closer to home and can be prevented and/or cured by the ordinary, caring woman. First, it begins in the home. Do you allow your child to be cruel to her pets or living things in general? Do you correct her when she's too free with her hands? Do you teach her to respect the belongings of others? And so on.

The next initiative falls back to governments again, which is to develop employment or training schemes for youth. How can you expect your children to grow into worthwhile, productive members of the community when there is nothing for them to do? As a parent, you can teach your children the work ethic, not in the way you had it drummed into you but in a more balanced way, a way that nurtures a natural love for learning and experiment in all things, not just paid employment. Better detention systems are needed, especially for the young, places that correct misguided patterns of behaviour while teaching positive life skills. The effect of love and caring discipline on offenders cannot be measured. Perhaps some were on an inevitable path to a life of crime, but you have no right to assume that about anyone. Expect the worst and you will get it every time.

Operate with love and your efforts will bear fruit. Not blind, unthinking love, but love from the heart, love that streams forward and cannot be hidden, even from the most hardened unbeliever. Haven't you ever been in the presence of a person who emitted goodness, who carried a light around with them and illuminated everything and everyone? It cannot be created by talking about God incessantly or going to church five times a day. Some of my strategies sound like recipes for Utopia, but they are all workable, although it will take a concerted effort on the part of all of everyone and a genuine desire to shape a better world.

Neighbourhood conflicts

Apart from noise, the main problems to plague you in your close home surroundings are the neighbours themselves, barking dogs and the threat of burglary. Neighbour relations should be cordial without ever getting intimate. It is quite understandable that a woman with young children who is at home all day may reach out for companionship to her near neighbours, but few can sustain true friendship over a long period of time. It is rather illogical that you are expected to like your neighbours, who are random strangers at best. Their proximity means that their bad habits will be pronounced and affect your quality of life. As was seen in the chapter on relationships, all human interactions are improved by honesty and clear communication; this holds particularly true in dealing with neighbours. As the expression goes, 'Begin as you mean to continue.'

Consider this example: Helen had just moved into a house with her two dogs. An ongoing problem she always had at new places was the penetrability of the fences with two large, mischievous dogs to keep in. On this particular occasion, she had overlooked a hole in the timber underneath some shrubbery and her two dogs had scampered through, proceeding to tear through the new neighbour's backyard. Helen heard him exclaim in a loud voice and colourful language that he was not going to have dogs running through his property. She took up the mantle and went next door, introduced herself politely and apologised for her errant animals. She stressed that this was not going to be a regular occurrence as she did not believe in allowing her pets to run freely in suburban areas. The neighbour was a little surprised at her forthrightness, but it broke the ice and put his mind at ease about the future of their interaction.

People who go out to work all day and leave their dogs howling in backyards, sometimes tethered, are utterly reprehensible. With a modicum of caring and concern, alternative arrangements can be made. The answer to people who say that they cannot afford or be bothered with these considerations is very simple—don't have a pet! Thoughtlessness in its many forms certainly creates stress and is unnecessary in most cases.

Beating the burglar

Burglary and home break-ins are a lot more serious than mere neighbourhood annoyance. The same factors that govern violence in general affect this social behaviour, but it is probably a lot more preventable than other crimes. Since it occurs in your domain, it is containable and controllable. There are practical measures you can take individually, without relying on outside help. Simple precautions like having well-secured doors and windows, always locking up after yourself and checking visitors at the door before you admit them can make all the difference. 'Neighbourhood Watch' is an innovative initiative that gives the power back to the people. Ordinary suburban residents take responsibility for their safety and privacy, banding together in a co-operative effort instead of complaining that the local police don't do enough. It is a perfect example of self-help that really works. Beyond these measures, carry insurance, leave lights on when you go out, secure your family home as far as your wallet will allow and then trust to the universe to protect you.

Money problems

Almost everyone, to some degree, has financial difficulties these days. Those on modest incomes worry about making ends meet, wealthy businesswomen are concerned about hanging on to their money and economists and investors watch the share market with trepidation. Some feel compelled to adopt negative solutions which, in turn, aggravate the problem, such as the family man who gambles away his pay in an attempt to stretch it a little. The trick is not to take it all too seriously. Money is a currency which means that it should keep moving. If you need to hold on to your money in order to feel secure in life, then your priorities are back to front. Unfortunately this view is not widely accepted in society and there are those who would say it is irresponsible to expound it. Wealth is an attitude of mind, and how much money you actually possess is not as important as what you think about it. There are paupers who live like queens in their minds because they enjoy all of life's free gifts, and there are millionaires who live tight, mean little lives because they love only their wealth.

Enjoy what you have, be thankful for your daily gifts, open your life up for more and more abundance, but do not be greedy, calculating, or desperate. Pay your bills with love, spend your money with joy, as long as you are not extravagant to the point of damage. Cultivate a prosperity consciousness; say affirmations about the state of your wallet such as, 'I am tapped into an endless source of wealth everyday.' And believe it. Do not make the mistake of identifying yourself with how much you own of anything. You are you. If you work hard and invest wisely, you can be financially comfortable. Just working in a nine-to-five job, banking a small amount each week and paying off a house will get your bills paid if you are careful and not interested in luxury. Some are not content with that, so they drive themselves a bit harder. The main thing is to know *why* you are doing it. Money represents different things to different people, and that is okay. It is only a problem if it becomes an obsession.

Do not let those with vested interests scare you into a lot of insurance and financial advice and investments you neither need nor want. Research your options, and then let your own judgment guide you. Rich people are not more important in the community; they have simply been endowed with more power because of dollar worship. There are things that money cannot buy, such as real friends, sunshine and good taste.

Cultivate in yourself and those under your influence those values that really matter, and enjoy the money you have. It is far better to do work you love doing than to be paid a packet for employment that is demeaning or unsuited to you. You do not have to worry about money if you do not wish to.

If you are short of money, ask yourself if you are blocking prosperity in your life. If so, why? You will usually come up with an answer if you are honest. Once you get your thinking straight, the problem and the shortage disappears.

Chronic pain and disability

Common complaints that cause discomfort and pain are headache, backache, menstrual pain and specific ailments such as ulcers and rheumatics. A lot was said in Chapter Three, so it will not be repeated here except to suggest that pain itself is both a signal and cause of stress. Excessive stress over a long period can manifest itself in unnamed but continual suffering such as constant migraines. You will tend to feel pain in your vulnerable area; let it remind you to pull up and take it easier for a while. There are some pains that cannot be whisked away by simple aspirin or meditation or mind-over-matter. A woman who is confined to a wheelchair and has to deal with physical, emotional and psychological realities every day lives with pain as a constant companion.

At a chronic pain support group I spoke to once, the issues raised were rather surprising. The key one was the fierce desire these men and women had to be respected as individuals and not just treated as patients with symptoms. They resented the fact that they were often not consulted about treatments or spoken to with any real compassion. Another point that was raised by those in wheelchairs was their need for ordinary human interactions such as sexual intercourse. A lot of doctors would not discuss this with them for fear of embarrassment, but they wanted to ask questions and have their doubts allayed. They were distinctly devoid of self-pity, but anxious to live as normal a life as possible under the circumstances.

If a woman becomes a paraplegic or loses her sight because of an accident, she has the plain choice of getting on with it or giving up, which is the same decision everyone has to make in the face of human difficulties both large and small. If, however, the cause was preventable or there is a cure available that you are not grabbing with both hands, then you need to ask yourself if you are on a self-destruct course and what you can do about it. The disabled are usually the strongest and most cheerful people of all. Is it a compensation for the losses they have sustained, or did they have the strength to start with and only revealed it when the need arose? The resilience of the human spirit and the fact that women are capable of living through the most terrible horrors and then come bouncing back is amazing.

The pragmatist emerges with a sense of the inevitable; what else is there but to continue? This view does not have to be a bleak one if there is also optimism and hope. We of able body and sound mind can learn a lot from those in pain. That is not to say the whole world is not bleeding, but the next time you are depressed, walk through a children's cancer ward in a hospital, and suddenly any problems you have will melt away like snow in the sun. Those of you who may be suffering from a chronic illness or terminal disease can still practise stress management because your attitude of mind will either increase or decrease your discomfort. Smile through your pain if you can and live every day as if it is the only one you have.

Death

Bereavement has been discussed elsewhere, but it is death itself that creates a lot of stress in people's minds from the moment they first understand its meaning. For some, the reality of death takes away the joy of life. It highlights the futility of existence— the old argument of, 'What's the point? We're all going to die anyway.' Your view should be exactly the opposite. If you are only on earth for seventy years or even less, the most important thing is to make a contribution, to leave a legacy of benefit to the world. Most women choose to do this by having children, thus guaranteeing a type of immortality for themselves.

Bereavement has another common side effect: it can cause an obsession with the notion of death, sometimes for years after the loss. Professional counselling and bereavement therapy is the only answer to bring things back to perspective. However, if you are afraid of the idea of dying or the loss of a loved one without having gone through the experience of death first-hand, then it is likely to be a philosophical issue. One suggestion would be to step back from the emotional arguments and consider some other viewpoints.

You could dread dying for many different reasons, possibly a childhood experience or your parents' attitudes. Think it through for yourself. It is illogical to spoil the years you have because of the uncertainty of the future. The unknown makes life such an adventure. If you have religious beliefs, they should offer comfort about life after death; if you hold the view that life is a random event with no pattern or purpose, then accept the time you have, enjoy it to the fullest and let go graciously when your life ends. Some people not only accept death, but relish a new beginning, further opportunities and adventures. When you are at peace with yourself, fear has no part in the playing out of your drama.

There are many philosophies about life and death. Almost the only absolute is that everyone will one day expire and your physical body come to an end. The individual spirit lives on, so death is a superficial conqueror at best.

Moving house

I have moved house a lot more than the average woman, due to a variety of circumstances. I get ribbed about it by friends and family who accuse me of being a vagabond. Funnily enough, I am by nature a homebody, preferring to do my quality living within my home rather than outside it. So how can I bear to keep putting down roots and having to dig them up again? This question puzzled me over the years until I figured out the answer. I *do* hate leaving behind a home that I have loved and tended and grown memories in, but *I* am my home, not the bricks and mortar that constitute the physical buildings. Wherever I go, I take my home with me. Also, there are people who are careless, those who are destroyers and those who are enhancers. I like to think I belong in the last category. It does not matter to me if I own a house or am renting or staying with friends, I look after the property in my care to the same degree. When I move on, I want to leave behind something better than I found, roses where there were weeds, green grass where there was just scrub, broken objects mended and love where there was neglect: the same in little things as in the grand scheme of life. Moving house is listed on stress scales as one of the highest rating of all human events. The two main reasons for this are: the emotional wrench many people experience at having to move out of their home, and the trauma of the move itself.

To combat the first reason, look objectively at your reasons for moving. If it is out of necessity and not by choice, that is the hardest, but life is mainly about change, learning and letting go. Often it takes a painful occurrence to make you realise this fact. Once you have let go, emotionally as well as physically, the future beckons you, full of promise and new hope. If you find the future anything but exciting and rewarding, it could be because you hang on to the past, blocking the way to new beginnings. This is especially true of moving house. Don't look back as you walk out the door, just straight ahead. That is a good motto by which to tackle everything in your life.

As to the moving day itself, there are several golden rules, and I should know!

- be organised before, during and after the day you move. If you are not normally a list-maker, cultivate the habit for this day as it will make the transition so much smoother. The lists should be categorised under headings such as 'Last-minute packing', 'Things to do before packers arrive', and 'People I have to notify'. If you just have one long mixed-up list, it will make things worse. Forgetting obvious details and essential items is very easy, like leaving the kettle in an immediately accessible place!

- packing should be started at least two weeks before the day so that there can be a co-ordinated, orchestrated procedure. Boxes of lesser-used items can be put away in the garage, which frees up more space inside cupboards and rooms. Decide what you are going to pack yourself and what you are leaving to the professionals.

- choose the best available help. Discount movers will cost you far more in the long run. This is not an area in which to try and save money. There is no need to have a miserable moving day if you have the right attitude yourself and surround yourself with caring, happy people.

■ engage the help of friends as many hands make light work on the day, but ensure that they are not more of a hindrance. Work as a chain gang, one or two unpacking at the new house while others keep things moving at the old. Get people with cars so that all smaller items can be moved separately.

Remember you are paying the moving company by the hour and every little bit you do yourself will take dollars off your final bill. Have a tight, point-by-point list ready for the big day and follow through systematically and calmly.

Life in the city

City dwellers are always assumed to be stressful people, what with the noise, the traffic to drive through daily, the crime rate, the air and water pollution and the mediocrity of suburbia. You dream of getting away from it all, into the rural paradises and green farms of your dreams. Of course, one way of life is not intrinsically better or easier than the other. It depends on personal choice and taste. Many modern pastoralists suffer financial hardships and have to sell off their properties or live with constant worry and privation. Rural conditions are physically hard; there are few luxuries and pleasures are simple. Country folk also do not have the diversity of entertainment and facilities that their city cousins take for granted.

So, before you sell that house in the suburbs, consider what you are giving up and what you are going to and you may change your mind. To make a success of farming or to live happily in a small country town requires as much of a commitment as paying off that mortgage in the city. Take the stardust out of your eyes and if you still want to 'go bush', then it is probably the right move for you. The main stress of living in the suburbs is the sameness and isolation, particularly for women stuck at home without transport and with young children. First, brighten up your immediate surroundings. Fill your house with colourful, cheerful things. They do not have to be expensive, just a piece of pottery in the corner or some fresh flowers can make an enormous difference. Pay equal attention to your garden or yard. Plant some scented and pretty shrubs that will greet you every time you step outside. Cover the house with vines and a protective fence of trees so that you feel safe and warm within its boundaries.

Put variety into every day—do not forget boredom, too, is stressful. Do things with your children, don't just endure them. Keep yourself informed by watching interesting television programmes, but allow 'soaps' as well because they offer harmless escapism; read books, join the local library with your children, form a mother's group in your neighbourhood and talk about everything under the sun, not just the mundane issues that fill your day. Never forget that you have needs that will not wait until your children grow up.

When people say they have nothing to do, they have not exercised their imagination. If you are married without children and live in the suburbs, do different things every evening. Don't just turn on the television at six o'clock and sit there until closing time. Start to live life and not just get through each day. Where you live has little to do with that, except in specific cases of nasty neighbours or lack of privacy (such as dreaded cul-de-sacs and some apartment complexes). City life can be great. Enjoy all that it offers.

An overview

The remaining common culprits that cause most of our stress problems are combined here as they have been discussed extensively elsewhere in the book.

Physical inadequacies

Unless physical inadequacies constitute serious disfigurement or disability, they are usually linked to low self-esteem, so concentrate on improving the latter rather than focusing in on the physical feature itself. Here is a good example.

Rod lived in a country town and had been tormented all his life because of a skin condition and a large nose. When he reached adulthood, he decided that he had had enough of being treated like a freak, so he had expensive cosmetic surgery done. Did the townspeople stop teasing him? Yes, but now they criticised him for having the operation! It was a hard lesson for him, but a useful one. Never do something just to win approval— it usually won't work.

Children

Children can be stressful, but remember you chose to have them. If you do not like your children, they are your creations so accept the responsibility for them. Be positive and loving in your dealings with them. Let them see that you are a human being with needs also. At all times, play fair, be as consistent with them as humanly possible and when you make a mistake or hurt them unnecessarily, tell them you were wrong.

Children want respect as much as you do. While parents love to scream about the respect they believe is owed to them, they rarely feel they should also give it. Children need and want discipline and boundaries, not kisses and hugs when you are feeling good and rejection when you are not. Love them at all times, give them your attention and lots of physical demonstrations of affection. They are usually 'naughty' and cause stress when they are under stress themselves. So, do not lash out, find out, and then deal with it. Remember that your relationships reflect your own inner life so create harmony and you'll be rewarded with children who are a joy. They have just as much to teach you as you could ever teach them.

Conflict

Conflict can occur in family circles, personal and work relationships and in daily activities (see also Chapter Five on relationships). Resolve the relationship that is causing you stress, heal the problem in yourself and the conflict will be removed. Conflict is created when you feel pulled in more than one direction, especially if you are fighting with your own instincts on a particular issue or course of action. Once you have identified the cause of anything you are halfway to a cure. Identify the source of stress and eliminate it if possible. At a seminar, a woman put her hand up after that very suggestion had been made and asked what she ought to do if it turned out to be her husband! Everyone laughed and, of course, the point was taken. You cannot always entirely remove the stresses in your life, but you can make changes that will reduce them.

Authority figures

Authority figures constitute bosses, parents, policemen, ministers, doctors, bank managers, teachers—the 'gods' of society. Some people choose their occupations specifically because they like to exert power. Many men like to lord it over women and keep them in subservient roles. Remember never to give others power over you. True assertiveness means not letting this happen; it is all tied up with notions of self-esteem and personal pride. Never be rude back to someone or lose your temper, otherwise you have lost the argument. Too much unearned respect is also given to people who wear uniforms and badges. Why let them frighten you? Why do people immediately start quaking when a police car pulls into traffic behind them? Why do people let their bosses treat them like dirt, deluding themselves with the thought that there is no choice. Everyone needs to rethink their priorities on this subject and consider before they act and react to people who hold positions of power over them. It is quite likely that upon closer examination you will find they have feet of clay and are imperfect like the rest of us.

There are endless sources of stress for the modern woman and no doubt stress comes in many shapes and forms, from really large, serious matters to small, insignificant triggers. If you drink too much, you get a hangover, which takes away all the pleasure of the previous night! Acne causes tremendous stress to teenagers; there is toothache and visiting dentists, operations and growing old, hiccups and insomnia, job interviews and taking exams, poor restaurant and shop service, ever-ringing telephones, waiting for results and waiting for the birth of a baby. But wouldn't life be dull without it?

Combating stress

To conclude this chapter requires a further examination of activities, philosophies and fun measures that can make your life more stress-free, or at least less restrictive and unhappy. Every technique known to humanity cannot be listed, but picked out here are some of the ones that will be the most helpful or that have been researched and thus deserve inclusion in a book of this kind.

Tai chi

People who have practised tai chi for a period have found that it is most effective in reducing stress. If you watch exponents enjoying tai chi on television you will envy the look of sheer pleasure and peace on their faces as they rhythmically and gracefully move towards a dawn sun. All sport and exercise is wonderful for stress reduction, but activities that engage the mind and spirit as well as the body have a lot more to offer. There are many martial arts, but tai chi is by far the most gentle and soothing. It is far less physical and much more a combination of all the senses, yet the slow movements strengthen each part of the body in a series of co-ordinated exercises. It would make an excellent inclusion in your stress management programme.

Meditation

The main point to remember about meditation is that it does not have to be undertaken in a spirit of Eastern philosophy: you do not have to chant or burn incense or wear flowing robes— it can form part of your overall lifestyle improvement package without all the trappings. The benefits are substantial, but as with most things you need to be serious about it. Set aside some time on a daily basis to sit quietly in your own space (for that is what meditation essentially is). Just before going to sleep is the best time because it relaxes you for the night's rest ahead and allows you to wash away any negative influences from the ending day. When you begin, it is best to have a set routine and a programme to follow. A meditation or relaxation tape is good. Once you are experienced, you will know what works best for you. All that is needed is a few deep breaths, some soft music, and a peaceful, uninterrupted atmosphere. Eventually, even these will not matter, and you will be able to meditate on a busy train if you wish. Many women have asked for suggestions on how to strengthen intuitive processes and work on self-esteem. Meditation is one of the best methods because it is at the subconscious level that you can most easily make changes in your psyche and ultimately your attitudes, thoughts and behaviour. Due to its quiet and tranquil nature, meditation is also an excellent stress aid.

Relaxation

Meditation can be part of a general relaxation programme, but relaxation itself encompasses an attitude of life rather than a particular activity. Some women are naturally more placid and calm, but everyone can be less stressed if they first change their responses to stressful situations. This choice is a conscious one and, once adopted, affects your daily existence in many ways.

Relaxation must engage the mind as well as the body. Many women think that because they have stopped bustling around and are sitting down with a book or some knitting they are 'relaxed'. Sitting down and turning on the television is useless if you are staring at the screen but your mind is on your shopping list or the fight you had with your son last night. That is a basic mistake a lot of people make. Work on your internal life. Within you there are no problems, no decisions to make or unhappiness to resolve, only miraculous, pulsing life. If you are unhappy or worried, that is a mind-game. Don't blame 'life'! Find out what is bothering you and change it. For example, if you are at a party you are not enjoying, leave.

There are almost as many methods for learning to relax as there are people, but mentioned here are some key ones. Apart from building your self-esteem, physical improvement is a great help. Try exercise that relaxes your body and your mind, like tai chi, swimming and walking. This works with any of the systematic and rhythmic forms of sport. All the stress management ideas offered to date will relax you if practised over a period. Maintain a balanced lifestyle. If you are out getting drunk every night and managing on two or three hour's sleep, eating poorly and not taking care of your body, you cannot expect to be a relaxed person. Practise meditation or one of the more conventional forms of relaxation exercises, such as deep breathing. Here is a fairly typical set that you can try at night or in the middle of a busy day, if you are feeling stressed.

RELAXATION EXERCISE

I

I surrender myself, (Slight pause)
My right arm is heavy—my right hand is heavy—
my right arm and hand are heavy—my right arm and hand are sinking into the ground. (Pause)
My left arm is heavy—my left hand is heavy—
my left arm and hand are heavy—my left arm and hand are sinking into the ground. (Pause)

My right leg is heavy—my right foot is heavy—
my right leg and foot are heavy—my right leg and foot are sinking into the ground. (Pause)
My left leg is heavy—my left foot is heavy—
my left leg and foot are heavy—my left leg and foot are sinking into the ground. (Pause)
My arms are heavy—my legs are heavy—
my arms and legs are heavy—my body is heavy. (Pause)
I surrender myself—my body is heavy. (Ten-second pause)

II

I surrender myself—my body is heavy. (Pause)
My right arm is warm—my right hand is warm—
my right arm is nice and warm—my right arm and hand are warm. (Pause)
My left arm is warm—my left hand is warm—
my left arm is nice and warm—my left arm and hand are warm. (Pause)
My right leg is warm—my right foot is warm—
my right leg is nice and warm—my right leg and foot are warm. (Pause)
My left leg is warm—my left foot is warm—
my left leg is nice and warm—my left leg and foot are warm. (Pause)
My arms are warm—my legs are warm—my centre is warm—
my centre is nice and warm. (Ten-second pause)

III

I surrender myself—my body is warm—my centre is warm. (Pause)
My pulse is calm—my pulse is steady and calm—
my pulse is steady—my pulse is calm. (Pause)
I surrender myself—my pulse is calm. (Ten-second pause)

IV

I surrender myself—my body is heavy—
my centre is warm—my pulse is calm. (Pause)
The air is breathing me—the air is breathing me—
the air is breathing me—the air is breathing me. (Pause)
I surrender myself—the air is breathing me. (Thirty-second pause)

V
My face is cool—my face is nice and cool—
my face is cool (Pause)
Make fists (actually make fists slowly and tightly, release slowly).
Take a deep breath, stretch arms, legs and body, yawn, stretch
fingers and toes, wriggle body. (Thirty-second pause)
Open eyes slowly.

This relaxation exercise takes about ten minutes.

Yoga

Yoga can be most beneficial to body and mind. It can help
you to lose weight because yoga teaches the correct posture for
the body. By aligning your parts you redistribute unsightly flab
and excess flesh. More importantly, it stills the mind and induces
a form of meditation. This is why yogis can reduce their blood
pressure to such low levels that they appear dead, and then
revive themselves at will. So, it is the perfect choice if you want
to increase the harmony between your mind and body, develop
better posture and a more relaxed demeanour, and improve your
physical health at the same time.

There are many misconceptions about yoga. Westerners
dismiss it as magical, mystical nonsense that is good for a laugh
when you get into intricate poses you cannot easily unravel.
Or they think it is for wimps—a soft exercise—when in fact
it is very physically demanding and challenging, albeit different
to football or hockey. Rough-housing is not the only form of
sport and prowess. Check out a yoga class. Go with a friend
in a spirit of learning and fun—you will end up staying and
perhaps going back for more.

Numerology/astrology

Although these are not specifically stress management
techniques, many women find comfort and insight through
them. It is a little absurd when people pronounce these studies
to be the 'work of the devil'. Taken in the broadest context,
they are considered to be part of the 'occult'. However, millions
of ordinary women throughout the world take an interest in
such subjects. As long as it does not constitute worship, there
can be no harm in it. Astrology is an amazingly accurate
discipline, not as when the local paper tells you that you are

going to fall over on Friday, but when a serious astrologer predicts trends that will affect your star sign as a result of planetary and stellar activity. Surely humanity is not arrogant enough to believe that, as one tiny part of a whole solar system, people are not affected by movements and conjunctions and the tides and the moon?

If you take up astrology as a serious study, you will find it utterly fascinating. If you read your horoscope with intelligence and commonsense, it can guide you and save you from unnecessary conflict and heartache. Of course, choose your astrologer carefully and make sure that they are reputable and not just a staff reporter in disguise.

Numerology is linked to an Eastern philosophy of numbers, specifically to the concepts of reincarnation and karma. Lifetimes occur in cycles and knowing what year you're entering helps you to determine what your best plan is for that year. Take the first year in the cycle. As you would expect, one is the number of beginnings so expect many stops and starts during a one year, much activity and bustle, new activities constantly but not too many conclusions. It will be a year of variety but frustrating in many ways because you seem to spend the whole year chasing your own tail and getting nowhere. You won't see the fruits of your labour until next year so just enjoy the interesting variety without seeking concrete results.

Other areas of your life are affected by numbers, such as the vibration of the number of your name and your birthdate. Letters have number equivalents and your governing numbers will determine the type of life you'll experience, although predestination is rather a choice made by your soul when you returned. In other words, there's no external God or Fate to blame for your misfortunes. For whatever reason, you chose everything you are and will be. Eliminate the element of blame and learn from your every experience and hardship for that's why you are here. There is simplicity and yet tremendous complexity in this philosophy. Investigate further the subjects that intrigue you.

Religion

Now to a more traditional source of help for stress. For those people who hold religious views, regardless of what church you belong to, praying and being part of a spiritual community is a great comfort, especially in times of trial. Do not just pay lip-service to your beliefs; do not be Sunday Christians or once-a-year church attenders. Ministers of religion hold the view that God is happy to see you any time you wish to drop in, but how many of you only go to church for insurance? That is demeaning to yourself, to God and to those people who sincerely worship. God is not something to carry around in your pocket as a stress management tool when you need it. Face your own troubles with courage and get yourself out of it. Visit God instead with joy and glad tidings. Would you visit a friend only when you have some whining to do? Then why go to church for that reason? Either have an ongoing relationship with your Creator, through good times and bad, or have the courage to say that you really do not want it. So much evil has been perpetrated through the centuries in the name of religion; the hypocrisy is disgusting. If religion is to truly help you be a better person and live a happier life, you have to practise it as you would anything else you want to perfect.

There are three fundamental things: it is what you do that counts, not what you say you are—your whole life should be a celebration of your faith; God is everywhere, in the trees, the earth, the wind and therefore, in you—you do not have to go to a church to find Him; different religions are but different paths to the Creator of everyone—there is no one true faith. If you are sincere, your religious fervour is a real and legitimate comfort and certainly reduces the stress of many of life's more difficult challenges..

Zen

This philosophy is included because it involves meditation but is a much more stylised and disciplined form. It certainly is not for everyone. A devotee once said that you cannot go out to seek knowledge of Zen, but are led to it when the time is right and if you are a suitable pupil. Zen involves stillness, meditation and communion with one's spiritual centre. The mind must be emptied of all thought in an attempt to find 'Satori', the meaning of all life. Zen embraces the philosophy that everything is good and death only rejoins you with all nature. The ego must be subdued for the sake of truth and tranquillity, an aspect of Zen that Westerners find difficult. This poem sums up best what Zen is all about:

Before enlightenment
chopping wood
carrying water.

After enlightenment
chopping wood
carrying water.

How beautifully simple and true. If you imagine that life suddenly becomes idyllic when you gain self-knowledge, you are in for a rude shock. What *does* happen is that because your attitudes change, you create less conflict and struggle for yourself, thus ensuring an easier passage through the days of your life. Struggle and unhappiness are not your inevitable destiny as many seem to believe. It is your choice. Overall, life can be a daily adventure, but you still have to carry water and chop wood unless you win the lottery!

Massage

It used to be thought that massage was either an erotic experience or it was for the self-indulgent or the injured. Not that there is anything wrong with being self-indulgent, but nowadays all sorts of women have regular massage. The benefits have been extensively chronicled and range from stress reduction to improvement of body functions (such as circulation and digestion) and muscle tone, loosening of body tension, and inducing a general feeling of relaxation and well-being. A massage is cheaper and more fun than drugs or alcohol or medical treatment. It should not be seen as an alternative to exercise, but rather a beneficial adjunct. Although not its primary purpose, massage is also useful for weight loss, particularly in cases of fluid retention as it breaks down the pockets of water that gather in the armpits and ankles. Massage is only beneficial when enjoyed regularly, as tension builds up quickly between visits and the masseuse has to start from scratch each time.

Aromatherapy and reflexology

Combine massage with oils made from flowers and herbal extracts and you have aromatherapy, which is a relaxing technique designed to please the senses while treating the body. Surely these are two of the more enjoyable methods of reducing stress.

Reflexology is specifically foot massage, but much more. The pressure points of the foot represent the parts of the body that can be treated by massaging the relevant areas of the foot. This can help to increase blood circulation and relax tension in the nervous system. It is also a diagnostic tool as problems can be identified through massaging the foot and finding painful spots that reveal the area of the body that needs attention.

Some orthodox medical practitioners dismiss such practices as reflexology and iridology, but they are gaining more recognition with time. Again, they should not be used to the exclusion of traditional remedies but in conjunction with them. These alternative methods of healing are based on the philosophy that a woman should be responsible for her own health and that self-help is the most effective way to combat stress and prevent disease.

Colour therapy

This is a departure from the tactile arts and into a realm that affects everyone. To one extent or another each person is influenced by colour, on them, around them, and within them. Gestalt and other therapies hold that you can visualise colours in your psyche that reveal the state of your consciousness and subconscious life. Most people would accept that certain colours are 'happy', like orange, yellow and bright blue, and that some are sad like black and grey. However, there is much more to colour therapy. You are affected psychologically by the colours surrounding you. The ones you choose to have near you reveal a lot about your personality and basic nature. There is usually a colour test on psychological profiles, for instance. Have you noticed that you go through stages with colours? The one you automatically reach for in a group is the right one for you.

Colour therapy is now being used extensively as a fashion aid. The right colour can make all the difference between success and failure in the overall effect you are trying to create with your clothes. Good saleswomen have been telling customers this for years, but not everyone buys from a shop that offers personalised attention. If you pull a dress off the rack that appeals to you, no matter how expensive it is, it may not flatter you because of its colour and texture against your skin tone. When you wear a colour that is right for you, you will know immediately because heads will turn and people will compliment you on your appearance. If you consult a colour analyst, she will tell you which spectrum of colours you look best in, and you can use this a guide when you shop for clothes.

Feeling good about yourself involves every aspect of your physical and emotional life, dressing effectively to express a statement you feel comfortable with is part and parcel of it. Living an unstressed life requires all the ammunition you can muster. Your physical appearance is a good place to start.

Rebirthing and flotation

Two other ideas you can try to combat stress are rebirthing and flotation. The latter is recommended as a wonderful release from stress. Since you can listen to music or motivational tapes while you float, it seems to satisfy even the most stringent criteria for a good stress management technique. Isn't it grand that there are so many things out there to help you nowadays? As long as you do not get lost in the hype and allow the range of choices to stress you! Read some of the many books available on rebirthing for specific information on that process.

Hypnotherapy

One stress management possibility that has not been mentioned to date is hypnotherapy, which should be used sparingly and only in cases where other techniques have not worked. It is particularly useful for those trying to give up smoking or lose weight, because stubborn patterns of behaviour can be shifted by the auto-suggestion process that takes place during hypnosis.

All sorts of everyday things are safeguards against stress build-up, such as leisure activities, entertainment, partying, travel, jokes, friendship and fun things like dancing. There is nothing like having a good time to release tension. Sometimes, when you are tired, you feel inclined to shut the world out and crawl into your bed to sleep forever. Rest may be the best remedy for fatigue, but the other option is to get your glad rags on and rush to where the action is.

Often, laughter and good company are the best medicine for

what ails you. Good humour is very therapeutic, and a hearty belly laugh is guaranteed to release tension. Laughter can brighten up the most miserable day and even cheer a very sick person or one in pain. Humour automatically relaxes people and puts them in a more receptive frame of mind.

Dancing, being a physical activity, makes you feel great in every way, and is very slimming! It has to be in the top ten list of best stress remedies.

Sports in general, sitting in a spa, lying on a sandy beach— all of these are simple, effective ways to relax and unwind from the busy demands of modern life.

Friends are a great help in times of stress, if they genuinely care enough to let you talk out your problems or worries. You do not always want advice, but value a sounding-board. Just by expressing your feelings in person or in a letter you release some of the concern, gain insights and put things back into perspective. If your problem is a very serious or personal one, it is sometimes easier to discuss it with a stranger, and that is where counsellors come in. Their job is to listen, canvass options and offer some practical strategies for change. No one sees a counsellor if she is happy with everything in her life, so change of some sort is inevitable if improvement is to be forthcoming.

The stigma of seeking psychological help is largely gone although some males still consider it a weakness to have to ask for guidance and help. Do not hesitate to see a counsellor if you are feeling stressed or are grappling with a specific problem. The solution may be close at hand, but you are too close to the situation to see it. An objective adviser may be all you need.

Animals are a marvellous source of comfort and offer a special brand of friendship. Recent research indicates that just stroking an animal's fur brings down blood pressure and lowers stress levels. Dogs, in particular, are now being used in homes for the aged. They have been effective in reaching isolated personalities that all the human coaxing available could not touch. A wet kiss and a furry hug make you forget your troubles. Of course, if you are not fond of animals or you are allergic to their coats, then they are not the right stress managers for you.

Television also, can be very relaxing, because essentially it is a mindless activity. There are some thought-provoking programmes on, but it is still a pleasure to be able to lie back and be entertained without lifting a finger. It is a nice contrast to the more physical suggestions offered, as long as there are both types of activity in your life. There is an awful lot of snobbery about television when, in effect, it is like everything else: use your common-sense, include a varied diet and do not get addicted.

Conclusion

In conclusion, I want to leave you with the thought that life is indeed what you make it. Stress management is an important part of living in the twentieth century, but it is only one aspect of the challenge in facing every new dawn. What makes life so wonderful is the element of surprise, but remember that around every corner is waiting just as much beauty, joy and goodness as there are disappointments, difficulties and sadness. The secret is to embrace it all and live life as a total experience rather than tiptoeing around as if in a minefield, waiting for bombs to explode. There is beauty in life and in people.

The information given to you throughout this book is not intended to be a definitive, theoretical study of techniques but rather suggestions and hints for better living. You may disagree with much of it, some of it will even offend you, but it has been offered to you in a spirit of love and sharing. With determination, patience and a little effort, you can benefit from the stories, experiences and information you have been introduced to. Remember, every day is a new beginning.

AFFIRMATIONS

There is no difference between what I wish and what I have.

The universe is now materialising all my desires.

When a wish can be willed, the means will follow (A. Christie).

What I can visualise, I can actualise (Richard Bach).

I am worth loving.

I trust the universe completely.

BIBLIOGRAPHY

Berne, Eric. *Games People Play: The Psychology of Human Relationships*, Penguin Books Ltd, 1964.

Byrski, Liz. *Pills, Potions, People: Understanding the Drug Problem*, Dove Communications, 1986.

Clarke, Michael & Dorothy. *Sexual Joy in Marriage*, ADIS Health Science Press, 1979.

Gawain, Shakti. *Creative Visualisation*, Bantam Books, 1979.

Gibran, Kahlil. *The Prophet,*Heinemann, 1926.

Greer, Germaine. *The Female Eunuch*, Paladine, 1971.

Hay, Louise L. *You Can Heal Your Life*, Hay House, 1984.

Kauz, Herman. *Tai Chi Handbook: exercise, meditation and self-defense*, Dolphin Books, 1974.

Kubler-Ross, Elisabeth. *On Death and Dying*, Tavistock Publications, 1970.

Linn, Denise. *Pocketful of Dreams*, Triple Five Publishing, 1988.

Meares, Ainslie. *The Wealth Within*, Hill of Content Publishing, 1978.

Morris, Desmond. *The Naked Ape*, Dell, 1980.

Pease, Allan. *Body Language: How to read others' thoughts by their gestures*, Camel Publishing Company, 1981.

Sisson, Colin P. *Your Right to Riches*, Total Press, 1986.

Untermeyer, Louis. *The Pocket Book of Robert Frost's Poems*, Washington Square Press, 1946.